WINGS 1

TYPHOON STRIKE

WINGS 1

TYPHOON STRIKE

Charles Anthony

First published in Great Britain 1995
22 Books, Invicta House, Sir Thomas Longley Road,
Rochester, Kent

Copyright © 1995 by 22 Books

The moral right of the author has been asserted

A CIP catalogue record for this book is available from the
British Library

ISBN 1 898125 32 5

10 9 8 7 6 5 4 3 2 1

Typeset by Hewer Text Composition Services, Edinburgh
Printed in Great Britain by Cox and Wyman Limited, Reading

Prelude

March 1942. Oberleutnant Karl-Heinz Ketelheim was fed up. He was lost, and hated it. He was flying a lumbering, fully laden bomber and hated that too. What he really wanted, what he'd really hoped for when he'd gone into the Luftwaffe, was assignment to a fighter squadron. He was, after all, a Prussian, he fumed, and Prussians were warrior-knights. His modern steed should have been one of Willy Messerschmitt's wonders, the Me-109. Then he would have turned to give battle to the Tommies in their vengeful Spitfires when they had bounced his attack force of twenty-five aircraft, instead of going into the wild, evasive contortions about the sky that had subsequently separated him from the main group.

In a way, he was lucky, he supposed. He had watched all the section leaders and the raid commander himself go down in the first attack. His own manoeuvre had enabled him to escape the deadly British fighters – so far. He glanced anxiously about him through the faired cockpit of the Heinkel He-111H medium bomber, looking for the fighters. The sky was empty. He hoped their luck would hold.

'Look out for those damned Spitfires,' he ordered

the other four members of his crew. 'And stay at gun positions.'

All non-commissioned personnel, each replied, 'Yes, Herr Oberleutnant.'

'What am I doing in this sitting duck?' he muttered to himself. If they made it back, he was going to request an immediate transfer to a fighter unit. He didn't care how many strings he had to pull.

He had never bought the ludicrous Nazi ethos, for whose practitioners – who included his entire crew – he harboured a well-concealed contempt; but he loved and believed in the glory of battle. In his mind, class was all and his connections were powerful enough, even these days, to get him the new assignment. He was emotionally more suited to fighters, he reasoned. He wanted the freedom to charge through the skies to take the battle to the enemy, the way the Me-109 escorts had. As was usual these days, however, the escorts had been too few.

'Müller!' he called to the bomb aimer, who doubled as nose gunner, in the lower nose section.

'Oberleutnant?'

'We're going to have to dump those bombs. We need more speed.'

'There's no target below. Just open fields. I think we're over Dorset.'

'He *thinks* we're over Dorset. Then we'll frighten some cows and deprive the Tommies of their breakfast milk.'

No one laughed.

'Get ready to dump when I tell you,' he snapped.

'Yes, Oberleutnant.'

Bunch of thick-headed peasants, Ketelheim thought

disparagingly. What was he doing flying with such people?

The black Jaguar SS-100 was in beautiful condition. The day was unseasonably warm and the hood was down. The twenty-one-year-old at the wheel, in civilian clothes, drove it at a gentle pace along the country road, his left arm about the shoulders of the beautiful young woman at his side. She was just six months past her eighteenth birthday. There was a happiness about them that was frighteningly vulnerable.

The car was not his, but his father's pride and joy, and was on loan for this the last day of their two-day honeymoon. Mindful of the shortage of petrol, they were not going far, only the five miles round the perimeter of the family's farm. It was the first time that the car had been out since the beginning of the war.

'Ah,' he said after a while. 'Here we are.'

He took his arm from her shoulders as he slowed down and turned into a narrow track that could easily be missed if one did not know what to look for, and was just wide enough to allow the car through. It rocked its way sedately along the bumpy ground, its exhaust rumbling powerfully. Soon they came to a small clearing, hidden from above by a canopy formed by the branches of tall trees. He brought the car to a halt, near the bank of a clear stream.

'This is it,' he told her, climbing out and waving an expansive arm. 'My secret place. I came here quite often as a boy. Walked across the fields.' He went round the side to open the door for her. 'Just right for our picnic. I wanted you to see it before I went back to the squadron. I've never brought anyone here before.' He looked at her anxiously. 'What do you think?'

'I love it.' She turned eyes, full of love, upon him. 'Thank you for bringing me to your secret place.' She put her arms about him, hugging him tightly. 'I feel I'm really part of you now, and that feels wonderful.'

'And I am so lucky,' he said, kissing her gently. 'Wife.'

It was then that they heard the faint sound.

He stiffened briefly, then relaxed. 'Must be one of ours. There's nothing of military value way out here. Let's get our picnic things.'

'Get ready to dump, Müller,' Ketelheim ordered. He knew the way home now. 'Then we turn for base.'

'Yes, Herr Oberleutnant.'

'All right. Now!'

He had listened to the growing sounds of the engines with mounting disbelief and anxiety. The uneven beat was too familiar; but because it did not make sense, he was slow to react. An instinct for survival, despite his own reluctance to accept that a bomber was overhead, made him yell, '*Megan! Move!*'

He had grabbed her and was dragging her unceremoniously, when the first bomb hit.

He came to, feeling cold and wet, and realized he was in the water. He got to his feet groggily and looked about him.

The Jaguar was in two pieces. Half, almost intact, was still on the bank. The other was a twisted mass of metal, wires and upholstery lying upside down in the stream. Bits of stuffing, looking like fluffy young chicks, floated aimlessly away. There was a big crater next to the remaining half of the Jaguar on the bank. Several trees were down, scorched and still smoking, the smell of their burning hanging in the air.

Of Megan, there was no sign.

'Oh my God!' he exclaimed softly, with mounting dread. A terrible fear began to envelop him, freezing his heart and chilling his blood, making him shiver with foreboding. He began to shout, a desperate wail in his voice. '*Megan! Megan!*'

He stumbled out of the water to begin frantically looking for her, a man demented, calling out her name over and over.

He found her eventually – pieces of her, scattered all over his secret place. There was not a mark upon him.

March 1944. The Typhoon, a great darting, predatory ghost, swept low over a landscape made deceptively tranquil by the drowsy twilight of the approaching dawn. The roar of its powerful engine ripped the tranquillity apart in a tearing bellow that was almost obscene. Yet the winged form that flitted between the trees, miraculously remaining unscathed as its silhouette appeared to shift insubstantially in the gloom, seemed remarkably graceful. This gracefulness belied its dreadful purpose, for there was murder in the heart of the man who piloted it.

The Hawker Typhoon 1B was a killing machine that was as dangerous to unwary pilots as it was to the enemy. Some of its pilots feared it so much that they tended to approach it with trepidation, knowing what it could do to them and already afraid of the possibility. They had good reason. Earlier versions had the disconcerting habit of shedding their entire tail sections, and despite the fact that these problems had eventually been ironed out, its pilots still viewed it with understandable caution. Many had not survived their first take-off. Others had nicknames for it, a good percentage of which were highly descriptive anatomically.

But the Typhoon was also a formidable weapon in the right hands, and Mike Pendrake loved it. He had flown both the sturdy Hurricane and the inimitable Spitfire in combat; but it was the Hawker monster that had stolen his soul. Much bigger and more brutal than the Spitfire, he called it the 'Beast' and felt he belonged to it. It had served him spectacularly.

It was noisy inside, the raw power of the 2100-plus horsepower Napier Sabre engine snarling its way into the cockpit he called the 'birdcage'. This had anachronistic side-opening doors rather like a car and he longed for the sliding bubble canopy of some versions, with its infinitely better all-round view; but he didn't care. What mattered was the thunderous power under his control, which, at his command, could unleash devastating havoc upon the enemy. Armed with four Hispano 20mm cannon and eight rockets, he deployed awesome fire-power. He could obliterate tanks, turn trains into starbursts of flame and steam, demolish buildings, tear roads apart, and convert railway lines into so much twisted metal and the sleepers into shrapnel. The more the devastation, the better he liked it.

He could drop bombs too, but the aircraft could only carry at most a pair of 1000-pounders at a time. He didn't like bombing missions. The drag and weight of the bombs slowed and restricted the manoeuvrability of even such a powerful aeroplane far too much for his liking. He preferred the current set-up. Once the rockets were gone he could take on even the Focke-Wulf Fw-190, which, with its top speed of 472mph in some variants, was still his meat. He hoped one or two would come out to play. This low down, they would be hopeless against him.

He banked the aircraft steeply on to a new heading, threading his way between a pair of tall trees whose very branches, barely visible arms, reached vainly for him. The dark shape of a building seemed to caress a wingtip as it flashed past.

'Hope I woke you up, you bastards,' he shouted into his mask. Darting fireflies of anti-aircraft shells, their tracers lighting up the gloom, followed him briefly. 'Too late, you dozy sods! You can't catch me!' He laughed. 'Better luck next time!'

Distorted by the mask, the strange noise did not sound like the laughter of a totally sane man.

He banked once more, then brought the wings level on to another heading. The parallel lines of a railway line gleamed dully before him in the pale light of the new day; but with the darkness at his back, he would not be spotted until it was much too late. He flew along the track so low it seemed as if he was about to land on it. Soon, just up ahead, he found what he was looking for.

The train was packed with ammunition and troops. Its importance was such that three flatbed anti-aircraft trucks were among its carriages. One of these was at the very end, to cover the vulnerable tail. The gunners were among the best, their weapons lethal. They were very alert. Even at this time of the day, only a very daring and perhaps foolish lone pilot would take them on and hope to achieve surprise.

But surprise was achieved.

It may have been a trick of the wind, but the deafening roar of the Typhoon did not come to them over the clatter of the train until far too late. A sharp-eyed gunner spotted the dark shape impossibly low and, disbelieving his own eyes, tried desperately to train his multi-barrelled gun, only to find he had run out of elevation. He could not bring the weapon to bear. *The target* was *too low!*

He yelled to his comrades in fear, rage and despair. He knew what was coming and, worse, knew he hadn't the slightest chance of being able to do anything about it.

Pendrake held the Typhoon steady as he swept down on them. He fired the rockets, watching as they whooshed off to explode along the length of the train. It had been beautifully done.

The rear anti-aircraft truck was lifted clean off the track, rolling in mid-air as its ammunition exploded as if in response to the rockets. Like a giant hand twisting a toy, it took the entire train with it. The ammunition wagons ripped apart, incinerating the carriages that housed the troops.

The Typhoon flew through a raging hell of fire, and Pendrake heard several thumps strike the aircraft. He knew no one had fired at him – they hadn't had the time – and assumed that bits of the exploding train had somehow reached him. But the aircraft felt OK. No serious damage, so far.

He banked away and wheeled round to survey his handiwork. Though he knew with the train off the track the anti-aircraft guns would be useless, he was still taking a chance. He was breaking his own rule of never going back to look. It was one of the best ways of getting pounced on by marauding fighters, out for revenge. There would also be survivors, and they'd be after his blood with anything to hand. Even a rifle bullet could down an unwary aircraft.

Yet he wanted to see.

His work had been terrible. The train was burning along its entire length. The engine lay on its side off the track, its steam shooting along the ground in a white jet before rising into the air, the last gasp of a dying behemoth. Then tracers began to reach for him. He swung away, out of range. No point wasting cannon shells. That train was going nowhere. The carnage on the ground and the haphazard nature of the firing had also shown that those lucky enough to survive had been very few indeed.

He felt good.

He kept the Typhoon low as he headed across the fields of Normandy for home. Behind him, the glow of the burning train was like a demonic sunrise. Despite the severe attrition of the years of war and their relative scarcity in the skies above France, there were still a fair number of enemy fighters around. It wouldn't take them long to come hunting. Pendrake kept a good lookout, while maintaining his ultra-low-level flight.

He did a thorough check of the aircraft. Everything was working as it should. Whatever had hit him, had done no damage.

Despite the increasing light of the day, it would still

be difficult to spot him, and his rush for home did not mean he would run away from a fight. If anything, he'd be happy to oblige; but there was little point in making it easy for them. Yet though from time to time he glimpsed tiny specks high above him, none came down to look and it was with a slight feeling of disappointment that he made it safely back across the Channel, keeping low above the choppy grey waters.

1

Major Jack Halloran, in the uniform of the US Army Air Force, sat quietly in the office of the Royal Air Force station commander while the group captain, the Honourable William, Viscount Fox, read through the papers in the black folder he had brought with him.

Halloran had arrived at the station gates at about the time that Mike Pendrake had destroyed his train so spectacularly. The guards, surprised by the uniform, despite having seen many of the different kinds worn by Allied and Commonwealth forces during the course of their service, still took no chances and intially put the major through stringent security checks. The major was unperturbed, insisting only that he be taken directly to the station commander. This was done under heavy guard. No one had been allowed to look into his briefcase, or take it away from him.

Halloran now permitted himself the faintest of smiles as he waited patiently for Group Captain Fox to finish. The guards may have considered their checks rigorous. They had little idea of what a really tough security check was like. They should meet some of the people *he'd* had to deal with.

The group captain glanced up briefly. Halloran's smile disappeared.

'Something to amuse you, Major?' Bill Fox, as he preferred to be called, queried mildly.

'Er . . . no, sir!'

'Good.' Fox returned to his reading.

Halloran, Fox had noted, though in the uniform of an air force officer, was conspicuously bereft of pilot's or aircrew wings. The American did, however, sport a chestful of ribbons. Everyone knew the Americans were rather lax when it came to dishing out gongs. His own pilots tended to claim with graveyard humour that you had to die first, before the RAF would deign to give you one.

Still, Halloran appeared to have people of some influence in his corner. No less august a body than the War Office had underwritten his security status, and the contents of the papers he'd brought pointed squarely to the fact that the good major spent much of his time behind enemy lines. However, the part that interested Fox most was the blueprint for a very special squadron, to be trained for a particularly difficult task. Halloran's people were looking for someone to command it. Even at this early stage, they had already given the squadron a name.

Fox looked up once more. 'Why Cobra Squadron?'

Halloran cleared his throat. 'Its mission is . . . er . . . part of an overall . . . er . . . strategy, sir.' If the group captain did not already know about Cobra, the plan that was part of the tactics for the eventual invasion of continental Europe, it was not his place to give that information.

'Major,' Fox began, 'when people clear their throats before speaking to me I know they're either lying, or holding something back. However,' he continued before Halloran could protest, 'you are quite right. If it doesn't concern my responsibilities to this unit, I don't want to know. That satisfy you?'

Taken aback, Halloran said, 'Yessir!'

'Good,' Fox murmured as he slowly closed the folder. 'The people who sent you already knew what they were looking for. I think we may have your man. He's out on a rhubarb at the moment . . .'

'Rhubarb, sir?'

Fox smiled thinly. 'Something you don't know about, Major? A rhubarb is a sort of prowling flight over enemy territory. We go out to make mischief. It's dangerous work . . . and the man I'm thinking of is on one at this very moment. He tends to get results. Bit mad, of course.'

Halloran was startled. 'Mad?'

'Ah. You're wondering whether a madman's the right sort of chap to command this . . . Cobra unit of yours.' Fox tapped at the folder. 'From what I've just read, that's exactly the type of chap you need. Mad, or suicidal. There are times when I think Flight Lieutenant Pendrake's both. There are also times when I think the people who dream these operations up are equally touched in the head . . .'

'It's my plan, sir,' Halloran said quietly as Fox paused.

Fox levelled upon the major the sort of gaze that one would expect of a scientist scrutinizing a laboratory specimen. 'Is it, by George? Astounding.'

'It *will* work, sir,' the major insisted. 'I've already got the backing. It's an operational necessity.'

'I've no doubt you do have, and I'm quite certain it

is. You would not be here, and I would not just have read the contents of your folder.'

'You sound as if you might be changing your mind, sir.'

'Good Lord, no. I'm more convinced than ever he is your man.'

'Because he's mad?'

'No,' Fox replied calmly. 'Because he's damned good. Strangely enough, he is a good commander. Once took command of a full squadron during the worst times of the air war over this country, when both the CO *and* the deputy CO bought it on the same day. He whipped the demoralized squadron into shape and they eventually went on to take a grievous toll of the enemy. He was only twenty-one at the time and they called him the *old* man.' Fox gave a soft laugh. 'I'm the really old man around here. Thirty tomorrow. He's now twenty-three and covered in gongs, though it's the devil's own job to get him to wear them at all. Always improperly dressed, that man.'

'Then may I ask you something, sir?'

'Please do.'

'If he's so good, why is he still a captain ... er ... fight lieutenant? It can't be because of his dress sense, surely.'

'Sometimes,' Fox began seriously, 'being brave is not always the prerequisite for command. Or so I've been told. By rights, he deserves his own squadron, though there are those who will disagree.'

Pushing his luck, Halloran asked, 'So you think he was unfairly treated?'

Fox, a tall, elegant man whose own uniform was hand-made in Savile Row, looked at Halloran steadily.

His triangular face, adorned by the thinnest of dark lines upon his upper lip, was given greater effect by the fact that his neatly trimmed hair was almost blond. His dark eyes radiated a calm that Halloran found, despite himself, oddly relaxing. The ribbons of the DSO and the DFC nestled in splendour beneath the pilot's wings, above Fox's left breast pocket.

By contrast, Halloran, though almost as tall, was more solidly built. His crew-cut, less militarily brutal than Fox had expected, gave him an air of boyishness that was very misleading indeed. Among his friends and colleagues in the French Underground unit to which he'd been assigned, he was known as a very dangerous man; as dangerous as the snake they'd chosen as his code-name: the *fer de lance*, the spearhead.

'Pendrake's wife was killed in a bombing raid,' Fox said, 'when she'd been a bride for just two days. Damned awful luck. They were out in the country on a picnic, well away from the danger of bombs. The last day of their forty-eight-hour honeymoon. Then this lone aircraft went over, probably lost, dumping its load any old where. Blew her to bits. Nothing touched him. He's been fighting his own war ever since.'

Halloran, a man who'd seen many shocking things, suddenly felt sympathy for Pendrake. He knew something of what he must be going through. There'd been a young French girl who'd been part of his team in France; then the Gestapo had got her . . .

Fox was looking at him interestedly. 'I do believe I may have struck a chord somewhere.'

Halloran nodded.

'When he came to us about a year ago,' Fox continued, 'he'd been in so many battles it seemed as if he was hanging on to his sanity by a thread. But he hasn't let up, and is arguably the best and most aggressive pilot we've got.'

'If you recommend him, sir, I'll pass that on to my superiors. But I'd like to see him first, if that's OK.'

Fox nodded. 'Wait till he lands. Stay for breakfast. I can't promise an American bounty, but I'm sure you'll find ours sufficiently substantial.' Fox stood up. 'Let's see what they've got on offer in the mess, shall we?'

'I happen to like an English breakfast, sir,' Halloran confessed with a straight face as he too got to his feet, 'though some of the guys might think me crazy. When I ask for tea they think I've really flipped.'

'Gone native, have you?'

'Something like that, sir.'

'Good man.'

As they made their way out of the office, Halloran added, 'You're sure he'll make it back? If these rhubarbs are as dangerous as you've said . . .'

'He always makes it back. Don't be put off by his manner when you first meet him. Strange thing, isn't it, Major?' Fox continued mildly. 'When a man wants to die, the gods almost never grant his wish. Quite, quite remarkable.'

Halloran realized that Fox was looking directly at him.

The bellowing roar of a fast-approaching aircraft made virtually everyone on the station interrupt what they were doing and listen. Some, out in the open and newcomers to the airfield, at first believed it to be an attack and were already priming themselves for a headlong rush to the nearest shelter, when they noticed that other people had stopped wherever they were, to stare in the direction of the sound. As yet, nothing could be seen.

In the dispersal area, pilots due to fly halted their pre-flight preparations to do the same. One very young airman paused in the act of heaving himself on to the wing of the fifteen-foot-high aircraft, trying to identify the direction of the swelling thunder. In the various messes, diners left their tables to have a look. Most of them already knew who it was and waited for what would come next.

Leaving his own table, Fox said to Halloran, 'That's Pendrake. Let's go and meet him, shall we?'

'How do you know?' Halloran demanded as he hurriedly followed the group captain.

Fox put on his cap as they emerged into the crisp, brightening day. There was no wind to speak of and no early spring rain had fallen during the night, though there was a slight patina of frost on the grass.

'Everyone who's been on this station long enough knows . . . aircrew and groundcrew alike.' Fox came to a halt. 'We can see everything from here. Look at the runway.'

From where they stood, the far end of the runway appeared to dip out of sight. The crescendo of noise was closer but as yet, there was still nothing to be seen.

Then Halloran gave a gasp of astonishment as the bellowing Typhoon seemed to rise from the very ground itself, to hurtle at what he was certain was a height of bare inches, along the length of the runway.

'My God!' he exclaimed. 'His prop will hit!'

Fox said nothing.

Miraculously, the aircraft did not slam into the unforgiving earth. Instead, it pulled up into a steep climb, rolling swiftly as it did so. After the third roll it stopped, pulled on to its back, flicked into a ninety-degree bank, hauled round tightly, levelled out and was nicely placed to land along the runway's centreline.

It was only when he let out his breath the Halloran realized he'd been holding it.

'The guy can fly,' he remarked with soft admiration.

'Got some trade too,' Fox said. 'He always does. That's what those three rolls were about. Come on. I'll take you to Dispersal in my car. Get your first impression of him in person.'

At Dispersal, where aircraft were parked in small groups, the young pilot, with the barely visible thin blue ring of the rank of pilot officer on his shoulders, stood gaping as the Typhoon taxied towards them. Another pilot, barely older and with the slightly thicker rings of a flying officer, sauntered up.

'Catch a fly in that if you're not careful.'

The pilot officer snapped his mouth shut in embarrassment. 'Anyway,' he protested after a pause, 'too cold for flies.'

'Never too cold for those pests. Took one up once. Wretched thing had got into the cockpit. I went high, hoping it would die of oxygen starvation.'

'Did it?'

'Of course not. The thing kept buzzing around infuriatingly and tried to get inside my mask; and then I had to go into a furious evasion manoeuvre when I saw an enemy approaching from my starboard quarter.'

'What did you do?' the young pilot asked breathlessly.

'Not an enemy aircraft at all. The wretched insect had pasted itself to the canopy. At that angle, the speck looked like another aeroplane.'

The young pilot was not sure whether to believe the story or not, but said nothing. He looked towards the Typhoon, which had now stopped some distance away, and saw the station commander's car heading towards it.

'The station CO's going to congratulate him for those three victories.' There was a touch of wistfulness in the young pilot's voice. He had yet to successfully down an aircraft.

'Not three victories . . .'

'But he did three victory rolls.'

'Victory rolls . . . yes, but not for three aircraft. When you've been here a while, you'll recognize Old Scarface's codes. Like everyone else, each slow roll is a kill. But Mike Pendrake's fast rolls mean something else entirely. One means a tank or tanks . . . usually several when Mike gets truly going. Two rolls and it's some other ground target . . . artillery pieces, radars, ammo dumps, so forth. Three, and he's got a nice fat, juicy train. Must have been a good one. He was particularly exuberant just then.'

'So the old man's going to tell him off for the low approach?'

'No fear, old boy. Mike's the only person who gets lower than Foxy the Viscount, though strictly, the station CO shouldn't really go on ops any more.

Now come on. Up you go. And stick to me. They still play very rough across the water.'

'Ye . . . yes. Yes, of course.'

The young pilot climbed into the cockpit of the Beast with trepidation.

The car drew up just as the huge propeller whirled to a stop. Fox and Halloran climbed out to walk slowly towards the Typhoon. Its ground crew were already beginning to busy themselves around it.

Halloran stared at the large aircraft with its aggressive, inclined stance, the brutish nose with its gaping intake beneath pointing upwards meanly. He moved closer to tentatively pat its flank as he would a wild, skittish horse that he half-expected to kick out at the slightest provocation.

'Ever flown one of these?' a strong voice, strangely cold, addressed him from above.

He turned to look. The helmet, with goggles raised, was still on and the oxygen mask, though now unhooked, still partially obscured the face. There was such a chill in the eyes that Halloran found he had to suppress a shiver.

'No . . . no,' he replied. 'I'm not a flyer.'

'I see.' It sounded like a condemnation. The eyes continued to survey him from their eyrie. 'American.' That sounded like a condemnation too.

'Yes. My name's Halloran.'

'Pendrake.'

'Yes. I know.'

If Pendrake thought that surprising, he gave no indication. 'I've flown with your compatriots when they were with the Eagle Squadrons. Good blokes.'

'I'm glad to hear it.'

'Of course, the Royal Air Force ironed out the rough edges.'

'Of course.'

Suddenly, helmet and mask came off. The face grinned. Halloran saw a long scar, like a sabre slash, running down the left side of the face from upper cheek to mouth, stopping just before reaching the corner. Yet the face, pleasant enough to look upon, was itself not distorted and almost handsome. Many women, Halloran decided, would find that scar dangerously attractive.

'Hullo, sir,' Pendrake called to Fox.

'Hullo, Mike. Got some more trade, did you?'

'A nice fat train. A pricey one, I think. Long job. Three flak cars, and lots of ammo. Went up like a gasworks. Must have been important.'

'It certainly sounds like it. Check with the Spy when you debrief. He may have had some news about it.'

'Will do.' Pendrake began to climb out of the Typhoon.

Halloran, his hand still on the aircraft, was apparently deep in thought as he watched Pendrake descend.

The pilot was of average height and slim, almost delicate. But there was an unnerving fire of such intensity burning within the eyes that it was enough to give an air of ferocious, relentless strength to his presence. His rich, dark hair bore faint streaks of premature greyness incongruous in one so young, low down on the temples near the ears. Like so many of his peers, Pendrake had grown up very quickly.

Halloran felt his hand move absently; then it came to a sudden halt. He'd felt something that was soft and sticky to the touch. He snatched his hand away, turning his head to see what it was.

'*Jesus!*' he heard himself shout.

Startled, both Pendrake and Fox turned to stare at him. Some of the ground crew rushed round.

Halloran had pulled a handkerchief out of a trouser pocket and was wiping his hand vigorously.

He pointed. 'Will you look at that?'

Everyone looked. A mangled hand was pulped to the fuselage.

'So that's what hit me,' Pendrake said calmly, as if it was something that happened every day. 'I flew through part of the explosion. The Tiffy rocked a bit and I felt some thumps. Thought it was bits of the train. Must have been flying bodies.'

'You flew *through* the explosion?'

Pendrake stared at Halloran. 'I was rather low.'

'I'll wipe it off right away, sir,' a horrified crewman offered.

'You most certainly will not!' Pendrake countered in a harsh voice.

The leading aircraftman stared worriedly at Pendrake, then glanced in appeal at the senior officers, before turning as a last resort to look at the non-commissioned officer in charge of the ground-crew team. Then it was back to Pendrake.

'Leave it,' Pendrake said.

'Sir, that's going to stink to high heaven . . .'

'Leave it,' Pendrake repeated, then turned to Fox. 'I'll be off to debriefing, sir, if that's all right.'

Fox nodded slowly. 'Give you a lift?'

'I'll walk, thank you, sir.'

Once more, Fox nodded.

Pendrake again turned to the aircraftman. 'Don't you dare wipe it off, LAC Thomas.'

He moved away without waiting for a reaction.

They all watched him go. Then Thomas turned to the group captain. 'What should I do, sir?'

'You heard the flight lieutenant, Thomas. Leave it for the moment. I shall be having a word with him.'

Leading Aircraftman Thomas looked relieved. 'Thank you, sir.' But he could not hide a look of revulsion as he glanced at the human remains on the aircraft.

'Are you going to let him leave that . . . that thing on there, sir?' They were on their way back to the car as Halloran spoke.

'Do you carry a rabbit's foot by any chance, Major?'

'No, sir.'

'Do you know anyone who does?'

'Well, yes, but . . .'

'And you have absolutely nothing which serves as one?'

Halloran took a few moments to reply. By then, they had reached the car.

He paused by the door. 'I have a small crucifix,' he eventually replied. 'It was given to me by a young girl . . . in France.'

Fox gave one of his thin smiles. 'I sense a few memories in those words.' He climbed in behind the wheel. 'Let Pendrake have his rabbit's foot. Slipstream and the weather will eventually clean it off. Get in, Major.'

'Grisly stuff, sir,' Halloran said as he obeyed.

'War is grisly, Major, as you well know.'

As the car started off, the NCO, who had been following at a respectful distance, saluted. Fox raised a casual hand to his cap in response. The man returned to supervise the servicing of the Typhoon.

Halloran craned his neck round to glance at them. They were leaving the mangled hand scrupulously alone.

'How did he get that scar?' Halloran asked. 'You said he was not touched when his wife was . . . er killed. Combat?'

'Combat caused the situation, but not the injury. The scar is the result of an argument he lost with the gun-sight of a Hurricane during a wheels-up landing that went very badly wrong. Considering the aircraft was blazing at the time, he's lucky to be alive. Not a burn on him.'

'You were right, sir. He *is* mad, but lucky too.'

'I doubt very much he'd agree . . . that he's lucky.'

'Lucky or mad, he'll do,' Halloran said.

'I had a feeling you might say that,' Fox said. 'Now to persuade him.'

'Persuade him? You expect him to refuse?'

'He'll not refuse a direct order, Major. But I'm not going to make it an order. This has to be his free choice.'

There was a long pause before Halloran said, 'An observation, sir.'

'Observe away.'

'You worry about him.'

'I worry about all my pilots.'

'You know what I mean, sir.'

'Are there none of your people across the Channel

about whom you worry especially?' Fox countered. 'The girl who gave you the crucifix, for example.'

There was another pause. 'The Gestapo got her,' Halloran said flatly.

'My dear chap. I am sorry.'

'Happened a while ago.'

'But you still remember.'

'Yes, sir.'

'I do think, Major,' Fox said after a while, glancing at him, 'that there is more in common between Pendrake and yourself than you'd care to admit.'

Halloran said nothing. In his mind's eye he could still see Jeanne-Anne's face. Although itself a vital part of the preparations for the eventual invasion, the mission was also for her. He would finally be getting the man who had betrayed her.

The 'Spy' was the unit Intelligence officer, a squadron leader called Stanley and whom everyone – including non-commissioned personnel – called 'Baldwin' out of earshot. It didn't help that his hair was rather thin on top.

Stanley had left the service and had already been too old for fighters when war had broken out. Undeterred by such minor problems, he had bluffed his way back in, lying about his age on rejoining, in order to get into combat. The acute shortage of skilled pilots during that fraught period worked in his favour. By the time the truth had been discovered, he already had five kills to his name. Unfortunately, reality had caught up and he'd been shot down, losing his right arm.

He considered himself lucky. His worst night-mare had been the thought of being trapped in a burning aircraft. He'd seen those who had got out too late.

Stanley looked up as Pendrake entered his small, standard-issue office, his eyes seeming bigger behind round, wire-framed spectacles.

'Hullo, Spy,' Pendrake greeted brightly. 'Use your phone?'

Stanley pointed to one of the two on his desk. 'Be my guest.' The other was the scrambler on which he received Intelligence reports.

'Thanks.' Pendrake picked up the instrument. 'This is Flight Lieutenant Pendrake,' he said into it as the operator answered. 'Get me Dispersal, please. Corporal Griffin.'

The was a brief wait as the call was put through and someone ran to find Griffin.

'Corp'l Griffin here, sir,' came the voice, slightly out of breath. Griffin had clearly been running.

'Ah, Corp. That little souvenir I brought back . . . cover it with clear dope, will you? That should hold it in place and kill the smell at the same time.'

'Dope . . . dope it over, sir?' Griffin sounded as if he wanted to vomit.

'We're not out of the stuff, are we?'

'No, sir. There's plenty around.'

Dope was the clear solvent used to stiffen the skins of those aircraft with fabric covering on their fuselages and wings. It was mainly for use on the station flight aircraft, some early-model Hurricanes allocated for the purpose of station air defence, should any raiders attempt to come over. Though the Hurricanes had their own pilots, the Typhoon boys always tried for a temporary swap, while the Hurricane men jealously guarded their mounts.

'Then do it, Corp,' Pendrake ordered.

'Yes, sir.' Griffin was obviously not happy about the idea, but he had little choice in the matter.

'Thank you.' Pendrake hung up.

Stanley was looking at him with interest. 'Souvenir? Smell? Caught a packet, did you?'

'You might say so.'

'Well, I'm not surprised. Got a report on your little jaunt, down the scrambler. I take it you were the one who hit that train?'

'Waste of time trying to surprise you, Spy,' Pendrake said. 'Yes. That's one of mine.'

Stanley passed him a form. 'Here. Fill in the details. Usual stuff.'

Pendrake took a seat and began to write. When he'd finished, Stanley compared the report with some notes he had made.

'It is the same one. The location and time match perfectly. You've raised merry hell over there. That train was full of reinforcements and ammunition for a vital rocket site. I'm not surprised you took some hits yourself. It would have been heavily defended. How many flak cars did it have?'

'I counted three.'

'You went after a train with *three* AA batteries? No wonder you took hits. You'll be pleased to know you've also killed a general, and several of his staff officers. They're going quite berserk and are seeking to take revenge on the French Resistance, whom they accuse of giving us the details of the train's movements.'

Pendrake said nothing about the 'hits' he'd taken.

Stanley would find out soon enough. It would be all over the station like wildfire.

'The Groupie wants to see you when you're finished here,' Stanley added.

'I'm hungry, Spy,' Pendrake pleaded. 'You know what it's like when I come back from a successful foray. I could eat ten horses.'

'He did say you could have breakfast first.'

'A generous soul. Any idea what he wants to see me for?' Pendrake was certain it was about the disembodied hand on his aircraft.

'He didn't say.'

Then Pendrake remembered Halloran. 'There was an American with him at Dispersal. Some US Army Air Force major, but not a pilot. Anything to do with that?'

'He didn't say,' Stanley repeated.

'Trouble with you, Spy, is that you never say anything.'

'Must be my high intelligence.'

'Ha!'

'Now there's a good chap. Run along to breakfast then dash off to see the group captain.' As Pendrake turned to go, Stanley went on, 'Oh Mike . . .' and when Pendrake had paused to look back at him, 'Good work getting that train. You really hurt them.'

'That's what I'm here for . . . to hurt the bastards.'

'How is it with Megan?' Stanley, knowing a little about the tragedy, enquired gently. He studied Pendrake's features with keen interest.

'She's still in my thoughts every day, Spy; every day for the last two years since it . . .' Pendrake paused, face stony, remembering. 'Exactly two years today,

28

you know. It was warmer too. That's why we went on that picnic. No time for a real honeymoon, of course . . . so the picnic was a sort of . . .'

Pendrake abruptly ended the sentence and went out.

Stanley watched him leave, and continued to study the retreating figure of the pilot through the crossed lengths of adhesive tape that starred his window. He knew and understood that Pendrake's outward mask hid an almost unbearable inner turmoil.

'God help you,' he said in a low voice. 'Poor devil . . .'

2

'Had a good breakfast?' Group Captain Fox asked.

'Yes, thank you, sir,' Pendrake answered.

'Sleepy?'

'Not at the moment. I can catch up later and be ready for my next flight.'

'No more ops for you today, Mike.'

Pendrake, still wearing the battledress he'd used for flying, looked surprised.

'But, sir . . .'

'No more flying today,' Fox told him firmly. 'There's an end to that.'

'Yes, sir.'

The group captain leaned back in his chair and studied Pendrake closely. 'How would you like your own squadron to command? Not temporary like the last time you took the job on, but fully confirmed. There's a half ring in it for you.'

Pendrake took this silently for some moments. 'Promotion, sir?' he said at last. 'And a squadron, to boot. Have I upset someone?'

'I can understand your cynicism, but this is genuine. Your talents are sought after.'

Pendrake gave a grim smile. 'Not grown tired of me, have you, sir?'

'You would know of it if I had. This is not an order. You are entirely free to choose.' Fox paused. 'I cannot tell you more at this stage – at least, until you've accepted. However, what I can tell you is that it will give you all the action you could possibly wish for.'

Pendrake looked interested. 'Dangerous?'

'Very.'

'In my place, would you take it on?'

'No. But then I don't have your talents.'

'I'm intrigued. This would not have anything to do with that American ... Major Halloran, would it, sir?'

'I've gone as far as I can, unless you decide to accept.'

'I'll take it.'

Fox nodded. 'Thought you would.'

'You knew I would, sir.'

Again, Fox nodded. 'Yes. But I'll give you one last chance to refuse. There's no going back once you've accepted and once I have told you, there'll be a total security blackout. You will talk to no one about it, except those specified by your orders. Is that clear?'

'Sir.'

'Do you still wish to accept?'

'Yes, sir.'

'Very well.' Fox paused for several seconds, as if making his mind up about something. 'You are to be given command of a special Typhoon squadron, with the confirmed rank of squadron leader. They will be highly modified aircraft. Though the squadron comes under the aegis of No. 100 Special Duties Group in Norfolk, you will in fact be based nowhere in that vicinity. You will also have a certain degree of autonomy – something which will be much to your liking, I shouldn't wonder. The Special Duties attachment is really for the purposes of organizational channels, and security.

'You'll be equally pleased to know that the new sliding bubble canopy you've always wanted will be on these aeroplanes. Like the Tempest, they are Tiffies with the bugs removed. In fact, they're virtually Tempest Vs but more powerful, more agile, and of course faster. But I've been told they are classed as Typhoons, designated "S" for Special.

'You'll be going to a unit deep in the wilds of Gloucestershire tomorrow,' Fox went on, 'where you'll be met by Major Halloran, who will brief you. Your aircraft, and pilots, will be waiting. You will be responsible for their training, and conversion to type if that proves necessary. When you are operational, the squadron will be moved to a forward operating base. You'll be given full details of the mission by Halloran. My part in this has now ended. Questions?'

'A few.'

'Fire away.'

'Why can't I pick my own pilots?'

'That's not an option. You'll have to work with what you find out there.'

'I'll need at least one person who I know can fly the Tiffy, sir. If I've got to get these unknown bods properly trained, I must have this one person I do know and can depend on. If these are such special aircraft, it would be folly to risk a high attrition rate in training. I'll need help. There'll be casualties enough without loading the dice even more.'

Fox thought about this and seemed prepared to agree. 'Anybody in particular in mind?'

'Bingo Wilson, sir. He's up at the moment on a ranger with young Braddock. If you'll give him the gen when they return . . . or I shall, if you prefer.'

'I'll do it. All right, you can have Wilson. But that's it. I'll have to square it somehow with Squadron Leader Mitchell. No squadron commander is going to like losing his star pilot, plus another who's shaping up quite nicely.'

'I did tell Halloran as he left,' Fox continued before Pendrake could reply, 'that if you did agree to take the job on, you might want to take someone with you and he hinted there was room to accommodate such a possibility.'

'Seems as if you had it all mapped out, sir,' Pendrake remarked drily, but managing to make it sound respectful.

'Can't watch over you for ever. I think you're just about ready for a move.'

'Is that what you've been doing? Watching over me?'

'Let's say some station commanders might not have understood you as I have.' Fox gave one of his thinner smiles.

'Am I that much of a problem?'

'Again, I'd prefer to say . . . a trifle unorthodox. Command will do you good.'

Pendrake gave one of his own rare smiles. 'I'll do my best.'

'Which is what I would expect of you.'

'I have a request, sir.'

Fox waited.

'I'd like to keep my current Tiffy,' Pendrake said.

'You mean you wish to hang on to that . . . that thing on the fuselage.' Fox did not look pleased. 'Besides, compared with your new aircraft, it will be under-powered, not as agile, and has the old canopy.'

'It can be modified, sir,' Pendrake insisted. 'They can bring it up to the same standard. It's practically new and has never been damaged in combat . . . and I'm certain work can be done to give it the new canopy.'

Fox was silent.

'I really would like to keep it, sir,' Pendrake added for good measure, pressing his case.

At last Fox said, 'I'll talk to Halloran, and he'll talk to his superiors. But I promise nothing.'

'Good enough for me, sir. Thank you.'

'Anything else?'

'If I can take the Tiffy, I'd like to fly it out. Bingo can travel by road with our gear.'

'Of course. And now, Squadron Leader designate, go and get some rest. Make the most of it. You'll be needing all the rest you can get where you're going.'

'Yes, sir.'

Fox got to his feet and came round the desk. He held out a hand. 'Good luck, Mike. And don't let the Hun get on your tail.'

They shook hands.

'Thank you, sir. I won't.'

Karl-Heinz Ketelheim had succeeded in his desire to be transferred to fighters. Having managed to escape back across the Channel unscathed, he had immediately put in for his transfer and had pursued his goal with single-minded determination. He had shamelessly pulled every string he could, until he'd got his wish. However, his string-pulling had annoyed a senior staff officer so intensely that the officer took revenge by having him posted to the Eastern Front, hoping the Russians would do what the British had not and put an end to his career – permanently.

But Ketelheim had thrived in the eastern theatre. He had revelled in his mastery of his Me-109 and had found the shooting gallery of the Russian front much to his liking. To the chagrin of the staff officer, Ketelheim had returned a highly decorated major sporting a couple of top-grade Iron Crosses, with fifty air victories to his credit, and worse, without a scratch on him. Mere days after Ketelheim's return, the staff officer was killed in a bombing raid while on an inspection tour of Luftwaffe units near the Ardennes.

Ketelheim was further promoted and was returned to France, having been given command of a new unit flying Focke-Wulf Fw-190s. In addition to its normal defensive duties, the unit had a special task: the defence of the airspace above a particular area of Normandy. Within that airspace was a château. He had been told that at all costs the area was barred to all aircraft, including those with German markings making unauthorized entry. All Allied planes were pounced upon with alacrity, and two light transport aircraft with Luftwaffe markings that had failed to obey the ruling on unauthorized entry had also been shot down.

Ketelheim took his task very seriously indeed.

Pendrake could not have known that of the two aircraft he'd spotted high above him after he had destroyed the train, one had been piloted by Ketelheim, the man who had killed Megan.

* * *

Bingo Wilson returned from the ranger mission. Braddock did not. Visibly affected by the death of his wingman, Wilson reported to Stanley.

'I warned him over and over, Spy,' he began. 'I told him to stick to me. Then he spotted a 190 stooging around low down. Instead of checking for another as he should have, he broke formation and went after what he thought was a sitting duck. He ignored my orders to return. He was desperate to get a kill, you see. The young fool.'

Wilson paused while Stanley, doing what he was very good at, listened and watched him intently.

'Then before he could even get a good line,' Wilson continued, 'this . . . this second 190 came down like a shark. One slash and Braddock was a flamer. He never got out. I told him . . . I *told* him,' Wilson ended softly.

'Can't blame yourself, Bingo.'

'I was the leader, Spy. My responsibility.'

'You could hardly have got out of your aircraft and dragged him back by the scruff of his neck,' Stanley pointed out reasonably. 'Happens all too often, old son. Eager young sprogs wanting to make a mark. Easy meat for wily veterans.'

A miserable Wilson nodded in agreement. 'Someone like that must have done it. No wasted action. It was down and *bam*, goodbye Braddock. Whoever was flying that 190 knew his business. And another thing, the one Braddock was after broke away with perfect timing, as if it had all been set up. It was an assassination.'

'Aces of some sort?'

'Must be. There was something else very odd too.

They just circled and then turned away, ignoring me completely. I can't believe they didn't spot me rushing down on them; but they weren't interested. They'd had a good start and I couldn't catch up. Besides, fuel was getting low. My Typhoon didn't frighten them. It was as if they knew there'd be another time.'

'Or were under instructions not to leave the area,' Stanley said mysteriously.

Wilson stared at him. 'What do you mean, Spy?'

'Random thoughts,' Stanley replied vaguely. 'All right, Bingo. Fill in the form then hop over to see the group captain.'

Wilson looked anxious. 'I'm being carpeted?'

'Good Lord, no. He wants to see you about something else entirely.'

'Any idea?'

'Why not wait until you see him? There's a good chap.'

Wilson gave up and began to write his report.

The WAAF officer opened the door to Group Captain Fox's office and announced, 'Flying Officer Wilson's here, sir.'

'Thank you, Miss Johnson. Send him in.'

'Sir.' Then the young woman stood back for Wilson to enter, closing the door after him.

Wilson, cap smartly on, marched in and brought himself to attention. He saluted briskly.

'At ease, Flying Officer Wilson,' Fox said. 'And don't look so worried, man. I'm not about to tear you off a strip. I heard about Braddock. Sorry it happened. Not your fault. I've lost a couple of eager beavers myself in

my time, for exactly the same reason. You're not the
first, and you won't be the last flight leader to lose a
man that way. Doesn't help the way you feel, I know.
But there you have it.'

'Yes, sir.'

'Well, Bingo. Think you're about ready to become
a flight lieutenant?'

Wilson, though ordered to stand at ease, was still
trying to maintain a smartly respectful stance. His eyes
grew round in surprise.

'Well, sir . . . I mean, sir . . . I . . .'

'Yes?'

'Well, sir, there are others of greater seniority on
the squadron . . .'

'Are you doubting my ability to choose whom I
wish to promote?'

'No, sir! And . . . thank you, sir.'

'Thank you, Flying Officer Wilson,' Fox said drily.
'You won't have to worry about offending anyone on
the squadron. You'll be leaving . . .'

His resolve weakened, Wilson broke his stance to
look aghast at the group captain. 'Leaving, sir?' He
sounded horrified. 'But . . .'

'Damn it, man! Let me finish.'

Wilson straightened sharply. 'Sir!'

'Yes. Well. Now where were we? Ah, yes, Mike
Pendrake is moving to take command of a new
squadron, with a new rank. He asked for you, though
God knows why.'

Wilson gave an unrestrained grin. 'Ah well, that's
different, sir.'

'I'm so glad you approve, Mr Wilson. I feel much
better now.'

Wilson glanced at the group captain warily, but his superior's expression gave nothing away.

'The necessary arangements are already being made,' Fox went on. 'You will be briefed by Pendrake. You will discuss this posting with no one. There are no exceptions, save those with the need to know, until you arrive at your new unit. Am I perfectly clear?'

'Yes, sir!'

'That's it, Bingo. You leave tomorrow.'

'Yes, sir . . . and sir . . .'

Fox waited expectantly.

'I've enjoyed being here. I've enjoyed being in this command.'

'I'm sorry to see you go, young Wilson. Look after yourself and look after Mike. Give him all the support you can.'

'You can count on me, sir.'

Fox nodded. Wilson again drew himself to attention, gave another snappy salute and went out.

The first thing he did was to go in search of Pendrake, whom he found in the mess.

'Heard about Braddock,' Pendrake greeted him. 'Sorry.'

Wilson nodded soberly. 'Mitch Mitchell's got another letter to write to one more family. I think I ought to . . . you know . . . write one of my own to them. More personal. After all, I was the last friendly person to see him alive.'

'If you can handle it, it's a nice thought.' Then Pendrake went on, 'I take it you've just seen the old man?'

'Yes.'

'And how do you feel about coming along?'

'Sounds interesting.'

'It will be. We've got brand-new special Tiffies.'

Wilson looked suspicious. 'And what have we done to deserve such largesse?'

'All in good time.'

'Ah. Dangerous, is it?'

'Would I lead you into danger?'

'Frequently.'

They grinned.

'Come on,' Pendrake said. 'Let's go and drink to lost ones. Tomorrow will come soon enough.'

'Yes. Let's.' Wilson knew what Pendrake really meant.

The Château de St Sauveur was a magnificent mid-seventeenth-century edifice secluded by thick woods, in the wooded heart of Normandy. A two-storey, U-shaped building, it stood serenely within perfectly landscaped grounds, an oasis of unmatched calm in the insanity of a war that was tearing the rest of the world apart. It was as if the years of madness belonged to a totally different world, for not a blemish marred its structure. No shell, no bomb, no bullet had touched it. But this air of wholesome perfection hid a far from pleasant reality.

The manicured gardens were dotted with anti-aircraft weaponry. A solid platform had been built at the back like an outward extension of the eaves, upon which were mounted two four-barrelled cannons, again for air defence. At the ornate gates at the end of the long drive, a company of Panther tanks stood guard. Positioned on each side of the approach road, their formidable 75mm gun barrels pointed menacingly along it. Anything suspicious coming along that road would be blown to bits within seconds. They had also perfected a routine whereby they could move from a defensive to an offensive posture with alarming rapidity.

Within the woods themselves, more tanks lay in wait for any force stupid enough to attempt an assault. These were backed by several platoons of battle-hardened, well-armed Waffen-SS troops positioned throughout the area in a series of concentric defensive rings. It was defence in great depth. The Waffen-SS infantry wore the standard grey-green uniform, sometimes with a camouflaged smock. All the tank crews wore black.

Within the immediate environs of the château itself, and responsible for its protection, was a praetorian guard of more black-uniformed SS men. By themselves, they could stop a small army. They were well aware of that fact and were arrogantly proud of it. Like their comrades in the woods outside the château, they displayed a contempt for the Allied forces that was matched only by their equally naked contempt for their own countrymen who served in the Wehrmacht.

But the true horror existed out of sight, deep within the bowels of the château. Dungeons that had two hundred years before been converted for the infinitely more civilized purpose of housing an extensive wine cellar had in part been restored to their former use. It was here that the local Gestapo went to work on their victims. There was something obscene about the horrors they perpetrated upon their fellow human beings, while from time to time drinking the rare and lovingly collected wines from cut glasses, commandeered from the legitimate owners of the château. The family of the

Baron de Malzey were virtual prisoners in their own home and were confined to one of the less attractive wings, under SS guard.

Two misguided attempts by some Resistance groups to rescue the family had ended disastrously, with heavy casualties and prisoners taken. There were other attempts, but for very different reasons. They, too, had failed spectacularly.

The new lord of the commandeered château was Emile Boucheron. Before the war, Boucheron had made a precarious living as a small-time garage owner and motor mechanic; but he had prospered enormously after the defeat of France. He was a man for whom the right time had come. Having decided he had found the winning side, he had readily offered to do business catering for some of the transport needs of the new overlords. This began in a small way, but soon burgeoned into a highly profitable operation. Before long, he was employing like-minded people. His influence with the invaders grew.

Then he discovered a source of even greater power. From the days when he had plied his one-man trade, he drew upon his knowledge of both the area and the people. He could tell with unerring accuracy those who would either support or be active in the Resistance, and those who would collaborate. He knew where they lived. He knew their families. He built up an impressive network of informers, people who owed him favours. His influence with his new-found friends became stratospheric. Soon, even general officers sought his company and advice on local matters. When the Château de St Sauveur was eventually acquired, Boucheron was installed as its new lord.

This arrangement served several purposes. The château provided the Gestapo with a handy operating base; it became an intelligence headquarters; it was a convenient and sumptuous location for the lavish entertaining of the Occupation elite; it gave visiting senior officers a place to stay; but most importantly of all, it afforded protection to Boucheron and his family, who could now never travel without a powerful escort. His enemies were many.

As the fortunes of the war began to turn against his protectors, so did he become more aware of his own vulnerability. A vaguely entertained hope that he would be taken to Germany soon died, and he was left with no illusions that his safety would be assured should a retreat become inevitable. It was therefore greatly in his interest that the Allies failed in their endeavours. To this end, he applied himself with great energy in ferreting out any items of intelligence that would be of use to his patrons, particularly anything to do with a possible invasion from across the Channel.

Boucheron's zeal surprised even the hardened thugs of the Gestapo. The more astute knew he was being driven by fear for his own skin but most merely made use of him and thought little more of it.

Boucheron had himself attended many torture sessions and had once actually outlasted his own SS bodyguards, who had been too sickened to continue watching and listening to the appalling screams. On that occasion, Boucheron had simply joined the torturers, between sessions, in depleting the stock of the baron's wine collection.

* * *

Jeanne-Anne Flahaut was just fifteen when she first met Halloran, two years before the outbreak of war, in Paris. One of the adventurous American students who had decided to 'do Europe' before settling into a pre-mapped career that had begun at an Ivy League university, Halloran had found himself warming to the quietly confident, green-eyed blonde he'd been introduced to by a group of new-found Parisian friends. She had seemed much older than her years.

A friendship had grown between them, but nothing more at that stage. Halloran travelled round France, doing odd jobs, living in different areas for a while and learning the language, which was eventually to stand him in good stead. He wrote to Jeanne-Anne frequently. He did not, like many of his peers, get involved in the civil war in Spain, and he was still in France when the first shots of the major war to come were fired on the Polish border.

In Paris he again met Jeanne-Anne, now seventeen. Everyone knew, she told him, that the war would eventually come to France and that if her country was invaded she would join the Resistance. People were already talking about doing so. It was also at that time that he found out that Jeanne-Anne was nearly eight years younger than him. Their friendship continued to remain platonic, much to Jeanne-Anne's annoyance. When the Wehrmacht inevitably stormed across the border, she was as good as her word and joined the Resistance. To celebrate doing so, she seduced him in an open field.

By now fluent in French, Halloran made his way to England and offered his services to the Crown, just as many of his compatriots were offering themselves as pilots for the RAF. His offer was taken up with alacrity. His knowledge of France and the language would be of great use, he was told. It was the beginning of a new kind of life he had never expected and one which turned him into Fer de Lance. It was also one that would eventually lead him to seek a terrible revenge upon the man into whose clutches Jeanne-Anne would subsequently fall.

Everyone at the Château de St Sauveur who had seen her would remember the day Jeanne-Anne was brought in. She had been arrested on a back road by two of the château's Gestapo men in a prowling car. They found material on her that indisputably linked her with the Resistance.

The SS guards in the grounds had stared in frank admiration at the proud and shapely young blonde, each with a sense of regret that she'd had nothing better to do with her time than join the Resistance. To them, it was a shameful waste.

Boucheron had been in residence that day and on seeing her brought in had intervened, saying he knew her. Perhaps he could help. He might get more information out of her, he suggested. The Gestapo allowed him some time.

He took her into a study. 'You don't remember me, do you?' he began.

He was a big man, and with his new status he had developed a passion for tight double-breasted suits that made him look like a Chicago gangster. His large face, topped by a head of lank, black hair, seemed permanently damp, as if the suit was trying to squeeze all the moisture out of him. His nose tended to shine when he got sexually excited and already it had begun to glisten. Once, twice, he drew his tongue slowly across his lower lip, as if priming it for action.

She stared at him. 'Should I?' she said. 'And why would I want to know someone who betrays his people to the Boche just so he can live in this place? What's it like? Stealing someone's home?'

Boucheron made a great show of being conspiratorial. 'Shhh! Keep your voice down! Many of them understand French, you know.'

'Why should I care?'

'You should. Because I can get you away from here.'

She laughed at him. 'From this fortress? With all your filthy SS infesting the countryside?'

'I have the authority of a general in this district,' he said pompously.

'The SS only listen to their generals,' she snapped back scathingly. 'They don't even obey the ordinary German generals. Why should they obey you?'

'They need me . . .'

'Yes. To betray your people! Collaborator!'

'Keep your voice down!' he hissed. 'And don't act high and mighty with me! I can help you. I am trying to save your life. But you must do something for me . . .'

'Of course,' she said contemptuously. 'And now it comes. Your eyes have been undressing me . . .'

'Don't be a fool! That was not what I meant. I can tell them you would be of better use to us if we let you go. You can become part of my network. I can tell them you will be our infiltrator. I will say I can

force you to work for me because I have something
I can use to pressure you.'

She stared at him. 'You have nothing. So how will
they believe you? And what makes you think I would
do anything once I am away from here?'

'I would not expect you to,' he said, genuinely
surprising her. 'I want you to let the Resistance know
I helped you escape . . .'

Understanding dawned. 'Your insurance policy. So
you do not believe your Boche are so invincible? You
are trying to save your miserable skin . . .'

'Listen! If I can get you away, I have much information that the Allies can use after the war . . .'

'So now you betray your friends.'

Boucheron had small, mean eyes. They became even
nastier. 'Don't play games with me, my girl. Have you
any idea what these people will do to you, a beautiful
young woman, to get you to talk? You will not die
quickly, I assure you. Aren't you afraid?'

'Of course I'm afraid.'

'Then you will do as I say. You must. Anything I
say.'

She said nothing.

His eyes studied her body. Again, his tongue stroked
his lip. 'You should know me, you know. Your father
stopped at my garage before the war, for fuel. Your
family was going to the coast on holiday. To La Baule.
You were a little girl then, just about to enter your
teens, but already very pretty. You, your father, and
your mother . . . a Jew.'

She paled. 'Wh . . . what?'

'You can't deny it. I know many things. People
gossip all the time. I know that your mother is dead.

47

She was pregnant that day. An unexpected baby. She and the baby died during childbirth. Your mother had married against her family's wishes and into another religion. They rejected her. You were brought up as a Catholic, your father's religion. But that won't save you if I tell my friends out there. To them, half a Jew, even a Catholic one, is still a Jew. After all, we all know with Jews the race is vested in the mother. They will treat you harshly enough as a member of the Resistance; but as a Jew . . .' There was no need for him to finish the sentence.

Jeanne-Anne had begun to tremble slightly.

Then Boucheron once more became reasonable. 'Listen to me. Do as I say. Let me help.'

There was a sharp knock on the door. 'Monsieur Boucheron! Are you all right?'

'I'm fine,' the Frenchman called. 'They're getting impatient,' he continued urgently to her. 'Well? Do you agree to my suggestions?' His eyes roved over her body yet again. Nose and face were glistening now. 'I think we should seal our . . . pact in a friendly manner. Don't you?'

There was no mistaking his intentions. Having exposed her secret, he now clearly thought she would do anything to avoid having it betrayed to the Gestapo.

She did what he never expected. She spat full into the large, moist face.

'Krötemann!' he yelled, reddening with anger as he wiped at the spittle with a large white handkerchief. The cruel eyes kept staring at her.

One of the Gestapo men came charging in, pistol drawn.

'Take the Jew slut down!' Boucheron ordered.

Krötemann stared from Jeanne-Anne to Boucheron disbelievingly. 'What? A Jew? Impossible.'

'You think she looks a picture of Aryan perfection?' he snarled. 'I know her family. Her mother was a Jew.'

Krötemann again looked from one to the other. Jeanne-Anne was glaring with unwavering contempt at Boucheron. With ludicrous correctness, he asked her, 'Is this true?'

'Yes,' she replied calmly.

Krötemann's correctness suddenly changed. '*Come on, bitch!*' he shouted. '*Move!*'

Boucheron followed them out. 'I'm coming to watch.'

In the dungeon, among all those bottles of rare wines, Boucheron watched as Jeanne-Anne was abused by her torturers. She was raped, her four interrogators taking turns, beaten, and raped again until her cries became piteous whimpers. It was this that even the SS bodyguards who had accompanied Boucheron could no longer stomach. In their minds, they still saw the beautiful young woman; not the mangled thing lying in her blood and urine, and who now whimpered like a badly injured puppy.

She never divulged any information.

Boucheron drank wine.

They did not finish the job of killing her. Instead, they took her out, flung her into a motorcycle sidecar and, under escort, drove her into the countryside. They dumped her by the side of a narrow road and left her there.

Several hours later a Resistance patrol found her

crawling along, an inch at a time. She'd been willing herself to stay alive. They took the wreck of her body to her beloved Fer de Lance.

She remained alive just long enough to tell him, 'Boucheron.'

'They're ready for you now, Major. *Major?*'

Halloran jerked out of his reverie as the hand shook him by the shoulder. He looked up at the young Wren officer, his eyes slowing coming back into focus.

She stared at him anxiously. 'Are you all right, Major Halloran?'

'Yes, yes,' he said, getting slowly to his feet. 'Sorry. I guess I must have fallen asleep or something.'

'You certainly looked as if you were a long way away.'

Without thinking, Halloran placed a hand to his upper chest and felt the shape of the small crucifix beneath his clothes. Strange, he reflected, suddenly remembering her like that; the way they had found her. He felt a sudden heat behind his eyes.

The Wren continued to study him anxiously and misinterpreted the look in them. 'You seem in pain, Major. Is it an old wound?'

'You could say that.'

She began to reach forward solicitously. 'Need any help walking?'

'No thanks. I'm really OK. Guess I'd better hear what the brass has to say.'

He followed her down the corridor to the room where the senior staff officers awaited him.

3

Pendrake was about seven miles from the airfield, with
the ancient city of Cirencester, at the junction of the
Fosse and Ermine Ways, passing his right wingtip. He
made his approach at full throttle – 'up the firewall' as
an American Eagle Squadron pilot once described it to
him – keeping the Typhoon low, almost skimming the
ground. They wouldn't know he was there until the
moment of his arrival.

Word had come from Halloran that modification
to 'S' standard had been approved. He was thus very
pleased that he had been able to take his own aircraft,
truncated hand included, to the new posting.

Even this far inland, he still kept a constant lookout
and it was during one of his repeated searches of the
sky that he spotted two specks bearing down upon
him, from the higher reaches. He was very aware
that pilots of other Allied aircraft, and the gunners
on the ground, sometimes tended to have difficulty
in recognizing the Typhoon.

It was not as familiar a shape as the Spitfire or
Hurricane, and he knew of at least one occasion when
it was misidentified as a Focke-Wulf Fw-190 and the
hapless pilot had found himself on the receiving end
of the concentrated attention of four Spitfires. Only

his flying skill had saved him, for by the time the eager Spitfire pilots had finally paused long enough to identify the RAF roundels, the Typhoon was no longer airworthy and the pilot had been forced to make an unscheduled descent by parachute.

Enraged, he had muttered bitterly when picked up that he should have given the Spits a dose of his cannon.

Pendrake kept a wary eye on the approaching aircraft, but did not alter his course. If they were Allied planes and they were incompetent enough to attack him, he would fight back. They *would* get a dose of *his* cannon.

They turned out to be Spitfires and, using the speed they had generated in the dive to catch up, peeled off beautifully left and right on either side of him, showing off the graceful, elliptical planform of their wings. They formatted on him, struggling slightly to keep up.

He waggled his wings at them as the greater top speed of the Typhoon began to leave them behind. They continued to maintain position, trailing him towards the airfield.

He took the Typhoon down to almost ground-scraping height as it bellowed its way along the runway. Then he broke smartly left, his wingtip making those watching gasp as they believed it was about to touch the grass beyond the runway, or that the aircraft itself would slam into one of the camouflaged buildings. But the Typhoon raced round the circuit to line up perfectly once more.

As he was turning, Pendrake saw that the trailing Spitfires had followed his approach pattern and had done the break in perfect formation, to follow him in for the landing. He lowered his wheels and landed smoothly. He was taxiing off the runway when the pair of Spitfires touched down.

On the break, he had seen a line of gleaming aircraft, positioned in a neat row in Dispersal. As he now taxied towards them, he saw they were the new S-type Typhoons. All were painted a uniform black, which gave them a powerful air of palpable menace, even as they stood waiting silently. Their bubble canopies glinted dully in the bright sun of a cold but clear day. Their RAF roundels and serial numbers were of such low visibility, the markings seemed to disappear into the paintwork. He realized that from the ground or in the air, it would be as if there were no markings at all. There were eighteen in all.

They were, he thought, absolutely beautiful and he felt a thrill of anticipation surge through him. Now that he had landed and had actually seen the aircraft, the full meaning of what had occurred barely twenty-four hours before began to make an impression upon him. These were *his* to command.

A member of the ground crew directed him to a parking position at the head of the line of black Typhoons. He cut the engine, removed his helmet and paused for a moment to savour the sudden quiet, then climbed out. As he did so, he was aware that two more of the ground crew had joined the first. They were staring at a spot on the fuselage.

'It's what you think it is,' he said to them.

They jumped at the sound of his voice, drew to attention and saluted. One of them looked ill.

He waved a hand at them to relax.

The ill-looking one, a senior aircraftman, said, 'It's not really a hand, is it, sir? It's one of those things you get in a joke shop, isn't it, really?'

'What's your name?'

'Henderson, sir.'

'Well, SAC Henderson, it's not from a joke shop. It comes from a German on a train. Not sure of his rank, though. It must not be removed. Understand?'

'Yes . . . yes, sir!'

The other two stared at him dumbfounded. He left all three to it and began walking. Before long, everyone on the station would know of the incident. It was what he wanted.

He'd only gone a few yards when a staff car approached. A short distance away, the two Spitfires that had followed him in were being marshalled to a stop.

The staff car came to a halt and a wing commander, almost three inches shorter than Pendrake, climbed out. He was not wearing pilot's wings.

The officer walked up to him. 'Squadron Leader Pendrake?'

Pendrake stood to attention. 'Yes, sir.'

'That was quite an approach. Impressive. You had everybody gawping. And you can relax. I'm not really CO here. You are. My role is to see that the administration of this unit runs smoothly, while you get on with whatever it is they sent you here to do.' The wing commander held out a hand. 'My name's David Rhys.' There was a pleasant manner about Rhys that Pendrake found agreeable.

They shook hands. 'Mike Pendrake.'

'Yes. We were advised. Hop in, Mike. I'll take you to . . .'

'Just a moment.'

Rhys paused to follow Pendrake's gaze. The Spitfire pilots were hurrying towards them, helmets still on, leads flailing as they jogged. Pendrake removed his Mae West as they waited, took his forage cap from a pocket and put it on.

The Spitfire pilots stopped when they had reached the car, whipped off their helmets and snapped to attention. Both had the rank of flying officer.

'Sean Kelly,' one announced with an American accent, grinning. 'Boston Irish. And next to me is Jim Dodson, Yorkshire terrier. We're your welcoming committee, if you're Squadron Leader Pendrake.'

They were trying not to stare at his scar.

'I am,' Pendrake said. He glanced at Rhys. 'Know these two?'

Rhys nodded. 'Flew in yesterday. I authorized their . . . patrol.'

'I see. At ease, gentlemen,' Pendrake said to them. 'I thought I was about to have been the victim of poor recognition.'

'And had you been, sir,' Kelly asked boldly, 'would you have fought back?'

'Let's put it this way, Kelly. You would have found yourself trying to dodge 20mm cannon shells. You might not have succeeded.'

Kelly stared at him. 'You mean that . . . er, sir?'

'I never joke about combat. If you are to be part of my squadron, you'll soon find that out. Have you two been assigned to me?'

'Yes, sir,' Dodson answered. 'We were told we

had been selected for a new squadron and to leave immediately. At least they let us take our Spits.'

'From now on, you'll be flying something else, gentlemen.' Pendrake pointed to the line of Typhoons. 'Those are to be your new mounts.'

'We've had a good look at them, sir,' Kelly said. 'We all have. They look like mean beasts.'

'They are. Possibly more powerful than anything you've flown before, and very different to the Spitfire. Do you have any Typhoon time? Either of you?'

Kelly shook his head. 'Hurrybacks and Spits.'

'I was on a Typhoon conversion course,' Dodson ventured. 'I'd come from Hurrys. Then I was sent on to Spits.'

Pendrake looked at him. 'Why?'

'Had a problem with the take-off, sir. I was always swinging to the right – couldn't seem to compensate in time.'

'So they send you back to something even more powerful?' Pendrake shook his head slowly in disbelief.

'Perhaps they thought every little would help,' the Englishman explained awkwardly.

'Perhaps.' Pendrake looked at Kelly. 'Earlier, you said "we all have". Are the other pilots all here?'

'They must be, sir. There's twenty of us.'

'Very well, gentlemen. As you elected to be my welcoming committee, you can now go and round up all pilots. I'll see them in the briefing room in one hour. I now have things to discuss with Wing Commander Rhys. See you then.'

'Yes, sir,' they said together.

Pendrake and Rhys got into the car.

As it drew away, Kelly turned to look at Pendrake's Typhoon. 'What are those guys staring at?'

Dodson looked. There was a small crowd by the aircraft. 'Let's see.'

As they approached, the men parted to allow them through.

Kelly stared at the object of everyone's attention. 'Is this for real?'

Henderson answered him. 'The squadron CO said it was, sir. Said it came off a German on a train. He was joking, wasn't he, sir?'

'I dunno, guys,' Kelly said. 'One thing I reckon our new CO doesn't do, that's make jokes like this. Came off a German on a train, you said.'

'Yes, sir,' Henderson replied. 'He also ordered us to leave it just where it is. If you look closely, sir, it's been doped over to keep it in place.'

Kelly peered at the remains. 'But how in hell did that get there? Did he just put it on?'

'I've heard his name before,' Dodson was saying thoughtfully. 'I think it was on my old Hurricane squadron. I heard someone talking about ...' he paused, looked at the ground crew and said, 'Sorry. We'd better leave you to your work.'

As they moved away, followed by uncomprehending stares, Kelly said, 'What's going on?'

'It may only have been someone shooting a line but if it's true, it's personal to the CO. I don't really want to gossip with the ground crew about him.'

'I get your drift. So? What's the story?'

'The way I heard it, he was married for two days when he and his wife got caught up in a freak bombing. Wasn't really a raid at all. Just one Heinkel, out in the country somewhere, I think. Story is it got lost and just dumped its bombs. She was killed.'

'The poor guy.'

'He went berserk in the air, killing anything with a black cross on it, moving or not.'

'Doesn't surprise me.'

'Mark you, I'm assuming it's the same Pendrake. Then on the Spit squadron, I heard he'd gone on to Typhoons and was a champion trainbuster. He's flown both the Spit and the Hurry, and now he's come here with a Typhoon to command his own squadron of Tiffies. It must be the same bloke.'

Kelly grabbed Dodson by the shoulders, turning him round. 'Now hold on. You're not telling me he attacked a train, it blew up, bodies flew through the air and one hit his plane?'

'Why not? He said it came off a train.'

'Aw, come on! He'd have to fly so low . . .' Kelly paused, remembering Pendrake's ultra-low approach.

Dodson watched comprehension slowly dawning on his companion's face. 'Exactly,' he said.

'Jeez!' Kelly said. 'What have we gotten ourselves into?'

'We're going to find out, Boston. We're going to find out.'

'Jeez!'

In the car, Rhys said, 'What would you like to do first?'

'I'll resist the temptation to inspect the aircraft immediately, sir,' Pendrake replied. 'I'll do that later. I want a quick check of the pilot records. What have they sent me?'

'A motley lot. Some very experienced, some fairly, and some not at all. You've got a mixed bag. In addition to the British contingent, you've got two Australians, a New Zealander, another American to add to Kelly, a Canadian, a Pole . . .'

'A Pole! Can he speak the kind of English that I can understand in the air? My Polish is . . . my Polish isn't.'

Rhys's features creased in a slow smile. 'He speaks it fairly well – when he wants to – and understands it exceedingly well – when he wants to.

'That's all I need.'

'Old Josef's a good type. Hates Nazis. Likes killing them.'

'Just the sort of man I want. Any more?'

'There's a Frenchman, and another Frenchman, only this one's from across the water. Quebecois. He's very fond of telling his fellow Canadian, Bill Mackenzie, that after the war Quebec will be free.'

'Does he actually mean that?'

'Oh, I believe as a French Canadian he enjoys ribbing Mackenzie. But you never know. This war will change many things. The world will change. Even in this country, things will never be the same again. The social strata will alter radically. It may not happen overnight, but it will do so quicker than many expect. But we've the job with the Hun to attend to first.'

There was a lull in the conversation as Rhys pulled over to allow a petrol bowser going in the opposite direction to pass.

'So practically half of my complement of pilots are Commonwealth,' Pendrake said as they began to move again, 'and Allied.'

'Will that cause you problems?'

'Absolutely not. All I want from them is the ability to fly the Typhoon without killing themselves, and to kill the enemy. To enable them to do that, I must turn them into hawks. Their souls will belong to me.'

Rhys glanced at Pendrake, noting how the scar seemed to have become a livid weal that faded again so quickly, Rhys thought his eyes had played tricks on him.

'Young Karen will help you with the paperwork,' Rhys went on. 'She . . .'

'Young Karen?'

'Yes. Karen Lewis. Section officer. She was sent to look after the bumf. Bright. Very bright indeed. I believe she was seconded from the Air Ministry. Powerful people are moving things for you. They got me here. I was staff officer to an air vice-marshal before this little lot. Karen's already arranged all the relevant documents for you. She's got an office next to yours. We're going over now . . . unless you'd prefer to go to the mess first.'

'No, sir. I might as well start right away if I've got to meet my pilots within the hour.'

'Fine. And by the way, no need for the "sir". I'm David. In reality, you probably outrank me. I'm actually a university lecturer. I'm thirty-seven. When they pulled me in, they weren't sure what rank to give me. I think they felt wing commander was just high enough, so as not to make things awkward.' Rhys smiled deprecatingly.

'I'm sure your rank is deservedly earned,' Pendrake said. 'But I'll compromise. In private, it's David. Before the men and any junior ranks, it's "sir".'

'Fair enough,' Rhys said awkwardly after awhile. 'But you're making this rather difficult for me. When I was with the AVM it was easy. I was the subordinate. Here, you're the operational commander. I know nothing about combat.'

'You've got skills I haven't, or you wouldn't be here. Let's do this together, and we'll be fine.'

'Fair enough,' Rhys said again.

'I'm expecting two others,' Pendrake said. 'A US Army Air Force major . . .'

'Ah yes. Major Halloran. He's actually on his way. An Anson's bringing him over. He should be here by the time you're ready to meet the pilots.'

'Good. Then there's Bingo Wilson. He's my deputy. He'll be coming by road. I expect him to arrive sometime this afternoon.'

'We'll look out for him,' Rhys said. 'Ah. Here we are.'

They had pulled up before a long, low building, brick-built and camouflaged.

'Your fully self-contained headquarters,' Rhys went on as they climbed out of the car. 'It's been furnished to meet all your operational needs. Your offices are at this end, close to the entrance. The briefing room's at the far end.'

'Someone's certainly been preparing for this for some time.'

'Oh, I don't think it was built especially for your particular mission. But it was here, and available. It's been used before, I believe, for other . . . special missions.'

Pendrake looked at the building and nodded. 'By the way, talking of missions . . . I don't think it's a good idea to leave the aircraft where they are. They look nice and shiny and impressive lined up so neatly for inspection. But I'd feel more at ease if they were split into pairs and dispersed haphazardly about the place, when they're not in the hangars being repaired.

'They make juicy targets as they are. I know we're well away from the bombers and that the old raids are now virtually non-existent. But there are still intruders. I've been doing single intrusions myself. It takes only one . . . and you never know where a bomb might come from. Believe me, I do know what I'm talking about.'

Pendrake turned from his scrutiny of the building to look at Rhys, who thought he saw a strange intensity in the pilot's eyes.

'I'll have it done,' Rhys promised.

'Thanks. And my own aircraft is to be modified to "S" standard.'

'That's in hand. As a matter of fact, they're moving it into a hangar as we speak.'

'Thank you, David,' Pendrake repeated. 'Do you see? You've already proved my point. The team's working. Now, let's meet Section Officer Lewis.'

Karen Lewis was a rare creature. Though aware she was beautiful, she saw little reason to preen, or to make a song and dance about it. She had scant time for make-up and the only concession she made to beautifying herself was a touch of lipstick that was less red than contemporary fashion dictated. Her male admirers, who were legion, fell into two camps. Some were of the opinion that hers was the face of an angel. The others, that the reality surpassed even that description.

Fortunate to have been endowed with flawless skin, jet-black hair and vivid blue eyes, she never failed to impress at the very first meeting. Her body, while not slim enough to be described as willowy, had an unconscious sinuosity of movement that generated awe. Her service shoes, built for utility rather than beauty, could do nothing to detract from the perfection of her legs. In the person of Karen Lewis, nature had won hands down. She was just nineteen.

It was thus something of a shock to Rhys when he introduced her to Pendrake that, though pleasant and polite enough, the pilot failed to register the slightest flicker of interest in her, other than in the question of her duties. And though from what he knew of her Rhys was aware she never traded on her beauty, he thought he detected a slight disappointment in her.

'I'll leave you to it,' he now said, glancing from one to the other. 'And I'll have those aircraft dispersed,' he added to Pendrake. He held out a hand. 'Good luck.'

'Thank you, sir,' Pendrake said as they shook hands.

Pendrake waited until Rhys had gone before saying, 'Well, Miss Lewis, shall we get started?'

'Yes, sir.' She had a warm, comforting voice. 'This is your office,' she continued, pointing to a connecting door. 'I assumed you'd want to see all the pilot records. They're on your desk, with the experience of each individual itemized and graded.'

'My word,' he said as they entered the surprisingly well-appointed room. 'This is better than the station commander's at my old unit.'

'I believe it was an American general's office, sir.

There were some people here last year, working on an operation.'

'Were they?' Pendrake was astute enough not to ask whether she knew more about it. 'Well, it's our turn.' He looked at the large desk, on which documents were neatly arranged. 'My pilots?'

'Yes, sir.'

He went over to the polished-walnut swivel chair with its padded leather seat and sat down, testing it with a couple of swings to left and right. 'Nice being an American general. Very pleasing. And now, the paperwork.'

She came across to the desk and stood next to him, looking over his shoulder. He sensed her glancing at his epaulettes. They still bore the two blue rings of a flight lieutenant.

'I know,' he said. 'I'm improperly dressed. No time yet to sew the new ones on.'

'I thought that might be the case, sir. I've got the new ones, so if you'll give me your battledress blouse, I'll have them put on.'

'You must be a mind-reader, Lewis. But you don't have to . . .'

'I'd be happy to, sir.'

Pendrake gave in. 'All right.' He removed the blouse and handed it to her. 'I'll look through these records in the meantime.'

'Very good, sir.'

He did not look up as she went out, already engrossed in studying the flying experience of the pilots he'd been given to command.

Lewis had done a thorough job of collating the information. Rhys was certainly right about her.

After a quick skim through the detailed breakdown by pilot, matters took a distinct turn for the worse; not because she had been inefficient, but because her remarkable efficiency had exposed to the light of day the motives of those who had set up the mission.

He waited for her to return, quietly fuming.

She entered with a smile that would normally have sent any man weak at the knees, carrying his newly be-ranked battledress blouse triumphantly. The smile vanished when she saw his expression. She paused uncertainly.

'Have I done something wrong, sir?'

'No, Lewis. You've done everything right.'

Still uncertain, she handed him the blouse. 'I don't understand, sir.'

'It's the information in here. I've got twenty pilots and if you add Wilson and myself, my complement's twenty-two. I've got eighteen brand-new aircraft, plus mine, making a grand total of nineteen. A well-equipped squadron ... almost too well equipped.' Pendrake looked about him. 'We've been very well accommodated, and I've got you to hold my hand. I should be happy. And yet ...'

'And yet, sir?'

Pendrake put his blouse back on and buttoned it as he considered his next words.

'And yet, Lewis.' He pointed to one of the neatly assembled files. 'Take Flight Lieutenant Keane. Australian, excellent combat record, shot down three times. Nothing wrong with that, except ... Keane's barely out of hospital. The third time, he was badly wounded. Right shoulder's still stiff, and gives him pain. Not much use if he's going to be doing some hard turning at low level with Jerry on his tail.

'Then our Canadian, Mackenzie. Also a good record, also shot down ... once. But over water, and he swallowed a lungful of oil-contaminated Channel. Though cleared for flying, I want to be certain those lungs are not going to be a liability. Captain Elmore, USAAF. Mustang pilot. Pranged. Not in itself a problem. I've pranged. Once. I was on fire. Elmore's pranged *three* times, none because of enemy fire. Noted for particularly heavy landings.'

Pendrake hunted out another file while Lewis watched him silently. 'Our New Zealander, Knowles, was on Mosquitoes. No single-seat experience what-soever. And as for the home-grown contingent, they've sent me *boys*, most of whom have flown nothing more powerful than an advanced trainer. Those Typhoons will have them for breakfast. It appears to me that with the exception of Wilson and myself, Kelly, Dodson, and our very own Pole, Josef Wojdat, who appears to have been trying to decimate the Jerry air force all by himself, I don't have a squadron. Now tell me something, Lewis ... Wing Commander Rhys has informed me that you're very bright. What does this smell like to you?'

'They've given you a bit of a job, sir.'

'I would have used stronger language, but I'm think-ing of a particular word, Section Officer Lewis.'

'What word is that, sir?'

'Expendable.'

The Avro Anson, a twin radial-engined light transport and training aircraft, banked sedately as it approached the airfield. Halloran peered down out of the oval window by his seat, to study the ground as it slowly moved across his field of view.

The place was much bigger than expected, until he realized it was rather like two separate units grafted together to make one. Yet both parts remained distinctly autonomous. The larger section, with its own runways, was a hive of flying activity over to the west. He'd been told that this was a major operational training unit, with a variety of aircraft in use. He wondered if that was where some of Pendrake's pilots had come from. As his window now passed over the Cobra Squadron section, he could make out the new Typhoons, haphazardly dispersed in pairs. He compared this with the neat lines of aircraft on the training unit.

His mouth twitched in a fleeting smile. Pendrake was already making his presence felt. Halloran approved of the precaution.

'You have seen something funny?'

Halloran turned to look at the speaker, dressed in civilian clothes, who was sitting across from him. The accent was French.

'Just observing a professional at work, Michel,' Halloran explained. 'The commander of Cobra Squadron has dispersed his airplanes, in order to minimize any damage that might be done by an unexpected strike against the airfield, even way out here.'

Michel Montcarneau nodded approvingly. 'I like the way he thinks. Perhaps we shall work well together.'

'I'd wait and see, Michel,' Halloran cautioned. 'I've met the guy briefly, just the once. But I've heard plenty. He's a tough customer.'

Montcarneau looked him straight in the eye. 'Someone once said to me when France fell, we are going to need some pretty tough customers.'

'Throwing my words back at me, Michel?'

'No. Just reminding you.'

The Anson throttled back as it lined itself up for the landing. Soon, it was settling itself gently on to the ground.

Rhys was waiting with his own staff car, with another nearby.

After introductions, Halloran said, 'Is the model ready, sir?'

'All taken care of,' Rhys answered. 'We've got a wide range of skills on site. Prior to our show with Jerry, some of the people who have worked on it had jobs requiring a very high degree of expertise, in toy factories. Others, like so many boys *and* girls, believe it or not, have built model aeroplanes since their childhood days. I've had both male and female personnel working on the construction. I think you'll be pleased with the result.'

'I'm sure we will, sir. Thank you. We'll check it out later. Better see our new squadron commander first. I see he's moved the airplanes.'

'Yes. Insisted we did so. Protection against surprise attack.'

'Understandable. It's what he's been doing to the Germans in Normandy. Be seeing you later, sir. We'll be on our way.'

Rhys pointed to the other vehicle. 'Car and driver at your disposal. Gentlemen.'

Halloran saluted. Montcarneau inclined his head

slightly. Rhys gave them a brief wave at his cap and went back to his car.

In his office, Pendrake had heard the aircraft go over and had listened to and accurately identified the noise of its engines.

'Sounds like an Anson has just come in,' he remarked to Karen Lewis after a while as he continued to study the pilots' records. 'Could be Major Halloran,' he went on grimly. 'He's early. All the better. I can see him before I meet the aircrew. I want a few words with that man. He's got some explaining to do. If not him, then whoever's responsible for this selection of pilots.'

'Sir . . .' she began in what sounded like an attempt to calm him down. 'You may be confronting officers of senior rank. A squadron leader of one day's standing will have no chance . . .'

The ringing of the telephone on his desk cut into any retort he might have been inclined to deliver.

He picked it up. 'Flight Lieut . . .' Then he remembered. 'Squadron Leader Pendrake.'

It was Rhys. 'Major Halloran's arrived, Mike. He's got a French chap with him.'

'Pilot?' Pendrake enquired hopefully.

'No idea, old boy. He's a civilian. That is, he's in civilian clothes.'

'*Civilian*? Why has Halloran brought him? And what does a *French* civilian want with me?'

'You're about to find out. They're on their way.'

'I see. Thank you, sir. You heard that?' he added to Lewis as they hung up.

She nodded.

'You'd better get out there to greet them,' he said unenthusiastically. 'Whatever they're about, it's probably not going to improve my view of the day so far. I'm beginning to think, Lewis, that I was much better off as a flight lieutenant roving on my own across Normandy at night.'

'Yes, sir.'

He looked at her. 'No arguments?'

'For the time being, no, sir.'

'I see. Thank you, Lewis.'

'Sir.'

She went out, a thoughtful expression on her face.

Not long after, Pendrake heard voices and got to his feet, composing himself for the coming meeting.

The door opened and Karen Lewis stood there. 'Major Halloran and Monsieur Montcarneau, sir.'

'Thank you. Please send them in.'

She stood back, and the two men entered, Halloran carrying his brown leather briefcase.

'Good to see you again,' Halloran began with a grin, 'and congratulations on the promotion.'

'Thank you.' Pendrake remained civil.

'This is Michel Montcarneau.'

Pendrake held out his hand. 'Monsieur Montcarneau.' He noted that the Frenchman was studying him hard.

They shook hands as Halloran continued, 'Michel will be working closely with you. You'll find his information, and his help, invaluable.'

Pendrake glanced at Montcarneau before returning his gaze to the American. 'I shall be better able to judge that when I know precisely what I'm doing here.'

'And I'm here to put you in the picture,' Halloran said.

'Fully?'

Montcarneau glanced at Halloran, his eyes seeming to telegraph a message. 'I think, Major,' he interrupted quietly, 'I shall wait in the outer office. I believe you and Squadron Leader Pendrake should discuss certain matters first, without my presence.'

He did not wait for either to comment. He turned, and went out to Karen Lewis's office.

'That's Michel for you,' Halloran said drily. 'Circumspect as always.'

'Has he reason to be?'

Halloran seemed to pause to take stock. 'I get the feeling you're sore about something.'

'How long do I have before this unit goes on whatever mission has been planned for it?' Pendrake countered.

'A little under three weeks.'

Pendrake stared at Halloran as if the other had taken leave of his senses. '*Under* three weeks! Is this a joke?'

'It's wartime.'

Pendrake's eyes bored into Halloran's.

'Out there,' he began in a quiet but hard voice, pointing in the direction of Dispersal, 'in addition to my own, I've got eighteen spanking new aircraft. An almost lavish supply of equipment. Now why, I asked myself, not give me the pilots to match such wonderfully shiny aeroplanes?' He brought a hand firmly down on the papers on the desk. 'Do you know what I've got instead?

'On the face of it,' Pendrake went on, before the

American could say anything, 'I've got a good complement of pilots. Twenty. Then there's Wilson, who's on his way and, of course, the squadron commander. Me. More than enough from which, with time, to fashion a good fighting force. Unfortunately, most of my aircrew appear to be invalids, indifferent flyers or inexperienced boys! Now you tell me I've got just *three* weeks to turn this bunch into a fighting unit that's supposed to not only do the job, but survive long enough to get it done!'

Halloran said nothing.

'Major? I'm waiting for some explanation.'

'I know what's biting you,' Halloran said at last.

'You do?' Pendrake remarked coldly.

'You've got your own private war with the enemy . . .'

'What the devil do you . . .?'

'You've got to let her go some time,' Halloran ploughed on. 'I know about what happened to your wife. You're not the only person, and you won't be the last, to lose somebody close . . .' Halloran stopped, seeing the look that had come into Pendrake's eyes. *I'm looking into hell*, he thought.

For a moment, Pendrake did not trust himself to speak.

'Who . . . what . . . what gives you the idea that you know anything about it?' he eventually said in a voice so devoid of warmth that Halloran again felt the slight chill he'd experienced when they had first met, only a day before. 'You're now inside my head, are you? You've persuaded yourself that you understand *my* feelings? You *know*, do you? You know what it means to watch the woman you love almost beyond life itself, blown into tiny pieces of flesh and bone, so that it feels as if someone has cut your heart out and stuck it in a lump of ice?

'Shall I tell you what it's really like, Major? You see her blood, flash-dried on the ground. Too late, you discover you've stepped on it. You see bits of white sticking out of scorched trees and you look and realize you're staring at slivers of bone with the flesh hanging off them. You see strips of blackened cloth that only moments before were part of the dress she wore.

'You see something like a dark ribbon hanging off a branch. It takes you a while to understand that what you're looking at is a length of her intestine. You see a ripped shoe. You pick it up and out falls this . . . *thing* of pulped, burnt flesh. And at last you've got to accept that the horrible thing from the shoe, the slivers of bone, the ribbon of intestine . . . *is your wife*. She's all around you; on the ground, in the trees . . . *and she wouldn't have been there* if *you* hadn't taken her in the first place.

'So you know all that, do you? Would you like to hear more? Do I hate the bastards? Yes, yes, *yes*! And unless you can give me an exceedingly good reason, I'm going back to what I know I can do well. *Killing* them. I may be waging my private war, Major Halloran, as you've put it, but I'm not going to be responsible for getting those pilots killed while I'm doing so. And I shall have no difficulty whatsoever about reverting to my old rank, if that's what it takes.'

4

In the outer office, Section Officer Lewis had found it impossible not to hear what Pendrake had said. In his torment, he had spoken loudly. She bit at her lower lip.

Montcarneau had been watching interestedly. A truly beautiful young woman, he'd been thinking. In his early thirties, he had been a railway worker before the war. A far more sophisticated man than his exterior proclaimed, he thought he understood clearly the reasons for the anxiety she displayed.

'You like this man,' he said to her, zeroing in on the truth with perfect accuracy.

Unable to help herself, Lewis blushed. 'Of . . . of course not. I only met him today. He's . . . he's my superior officer.'

'So? That prevents you from liking him? You met him today, but you have known of him before. Yes?'

'Ye . . . yes.'

'Let me tell you something.' His eyes never left her. 'Five minutes after I met my wife, I knew she would be my wife. You have had some hours already.'

His directness was throwing her into confusion.

'Your-your-your wife. What has that . . .?'

'To do with your present anxieties for the brave but

emotionally wounded squadron leader?' Montcarneau smiled. 'Who knows?'

'And where . . . where's your wife?'

'Serving France, as I am.'

In the squadron CO's office, an uneasy silence now reigned. Pendrake and Halloran were eyeing each other like a pair of stags marking out territory.

Then Halloran said, 'Let's sit down, for God's sake. I know nothing about the type of pilots they sent you. What do I know of pilots? I know what kind of man I wanted to command the squadron, that's all. The pilots were someone else's job. Like you, I've got to take what I get. If there's been a foul-up with them, there was nothing I could have done about it, and there is nothing I can do about it now.

'I can raise the matter with Personnel, if you want; but I don't hold out any hope. They'll say they gave us new airplanes and why do we think we deserve the best pilots too? Everyone wants top pilots right now. There's a lot of stuff going on. Things are hotting up. We're just a very small part of the whole picture.'

Halloran paused and absent mindedly felt for the small crucifix beneath his shirt to briefly pat it.

'Look,' he carried on in a reasoning voice. 'I'm sorry about what you had to go through. What more can I say? I'm not going to pretend I can begin to understand how you feel; but I've had my tough one too and, like you, I wanted to go out and shoot every goddam one of them by myself, all the way to Berlin. Believe me, I really felt like doing that. Stupid, of course.'

Halloran fell silent and became introspective. Pendrake kept his own silence and waited.

Then very quietly, almost as if talking to himself, Halloran told Pendrake about Jeanne-Anne. Frequently, he touched the crucifix beneath his shirt, as if searching for reassurance.

When Halloran had finished, Pendrake said nothing, but slowly took his seat. Halloran grabbed a chair, dragged it close to the desk back towards Pendrake, straddled it and sat down.

'Just as you blame yourself for your wife's death,' he said, 'I blame myself for what happened to Jeanne-Anne. I could have prevented her from carrying those documents that day. She would not have thanked me for it . . . but I could have stopped her.' He paused, seeing again in his mind's eye the wreck of the body that had been brought to him. 'We never had the chance to get married. I wanted it, but she didn't. Not in wartime, she said. I wanted what you had. I believed you should take everything that's handed to you today, in case you lost it tomorrow. Each of us, in our own way, still ended up losing what we valued most. So perhaps there's no difference. We each took our chances.'

Another silence fell.

'After that day,' Halloran continued, 'I wanted to attack the château with everything we had. Crazy, of course. We wouldn't have got near it. Other Resistance groups have tried before. They're probably still where they fell. But we have people working for us in there. That's how we've gotten to know what had really happened to Jeanne-Anne.' Halloran drew a ragged breath as he remembered. 'I saw her face every day. You know that? Every hellish day. I still do. Then at last, a chance came to strike back.' Halloran stood up. 'Come with me. I'll show you what your squadron is about to do. We're both going to pay those bastards back.'

'Your target,' Halloran said.

The accurately scaled model of the Château de St Sauveur and the surrounding landscape for miles around was on a large raised platform that seemed to fill the entire room. It was like a giant billiard table, with shaded overhead lighting hanging above it. There was just enough space to allow free passage around its perimeter. Outside in the corridor, armed guards stood on either side of the closed door. There were no windows.

Pendrake stared at the model. All the important trees, their respective heights marked on small flags, and every hill, mound, valley and river or stream, was represented. Every gun emplacement, every flak tower, every group of soldiers, every tank and scout car was in place. Whoever had supplied the information had done on incredible job.

As if he knew what Pendrake was thinking, Halloran said, 'It took a year to get all the information. The local terrain is well known by our group. We gathered the rest from ordinary people going about their business and who happened to notice an emplacement here, a tank there; but most of all, we got valuable details from Michel, his wife – who's in the château . . .'

Pendrake was astonished. 'In the château?'

'Why yes. It's her castle. Well . . . her family's. Michel worked on the railways and kind of married above his station.' Halloran smiled at Montcarneau, who smiled fleetingly in return.

Pendrake looked at Montcarneau. 'Don't the Gestapo know you're her husband?'

'Was.'

'Was?'

'She's a widow.' Montcarneau gave another brief smile. 'Safer for her.'

'We've also got others in there,' Halloran rejoined. 'Boucheron's cousin, for one. To the Gestapo and Boucheron himself, and even the local people, he's a fervent collaborator. It was he who got word to us that on one of their regular sweeps, the Gestapo picked up a very senior district commander in the Resistance.

'Thing is, they have no idea they have him. He's simply someone among others they've arrested in a reprisal raid, and who looks like just another ordinary old man. He's been in one of the dungeons for months while they decide what to do with him. We've even thought they were going to release him. They sometimes do that with people they take so they can keep tabs on them, hoping they'll lead to bigger fish. At least, he'd be out.

'But his health is failing and if they go to town on him, he may not be strong enough to hold out. He knows too much. When I had the situation relayed to the Intelligence services, they came up with a suggestion to help both the plans for the eventual invasion, and ourselves. They asked me to come up with a plan of execution.'

'Execution,' Pendrake remarked drily. 'Sounds appropriate. And those imprisoned in the château?' he asked. He was walking round the model, studying it, searching out the best approach for a successful attack. He did not look up as he spoke.

'Casualties will be inevitable; but if you carry out the attack well, we might get lucky.'

Pendrake stopped to look at Montcarneau. 'What about your wife?' He thought it grimly ironic that his actions might do to the man's wife what the unknown enemy pilot had done to Megan.

'This is the family wing,' Montcarneau said, pointing to a section that had been painted red. 'You do not attack there. They have been given times of the day when they should all be in that part of the building. This will be the same period of time as your attack. From today, they will be doing this for the next four weeks. It will become a routine and their guards will not be suspicious. Also, one of the girls who works as a maid has got one of Boucheron's SS bodyguards interested in her. It was he who told her of what happened to Jeanne-Anne. Even they could not stomach what was being done; but Boucheron, the pig, stayed to watch and drank wine as he was doing so. The animal.'

'It will be a pre-dawn attack,' Halloran said evenly with some effort, clearly not wanting to think of Jeanne-Anne. 'That should ensure the Malzeys and those others working for us will be in the family wing. We'll never be absolutely sure, of course. Anything can happen. There are sometimes special evenings, when the local commanders are invited to dinner or a general comes visiting. The family are obliged to attend. As these things can go on all night, we've just got to hope the day you attack is not one of those; or that they'll find a way of getting back to their section of the château in time.'

'And the Gestapo prisoners?' Pendrake asked again, still not looking up.

'They take their chances. We can't risk warning them. They may talk under interrogation.'

Pendrake looked up. 'Bit tough on them.'

'It's tougher where they are. My Resistance group will think of a way of helping them on the day.' Halloran sounded as if he did not want to discuss it further.

'The Waffen-SS forces defending the area,' he went on, returning to the main subject, 'come from the 1st Waffen-SS Panzer Division. We'd like to keep them tied up there, permanently, so that they can't be used to reinforce their comrades in other areas. This is vital. In short, they must be pushing up daisies. The Resistance will mop up what you leave.'

Pendrake was again studying the model. 'This place is a fortress,' he said. 'We'll be running a gauntlet all the way in, and all the way back.' He moved along a side of the platform until he came to where an airfield had been positioned, with fighter aircraft upon its runway and in the dispersal bays. They were Fw-190s. 'And these fighters . . . I assume they're stationed so close in order to protect the airspace?'

Halloran nodded. 'I leave you to decide how best to sort them out.'

'I'm glad you're leaving something to me. Tell me . . . do the people who've sanctioned this expect any of us to come back alive?' Pendrake looked up once more, his eyes surveying the two men steadily. He'd made the question sound almost conversational.

Halloran and Montcarneau stared back at him silently.

'Just wondering,' he said, returning to his scrutiny of the model.

His brow furrowed as he began to visualize the tactics he would use to give the squadron the best possible chance of success, with the least number of casualties. In the ensuing silence, it was as if the others had ceased to exist as he immersed himself in the problem. They stared at him, watching as he moved round the table from time to time, sometimes stooping to peer along the edge of the platform, studying the various possible directions from which to mount the attack.

Lewis, her eyes fastened upon him, stared palely from a shadowed corner.

At last, he stopped prowling around the model and straightened, his attention on Halloran. 'Six more aircraft.'

'*What?*'

'I want six more aircraft.'

'You've already got *eighteen*. Brand new! Then there's yours, which is being modified. I had a hell of a job convincing the brass to let you take it. Now you want me to go back to them and say you want *six* more? They'll have my neck.'

'*We'll* be losing our necks if I don't get my aircraft. I need those extra Typhoons to make this thing work. No Typhoons, no mission. It will be a waste of time, and lives.'

Halloran stared at him in astonishment while Montcarneau looked on with clinical interest. In the gloom of her shadows, Lewis's eyes seemed hooded as she continued to fix them on Pendrake.

'Why six, for Pete's sake?' Halloran demanded.

'I want eighteen aircraft in the air on the mission. We're bound to suffer attrition during training, and on the practice runs. The extra six will

81

give us sufficient margin. I must have eighteen fully operational Typhoons on the day. You want this job done, you get me my six aeroplanes.' Pendrake glanced at his watch. 'Time to meet my squadron.'

He went out, leaving them staring after him.

'How do you like that?' Halloran said, his eyes on the closing door. 'What does he expect me to do?'

'I would get him his six aeroplanes,' Montcarneau suggested.

They got to their feet in a rumble of chairs as Pendrake entered and climbed the low dais.

'Please take your seats, gentlemen.'

They complied, faces expectant, eyes questioning, most looking anxious and uncertain. The majority wore RAF uniforms, with those from the Commonwealth or Allied countries wearing the shoulder titles of their respective homelands. The Frenchman and the Pole wore their nations' uniforms while Elmore, the USAAF captain, had the exotic mix of an RAF pair of trousers topped by a USAAF tunic. Four of the British contingent were sergeant pilots. They looked very young and more anxious than most. They were the ones, Pendrake already knew, with the least experience.

There was another NCO pilot, a flight sergeant and slightly older, who had flown Hurricanes in combat and who had two kills to his credit. Pendrake had decided to put him in charge of the young sergeants.

'My name is Pendrake,' he began. As he started speaking, he was aware of Halloran, Montcarneau and Lewis entering the room. His eyes zeroed upon the USAAF officer. 'Captain Elmore, isn't it?'

Elmore got slowly to his feet. 'Yes, sir,' he drawled.

'Captain, you're improperly dressed.'

'Well, sir, it's like this,' Elmore began to explain in his Southern drawl. 'These here are my lucky pants. Had them since I was in the Eagle squadron. Never a scratch on me.'

'Did you wear them when you were transferred to the US Army Air Force?'

'No, sir.'

'Were you . . . scratched?'

'No, sir.'

'Captain, if you're going to remain with this unit, you will either find yourself a full Royal Air Force uniform with a relevant shoulder title attached, or find a proper pair of trousers to go with that tunic. This is not a carnival. Am I quite clear enough for you?'

Elmore, seeing a compatriot in the room and a major at that, looked to Halloran for guidance. Halloran gave him a cold stare in return.

'I'll be properly dressed, sir,' Elmore finally said.

'Good man. You may sit down.'

'Sir.'

'These two gentlemen,' Pendrake continued as Elmore resumed his seat, 'are Major Halloran and Monsieur Montcarneau. You'll be seeing them from time to time. Section Officer Lewis I'm sure you all know.'

The entire group beamed at her, including the fearful boy-pilots.

'Thank you, gentlemen,' he said drily. 'I see you do know her.'

They gave him nervous smiles, the tension easing.

'You may well be wondering what this unit is about,' he went on, 'and why you were chosen. You have come to Cobra Squadron. Its purpose is totally secret, and you will be given such information as is necessary at the appropriate times. You will discuss nothing about this unit to anyone. There are no exceptions. If any of you makes the slightest reference to the squadron outside these requirements, disciplinary action will be taken, and you will be replaced. This is the only warning you will receive.

'The job in hand is dangerous. I'm not going to pull punches. I want pilots who know what to expect from the outset, and who can carry the job through. You will undergo rigorous training. You will fly better than you have ever flown before, and you will fight better than you have ever done before.

'You will all have seen the new aircraft. They are powerful beasts and they'll have you for breakfast if you do not first learn to master them, then merge with them. Make them extensions of yourselves until fighting with them becomes second nature. To survive at all, you will need to achieve that level of competence. Then, and only then, will you be ready to tackle the mission. Today is your day of rest. Make the most of it. From tomorrow, training begins in earnest. Any questions?'

Elmore was on his feet.

'Yes, Captain?' Pendrake kept his voice neutral.

'Well, sir . . . I've heard that these ships . . . these Typhoons have gotten a habit of losing their tails, or suffering a sudden disintegration. Imagine that happening with a Nazi on *your* tail. One kill to him without a shot. Friend of mine was flying in a squadron when the plane next to his simply came to pieces. They were not being fired upon by the enemy at the time.'

Pendrake noted that the boy-pilots looked decidedly queasy.

'In the first place,' he replied calmly, 'this no longer happens, and our aircraft are not ordinary Typhoons. They are solid, and I'd rather be in one of them under fire or in a hard fight, than in anything else flying today. However, if one does break up around you, come back and I'll give you another.'

There were slow smiles that turned into chuckles that turned into laughter at Elmore's expense. He sat down ruefully.

'Any more questions?' Pendrake asked when the laughter had subsided.

No one else raised a query.

'Very well,' he said. 'That is all for now, gentlemen. Thank you.'

They got to their feet as he left the dais and went out, followed by his three companions.

'You handled that well,' Halloran said as they walked back to the squadron offices. 'Nice and short. You slap Elmore down twice, but without rubbing his nose in it. Then you give them the old one-two, soft and hard. Everybody knows who's in charge. They know your bite is worse than your bark, but they also know you'll be fair. Not bad going for a new CO. They'll all be bracing themselves for what comes next, minds concentrated. It will be a matter of pride to succeed. That was pretty good going.'

'Early days,' Pendrake commented. 'I took the initiative. It doesn't mean it will hold. They're still in shock. Let's see what evolves.'

'I'll try for your planes,' Halloran announced suddenly.

Lewis, walking behind with Montcarneau, glanced surreptitiously at the Frenchman, who smiled vaguely.

'Excellent,' Pendrake said. 'I knew I could count on you.'

Halloran stopped, forcing the others to an abrupt halt. 'Well, I'll be . . . You play a mean game, Squadron Leader.'

'Not a game, Major,' Pendrake said. 'Never a game.'

The big green Mercedes 540K open-topped sports car roared along the approach road to the château. Its driver knew where each group of soldiers, tanks and armoured vehicles was positioned in the woods.

A patrol of twelve Waffen-SS, six to each side of the road and commanded by a lieutenant, paused when they heard the approaching car and turned alertly. The lieutenant recognized the car and ordered his men to attention. They snapped rigidly erect. The lieutenant gave a sharp salute as the car passed. The driver brought a hand to his elegant cap as he drove past.

'A fine body of men,' his passenger, Oberstleutnant Ketelheim commented. Ketelheim, resplendent in his Luftwaffe uniform, turned to glance back. 'Very smart, Franz.'

Franz Meckler, of equivalent rank in the Waffen-SS and an old friend, smiled proudly. 'My men are the best in the whole of the 1st Waffen-SS Panzer Division.'

'And of course, you're not biased.'

'The truth is not biased.'

They laughed.

Sitting with his left arm resting on the back of the driver's seat, Ketelheim looked at his friend.

'It's really good to see you, Franz. Who would have thought we'd meet up in Normandy? We spent all that time on the Eastern Front and never saw each other and now I find you're commanding a unit in the very area my planes have been sent to protect.'

'On the Eastern Front, there was the little problem of the Russians getting in the way.'

They laughed again.

'But we made them pay,' Ketelheim said with a chuckle.

'I can see by those Iron Crosses,' Meckler observed, 'that you extracted a high price.'

'You haven't done so badly yourself. A lieutenant-colonel at your tender age. And what that's I see? A Knight's Cross with Oak Leaves.'

Meckler grinned. 'I'm only a month younger than you are. So spare me the ancient sage act. So . . . from bomber pilot to fighter ace. How did you manage it?'

'Friends in high places,' they said together, laughing a third time.

Ketelheim gave the dashboard a pat. 'And your car! The times we had in it! How did you manage to get it out of Germany?'

They looked at each other. 'Friends in high places!' they chorused once more.

'And a few low ones,' Meckler added for good measure. 'I have a transport sergeant who can arrange anything. He has more brains than some generals I could mention.'

Ketelheim gave him a serious look. 'That's a change from the Franz of old.'

'Since the Eastern Front, Franz has changed a lot,' Meckler said, momentarily speaking of himself in the third person. 'I know you have never given much credence to the Party's ideals, Karl-Heinz. Yes, yes, I know. No use denying it to me, your oldest friend. When you have known someone from childhood to manhood, you understand a few things about him. I know also, you considered I was foolish to join the Waffen-SS ... perhaps even disappointed in me. What would you have called it? Intellectually shallow. You used that term when we were students. You were talking about the SA Brown-shirts then.'

Ketelheim said nothing, waiting for his friend to continue.

'Well,' Meckler went on, 'I am going to shock you. You may have been right. The things I have seen on the Eastern Front. The things we have done ... Oh, don't worry. I'm not suddenly going to throw away my uniform and shout I repent, I repent. It's much too late for me. But I will fight as ferociously as ever, with one important difference – it is no longer for an ideal. I will fight to save Germany. And we shall need to fight, Karl-Heinz. We ... Germany, will be made to pay severely for the things that have been done in our name. Things we have done in our name.'

There was silence between them for a while as the car's exhaust note bounced off the trees.

Ketelheim was indeed shocked to hear such sentiments from his friend. He could well remember Meckler's first home leave in the smart new uniform of a junior officer in the Waffen-SS, and the piratical air with which it had been worn. Now, as a highly decorated senior officer and combat veteran, though the piratical air could still be discerned, there was a new attitude that seemed a contradiction to all that he thought he'd known about the man.

'Be very careful to whom you say these things, Franz,' Ketelheim now cautioned. 'That uniform, the rank and the Knight's Cross will be no protection if the boys in the black leather coats come sniffing.'

'I am a highly decorated senior officer in the 1st Waffen-SS Panzer Division,' Meckler said proudly. 'I command the forces in this area. I am the protection for their château. They need me. They would also have a rebellion on their hands. My men would take a terrible revenge on the corporal's thugs.'

'And don't let them hear you call the Führer the corporal,' Ketelheim said urgently, giving the impression of half-expecting to be heard, even in the car.

'The whole division might have something to say about it too,' Meckler said, as if Ketelheim had not spoken. 'With the rumours and counter-rumours flying about of an Allied invasion being imminent – though no one seems to know precisely *how* imminent – I don't think he would want to lose one of his best divisions. And we are one of the best . . . probably the best.'

'Just be careful, Franz.'

'There are other rumours,' Meckler said tentatively.

'What other rumours?'

'Rumours about saving the Fatherland from the current madness.'

Ketelheim stared at Meckler. 'I've been hearing rumours too, but I'm keeping well out of it. I'd advise you to do the same. I'm not interested in any coup, nor should you be . . . especially as a member of the Waffen-SS.'

'It's all right, Karl-Heinz. I'm not canvassing.'

'It still sounds to me as if you've been talking to some very dangerous people . . . dangerous to your continuing survival. As I've said, that uniform will be no protection.'

Another silence descended. The 540K's exhaust boomed its arrogance. In the woods on either side of the road, the unseen eyes of the SS troops observed their passage, radioing on ahead, warning other troops of their approach. Every so often, they passed a foot patrol on the road, a motorcycle and sidecar, or troop carriers going in both directions, returning the salutes that were sometimes given.

'Change of subject,' Meckler said. 'When and where do you think the Allies will invade?'

'It's anyone's guess. Their aircraft are very active all along the coast, so they're gearing up for something big. That much is obvious enough. The *where* is as important as the when.'

'Yesterday,' Meckler said, 'the Wehrmacht took a pasting.' He spoke with thinly veiled contempt. 'In the early hours, *one* plane took out an ammunition train that was also full of troops, rocket fuel and staff officers. From what I've heard, they never even saw it coming until too late. They had *three* flak cars on that train. Not one fired. I can hardly believe it.'

'I had some action too, yesterday,' Ketelheim remarked. 'A pair of Typhoons. One of them made the classic mistake of going after a decoy. My wingman, Hauptmann Schiffer, played it beautifully. I came down and the Tommy was finished. He was not very good. I think he must have disobeyed his leader as I cannot believe any flight leader would have been so stupid.'

'What did the other one do?'

'Brave man. He came for us, but as we were just outside our area, we let him live. There'll be another time.'

They were now approaching the section where the tanks stood guard. Ketelheim looked at them with great interest as the snouts of the gun barrels appeared to be pointing directly at him.

'The way you've got this area locked up, it would be suicidal for anyone to try an assault. Those Panzers of yours send shivers down my spine.'

'Then think of what they will do to the enemy,' Meckler said, grinning. The pirate of old was back.

'Herr Oberstleutnant!' someone called from a tank, saluting. There was a great deal of warmth in the voice.

Meckler touched his cap in a casual salute.

'Your men clearly think highly of you,' Ketelheim observed.

'You'll notice that the man who shouted used the military rank. None of that political Obersturmbannführer stuff for me. Not any more. In my command, we use the military ranks.

'You'll also have noticed that all my Panzer and other armoured crews, like my motorized infantry, use the field-grey or camouflage, instead of the black favoured by some other commands. Very pretty, the black uniforms, but excellent targets in combat. Favourites for snipers. They'd stand out in these woods. My men are all completely loyal. Imagine what would happen if those fancy-dress merchants at the château moved against me.'

'No one minds about your use of the military rank?'

Meckler laughed sourly. 'I'm a hero! They humour me. The Gestapo specifically asked for my command for this duty. My men have a reputation for ferocity in battle. Now tell me, Karl-Heinz. Your pilots . . . what do they think of you?'

'I am fortunate in having an excellent bunch.'

'Then between us we can give the enemy a few nightmares.'

They laughed, their good humour returning. They continued laughing as, a short while later, they arrived at the château gates. The two black-uniformed Totenkopf SS guards on either side clicked to rigid attention and gave arm-wrenching, outstretched salutes. A third raised the barrier, while simultaneously giving his own salute.

'*Heil Hitler!*' they barked in unison.

''Hitler,' Meckler responded in an indifferent mumble and waved a lazy hand at them. 'Concentration camp lackeys,' he muttered in a low voice to Ketelheim disparagingly.

Ketelheim gave a proper Luftwaffe salute.

The guards lowered their arms and the barrier, and

gazed after the car poisonously as it rumbled its way up the long drive.

'They hate everybody,' Meckler added.

When he was summoned to the château and told he'd be picked up by the area commander of the Waffen-SS unit, Ketelheim had been astonished to discover it was Meckler. No one had seen fit to tell him before, nor had Meckler known Ketelheim was in command of the air element of the defensive screen.

Now, as a curve in the drive gave them a full view of the building, Ketelheim said, 'Someone's done well for himself. Whom are we going to see?'

'At least one general, possibly two.'

'Waffen-SS?'

'Wehrmacht,' Meckler replied. 'But the second general may be Waffen-SS. I don't know who it might be. Neither general lives here. This is more of a Gestapo headquarters. There are plenty of documents in this place that could hang a lot of people. Resistance if we remain in control, Germans and collaborators if we don't. Quite a den of iniquity.

'The actual resident of the château is a collaborator of some importance, and carries the honorary status of general.' Meckler sounded as if he wanted to spit.

Studying the building as they drew nearer, Ketelheim said, 'I'm not surprised he's a collaborator. This place is beautiful. He doesn't want it destroyed and has obviously managed to arrange a situation that would enable him to keep an eye on it.'

'Oh, *he's* not the owner. That's the Baron Malzey and his family. The good baron looks upon us with civilized contempt. The entire family is more or less under open restraint. It makes the Resistance behave. They tried a couple of rescues, but my troops wiped out both forces easily. They were then warned by the Gestapo that further attempts would result in the death of the family. They've behaved themselves after that; at least, for the time being.'

'You expect more attempts?' Ketelheim was surprised.

'Who knows with the French? In their place, I would try. So my men are always on the alert. As for the so-called 'general' in residence, Boucheron . . . before this, all he owned was a broken-down garage on a road that leads to the coast. In Germany, I would shoot such a man myself. It's no surprise the Resistance want his head. War elevates all sorts of people . . .' – Meckler paused – '. . . even corporals.' He grinned as they came to a halt.

Two more SS guards came up and gave the Nazi salute.

Ketelheim looked at Meckler warningly as they climbed out. Meckler waved a hand at his cap and strode past the guards in the manner expected of an officer of his rank in the Waffen-SS. Ketelheim followed suit.

They were met by a bare-headed Wehrmacht major as they entered. They removed their caps.

'Gentlemen,' the major greeted them. 'The generals are waiting for you. Please follow me.'

As they walked along a wide corridor hung with priceless paintings, two civilians in long black leather coats went past on their way out. Meckler gave Ketelheim a knowing glance.

They were shown into an ornately furnished

room where the generals were waiting. One was a Wehrmacht lieutenant-general, the other a Waffen-SS major-general of the 1st Panzer Division, whom Meckler recognized as his own corps commander.

5

Pendrake had checked every one of the new aircraft and had decided to take one up on a test flight. Halloran had taken off again in the Anson, on his way back to persuade his bosses to supply six more Typhoon Ss as Pendrake had requested. Montcarneau had been found a room in the officers' mess, but was currently in the model room inspecting the target to see if modifications would be needed. His job would be to talk Pendrake through every aspect of the area until he knew it almost as well as the Frenchman himself.

A sheet of paper in one hand and flying gear in the other, Pendrake went through the connecting door of his office and into Lewis's. She looked up from her desk as he entered and began to rise from her chair.

He waved the hand with the paper briefly to stop her. 'You don't have to do that every time I come in here. I'm going to take one of the aircraft up. Might as well show the motley bunch that these particular Typhoons do keep their tails intact.'

'You won't take any chances, will you, sir?' she said quickly, stopping suddenly as if the words had come out before she'd realized what she had said.

She found her eyes drawn almost without volition to the faint scar that made him look irresistibly dangerous.

Yet she also sensed a strange vulnerability that was brought on, she knew, by the pain he kept deeply hidden within himself but which, as she had gleaned from his records, tended to find explosive release in the powerful rage of combat.

'What's the matter, Lewis? Not worried about me, are you? Major Halloran would be singularly annoyed if I went in. So would I, for that matter. Keep the faith, Lewis,' he added gently as he handed her the paper. 'I want the doc to see these men. Organize it, will you? And tell him, he must be ruthless. Anyone who flies must be absolutely fit to do so. He is also to annotate those he believes will be fit to fly at a later date.'

'Very good, sir.'

'And Bingo Wilson . . . if he arrives while I'm up, look after him, will you? He's got all my gear.'

'Yes, sir.'

He turned to go. 'Oh . . . have I got a car?'

'Parked in the CO's spot.'

'You're a treasure, Lewis,' Pendrake said as he went out.

'Yes, sir,' she said.

But the door had already closed. She stared at it for a while, then turned to the sheet of paper he had given her. She studied the names he had written, and picked up the phone to speak to the medical officer.

Captain Elmore was in the crew room trying to explain the intricacies of baseball to two of the sergeant pilots.

'It's rounders,' one said.

'Why is it whenever I try to explain the game to you guys,' Elmore complained, 'you always call it rounders? Like when I was with the Eagles. Our British ground crew used to say the same thing.'

'Because it is,' the other sergeant reasoned.

Elmore shook his head, as if in sorrow. 'I give up.' He glanced out of a window and saw Pendrake getting into the car that had been allocated as the squadron commander's vehicle. 'Hey ... lookee here,' he went on softly. 'The old man's got his flying kit. This I want to see. Find the others. Let's get to Dispersal.' He hurried out of the room.

The smell of freshly made coffee greeted Meckler and Ketelheim as they entered. It was real coffee, not the ersatz stuff with which ordinary people had to make do back in Germany.

'Franz!' Waffen-SS Gruppenführer Friedrich Herrenbach came forward with a huge smile, hand outstretched. 'Good to see you.'

'Pleasure to be here, sir,' Meckler responded as they shook hands.

'And this,' Herrenbach continued looking at Ketelheim, 'must be the famous fighter ace, Oberstleutnant Ketelheim.' He shook hands with Ketelheim. 'Franz will hate me for saying this, but he brags about you a lot. I am very glad you're watching the skies for us.'

'Thank you, sir.'

Herrenbach turned towards his superior officer. 'May I present Generalleutnant Manfred von Stahlenbüren of the Abwehr.'

The Army Intelligence lieutenant general shook hands with each man as they brought themselves to attention, clicked their heels and gave him sharp little nods of respect.

Von Stahlenbüren indicated a gleaming seventeenth-century table with four chairs already in place. 'Please sit down, gentlemen.'

Next to the table was a smaller one with a coffee pot, milk and cream jugs, spoons and cups of pristine silverware. There were also spotlessly clean white napkins, and gilt-edged place mats bearing eighteenth-century maritime scenes.

As they all sat down a young civilian woman entered and laid the table, then poured coffee for each, waiting as they made their choice of milk or cream.

'Thank you, my dear,' von Stahlenbüren said to her in impeccable French. 'We'll take it from here.'

She gave him a pretty, dimpled smile and went out.

'Shame to think she'd heartily slit all our throats,' he remarked conversationally, 'given half the chance.'

'Surely not, sir,' Ketelheim began, finding that difficult to believe. 'She looks so . . .'

'Pretty? Don't let that fool you. Do you have a sister, or a girlfriend, or wife back home?'

'A wife and a sister, sir.'

'And if the French were in Germany, doing what we're doing here, what would you expect them to do?'

Ketelheim said nothing.

'Precisely,' the general said. 'Now drink your wonderful French coffee, gentlemen. I know many people back home who would give anything to taste this.' He took a swallow, then put the cup down. 'And now to business.'

'You will both be well aware,' he continued, breaking their expectant silence, 'that the Allies are planning a major invasion. For months, they have been carrying out probing attacks under the cover of normal bombing raids, on all fronts, to keep us guessing. My Abwehr believe we should be alert all along the western coasts, from Denmark to the Spanish border; but we do have our favourite candidates ... here in Normandy, or the Pas de Calais. The general consensus is the Pas. It makes more tactical sense. It's also a more direct route to the Reich, their ultimate objective.

'As a result of this, I am virtually certain you will get your fair share of interest down here. There will also be increased activity from the Resistance. You, Ketelheim, must ensure that your aeroplanes are secure on the ground and you, Meckler, keep your boys on their toes.'

'They always are, General.'

Von Stahlenbüren nodded. 'So Friedrich has been telling me. Keep up the good work. And as for you, Ketelheim, I am certain you will take care of any Tommy or Ami aircraft foolish enough to come into your pasture.'

'Count on it, General. Our Luftwaffe infantry are permanently on the alert, guarding the airfield and the immediate area outside its perimeter.'

'Good,' the general said approvingly. 'The Abwehr has authorized its own probing flights, by night and by day, over Britain. We also use the cover of nuisance bombing raids. We're looking for units that are out of the ordinary, and use all kinds of aircraft for this work. Fighters on low-level search patterns; medium bombers to destroy identified special groups or airfields; parachute drops, E-boats and submarines making landfalls under cover of darkness to disembark specialist teams; even slow but quiet Storchs to drop agents to find out what's going on over there.

'Infiltrations are not easy. Although we have had our *Vertrauensmänner* in different countries – there are many here in France, for example, especially those used by our friends the Gestapo – it is not so easy with the British. Many are caught by the Tommies; but we still have a few at large. Your organization's own security units, Meckler, from the Security Service, like ourselves and the Gestapo, have made good use of these people who would earn the trust of their own kind, then betray them.'

The general gave a grim chuckle as he continued, 'The "trustful men" seems an ironic way to describe them. Good for us, bad for their own people. The hope is that these *V-männer* can send us information of the proposed invasion site and the date, in time to give us the opportunity to prepare the warmest reception.'

Everyone grinned at this. A meaningful silence then fell, causing both Ketelheim and Meckler to look questioningly at the two generals. It was Herrenbach who eventually spoke.

'You have also been probably aware,' he began, 'that certain rumours have been circulating.' He paused, watching their faces keenly for a reaction to his words.

Both subordinate officers stiffened slightly. They knew exactly what he meant.

'We've heard some loose talk,' Meckler finally offered cautiously.

'Loose talk.'

Both younger men were suddenly aware that the generals were looking at them very closely, definite messages in their eyes. They knew nothing more would be said in this Gestapo den; but they were also left in no doubt of the import of what had been disclosed, despite the apparently innocuous nature of the conversation.

'Be very careful, Franz,' Herrenbach advised, 'who you listen to. You too, Karl-Heinz.'

'Yes, sir,' they both said together.

'And now,' von Stahlenbüren said brightly, 'let us finish our coffee. Stay with us till evening, gentlemen. There is a dinner tonight. You will meet the owners of this beautiful *Schloss*, and other . . . interesting people. Meanwhile, enjoy the pleasures of the place. There are wonderful grounds, and very rare paintings. We shall see you both later.'

They all stood up, the junior officers springing to attention. All four shook hands, then Ketelheim and Meckler went out.

In the corridor, Meckler said in a low, urgent voice, 'Herrenbach's involved? And so cosy with the Wehrmacht, even though it is the Abwehr. I can't believe it!'

'We don't know that he is,' Ketelheim countered.

'I know my commander. It's what he doesn't say that matters in a situation like this.'

'In that case, let's take his advice. We know nothing, and we watch our step.'

Two black-uniformed SS came smartly towards them, boots gleaming.

'*Heil Hitler!*' they said, and stomped past.

''Hitler,' Meckler responded in his customary

clipped way, pretending to be so fully absorbed in his conversation, he had barely registered their presence. 'I agree with you,' he added to Ketelheim when they were safely out of earshot.

Pendrake got out of the car, picked up his Mae West and slipped it on. He then got the helmet with its goggles attached and shut the car door. He began walking towards the nearest Typhoon, helmet in hand. A sergeant in charge of a servicing crew was standing nearby, supervising a couple of crewmen at work. One of the aircraftmen was in the cockpit.

The sergeant, having heard the car approach, had turned to await him. The sergeant saluted.

'At ease, Sarge,' Pendrake said. 'You are . . .'

'Sergeant Ransome, sir.'

'Right, Sergeant Ransome.' Pendrake placed his helmet on the wing and began to secure the life-jacket. 'This aircraft serviceable?'

'They all are, sir,' the NCO replied proudly. 'Just doing some extra checks. Nearly done.'

'Ready to fly, is she?'

'Yes, sir.'

'Armed?'

'Full load of ammo, sir. No rockets though, as you can see. But I can have them put on.'

'No need, Sarge. Won't be needing them. I'm taking her up for a test, but I hate flying an aircraft without teeth, irrespective of the flight. Never can be too careful.'

'Know what you mean, sir. I checked the cannons myself. She'll bite if you ask her to.'

'Good.' Pendrake looked up at the cockpit, where

the aircraftman, head down, was still at work. 'Now if he'll get out of the office, I'll hop in.'

'Right you are, sir,' Ransome said. He looked up at the cockpit and bawled, 'Millar!'

'Yes, Sarge!' came the muffled acknowledgement.

'Get out of there! The CO needs the aeroplane!'

'Right away, Sarge! Just finishing.'

'Jump to it, lad!'

There was a brief pause, then, 'I'm done!'

Millar climbed out quickly, saw Pendrake waiting, and athletically slid down the wingroot to the ground.

'Sorry, sir,' he said to Pendrake, bringing himself to attention.

'Relax, Millar. It's all right. Do you recommend that I take her up?'

'Yes, sir! I've just been adjusting the throttle movement. Smooth as you could wish, sir. Like a hot knife through butter. I've done all the others. This was the last one.'

'He is good with the throttles, sir,' the sergeant confirmed. 'Got the touch. Makes them work like magic.'

'Then I shall have to find out.' Pendrake retrieved his helmet, put it on, then did a rapid but detailed pre-flight check.

The bigger wing of the "S" version enabled the four-cannon fit – two to each side – to be deeply recessed, instead of sticking out aggressively. They were still aggressive, but almost seemed to peep out of the leading edges by comparison. The rear fuselage was also bigger yet sleeker, and the tail more gracefully curved at the fin. The nose was longer too, with the cockpit set further back. She looked good.

Satisfied with his checks, Pendrake climbed aboard the black Typhoon. The parachute was already in the seat, which made life immensely easier, as scrabbling up to a cockpit which was nine feet off the ground while lugging the pack was hardly the stuff of elegance.

The crewmen moved back, two of them crouching some distance from either wing, holding on to lengths of rope to which the wheel chocks were attached.

Pendrake settled himself in, secured his harness, then looked right and left to make certain the aircraft was clear of obstructions. He immediately appreciated the unrestricted view the new bubble canopy afforded.

This is more like it, he thought.

He clipped on his oxygen mask and began his preparations for engine start. Throttle lever to starting position, propeller pitch control lever set, all fuel tanks full, centre fuselage selected, twin engine pumps low down on the right of the instrument panel set, starter cartridge inserted, starter button pressed . . .

The massive engine exploded into a powerful wall of sound and though Pendrake was familiar with the Typhoon bellow, the modified engine seemed to him to roar its challenge to the world.

'My God!' he whispered, enthralled. The ferocious power of the new engine was awesome. Yet it settled down to a remarkably smooth, but daunting rhythm. 'This will frighten the kids,' he added, thinking of the boy-pilots, 'but it's putting hairs on my chest!'

He checked his immediate environs once more, noting that the crewmen on the chocks were awaiting his signal. He also saw a group of people approaching, to stop a safe distance away. His pilots had come to watch him and almost certainly to pass judgement. All the better.

He moved the throttle forward, easing it gently. The engine roared gleefully in response, while he held the aircraft on the brakes. Millar had not exaggerated. The movement was smoother than anything he remembered on any Typhoon, or any other fighter, for that matter. He'd have to caution the new pilots about being over-eager with its use until they got to know the aircraft better; or it would run away with them.

He brought the throttle back. The engine responded without a hiccup. No tell-tale, oily smears on the windscreen. Forget the old Sabre. This was a beauty. He hoped the modifications to his own aircraft would be as good.

He gave a sharp outward wave with both hands and the chocks were hauled away. Aware that all eyes were on him, he taxied smoothly towards the runway, then lined up for take-off. He slid the canopy forward. It moved equally smoothly and clicked home, cutting out much of the engine noise, but still leaving enough to let him know it was there. A powerful vibration coursed through the entire airframe, making the Typhoon feel like a living being. Trifle with me, it seemed to say, and you're dead.

'Homebase, Homebase,' he called on the radio to the control tower. 'Cobra One calling. Scramble? Over.'

A green flare arced skywards. Time to go.

He opened the throttle wide. Now the beast was truly alive. The Typhoon hurled itself forward with an acceleration that almost took him by surprise. It did so much more rapidly than his old mount. He watched for the notorious rightward swing of all Typhoons. It was still there and as he applied left rudder to counter it, he realized he needed much less effort. The swing had not been totally eradicated, but it was much more subdued. There was none of the wild crabbing that had trapped so many novice pilots, some terminally, despite the fact that the Typhoon was a tough bird that could take amazing punishment. Even so, the less experienced pilots would have to be coached into using the correct trim inputs so as to make the best use of the aircraft's almost benign new trim set-up.

He eased gently back on the slimmed-down column with its familiar, laterally pivoting upper half and spade grip. The Typhoon surged into the air, eager to go. He brought the wheels up and held her at low level, letting the speed build. He glanced about him. The view out was quite a revelation.

At last. This was what he'd always wanted! Now he really could see the sky about him.

On the ground, the Cobra pilots were spread loosely in little groups. All followed the progress of the Typhoon keenly.

'He was wearing his Mae West,' one of the younger sergeant pilots remarked. 'He's not going over water. Why bother?'

'Why not ask him when he gets back?' someone else suggested.

The sergeant turned, and found himself looking into the steely blue eyes of the Australian, Dominic Keane.

'Oh. Hello, sir.'

'Benson, is it?'

'Yes, sir.'

'Well, Benson. How old are you?'

'Nineteen, sir.'

'How old?'

Benson looked embarrassed. 'Um ... still three months to go, sir.' He had a rich Midlands accent.

'If you want to make it even to nineteen, Sergeant Benson, I'd advise you to wear yours at *all* times, even over land. I once got into a fight over land, but found myself over water. Like an idiot, I had not worn my Mae West. Scrambled without it. I was very glad not to have been shot down that day. It was a lesson I have never forgotten. Today you're getting it for free.'

'Yes, sir.'

The roar of the Typhoon was growing louder and they both turned to look.

'Where is he?' Benson asked.

'Search me.'

Then a black shape hurled itself from between two hangars and came at them.

'He's ... he's going to hit!' Benson stammered and dropped to the ground.

Keane remained where he was and watched the great nose of the aircraft grow bigger. Then suddenly, it yanked upwards to fling itself into a steep climb. A series of fast rolls in the climb followed.

'You can get up now, Benson,' Keane said, staring upwards at the fast-diminishing shape. 'If that tail was going to come off, it would have done so just then. I think our CO's proving to us that this baby is going to stay in one piece whatever we do to her. Enjoy the fun.'

They all watched, many open-mouthed, as Pendrake put the Typhoon through its paces.

He was in his element. He pulled over the top of a loop and plunged earthwards. The powerful engine gave its howling bellow as the Typhoon hurtled down. The bigger wing gave it much-improved agility. He could see the airfield plan etched upon the ground beneath, as if on a model in an ops room. It continued to expand perceptibly as he lost altitude.

He began to ease back on the stick, progressively applying the pressure. He did not want to reach a speed where the controls became so stiff that he would be unable to pull out before hitting the ground. It had happened to many pilots.

But the control forces were well within the limits. The nose came up, the scything disc of the massive four-bladed propeller began to slide up the background of the sky as if greased on its surface, as the seven-ton aeroplane began to haul itself upwards. The forces of the pull-out pushed his head and neck towards his shoulders; a slight greying touched the edges of vision. He was experiencing forces of gravity under which, in later years, other pilots would wear special equipment to help increase the tolerance of the relatively frail human body.

Pendrake gave a heart-stopping display for about five minutes, throwing the aircraft about the sky with seemingly wild abandon. Then the Typhoon was shooting upwards once more. He pulled it on to its back, then rolled upright. At five thousand feet, he headed north-east from the airfield.

Elmore briefly removed his cap to scratch the back of his head.

'I'll say this for him,' he announced to Dodson, who was close by. 'He sure can fly.' The captain was now wearing a complete USAAF uniform.

'And if that kite was going to bend,' Dodson pointed out, eyes still on the Typhoon, 'it would have done so after what he's just put it through.'

'Yeah, yeah. I get the point. Hey. Where's he going?'

'As long as *he* knows, that's all right with me. A man who flies like that is going to want a lot out of us.'

'Yeah. Just what I was thinking. The blood from our veins. But that plane did sound real good. Reckon I'd hate to wash out of this outfit.'

'I'm certain he'll be pleased to hear that, Yank.'

'I'm no goddam Yankee. How'd you like it if I called you Scotch?'

'Scotch is a drink . . . the nectar of the gods. And I'm not a Scot.'

'See what I mean?'

The two Messerschmitt Bf-109Gs, coming from Cherbourg, had crossed the coast high above Lulworth Cove. They should have been spotted, but weren't. Flying at height to conserve fuel, they had each used an extra capacity ventral drop tank of 500 litres instead of the usual 300. With the tank in place, they had staggered to altitude over France, their performance improving as the fuel was used up and their all-up weight decreased. For the high transit over to southern England, they stayed on the ventral tank.

They were fortunate in not being caught by patrolling Spitfires, or Hurricanes. Their manoeuvrability would have been seriously compromised with the tanks still attached. Without them, the loss of the extra fuel would have made their return to base highly unlikely once they had become engaged in a fight.

Their mission objective effectively meant that getting into a dogfight would be a desperate, last resort. They were on a reconnaissance prowl and while they could attack ground targets with their cannon, dogfights were only to be entered into as defensive measures, if that proved to be the only means of escape.

This particular pair had survived many successful missions. They had caught out single Allied aircraft, shot up coastal airfields, sunk special forces assault craft training in British coastal waters, and even big Sunderland flying boats had been caught at their moorings. Intelligence supplied them with particular coordinates, and they would subsequently hunt down the target. They came from one of the type of units von Stahlenbüren had been talking about.

Today, however, they were tasked with searching out a special British unit. The information had been imprecise. There was no certainty that such an establishment even existed and their job was to either prove or disprove this, and get back to tell the tale. Definite confirmation would mean a night bombing raid by twin-engined Messerschmitt Bf-110 fighter-bombers.

They were passing high above Chippenham when they began their rapid and steep descent, engines throttled back, as if coasting down a precipitous hill. There was still some fuel left in their ventral tanks. Low down, they cruised towards their objective, their pilots marvelling that they had so far been undetected. No one had expected an intrusion from that direction, it seemed.

The pilots armed their specially mounted under-nose cameras, in preparation for a filming pass, if they did find the unit. They checked the sky about them. So far, so good.

Pendrake was making for an extensive beech wood in the Cotswolds. He intended to use it as a training area, deciding it would be a good place to introduce the squadron to the rigours of ultra-low flying.

'Assuming they can fly the aircraft in the first place,' he muttered to himself.

He went down to a thousand feet and covered the woods in a wide circle, examining landmarks and the narrow valleys. He did that twice, discovering areas where he could fly below the treetops. There was even an old, ruined manor house among the trees which could serve as a stand-in for the château. He was on his third circuit, when a fast movement over to his right caught his eye.

At first he refused to believe it. *Two* 109s were passing within less than a mile of him, coming from the south-east. They had clearly not seen him, for they made no alteration of course and appeared to be heading in the direction of the airfield.

He did two things almost simultaneously. He slammed the throttle to the wall and radioed the airfield. The Typhoon seemed to leap forward as its engine smoothly gathered power. Millar's magic was working nicely.

'Homebase, Homebase,' he called urgently as he prepared himself for combat. 'Cobra One calling. Two bandits. Repeat, two bandits heading your way. Am giving chase. All Cobra Squadron pilots, do *not* take off. Repeat, all Cobra Squadron pilots do *not* take off. I want no dead heroes. Inform Keane. Over.'

'Roger, Cobra One. Receiving you loud and clear. Understand bandits approaching. No Cobra pilots to scramble. Inform Keane.'

'Cobra One, out.'

The Messerschmitts were still holding a tight formation. Pendrake saw the belly tanks as he curved in behind them, gaining rapidly.

Now to see how the Typhoon S really performed.

Keane watched the startled expression that appeared on every face as the sirens went.

'What the devil?' someone exclaimed. 'Must be a drill. Can't possibly be a raid.'

Then the Tannoy came on. '*Airfield defences man your guns! Man your guns! All other personnel to shelters! I repeat. All other personnel to shelters!*'

'I'm scrambling!' someone shouted. 'Give me a helmet! Give me a helmet! I'll take one of the Spits!' It was Elmore.

Just then, one of the corporals ran up to Keane. 'Message from the control tower, sir!' he reported, wheezing from his run. 'It's from the squadron leader. No pilots are to take off. No dead heroes, he said. Message was for you specifically, sir!'

'Righto. Off you go, Corp.'

The corporal shot off to find a shelter.

'Hold it, Elmore!' Keane bawled at the American. 'To the shelter!'

'But . . .'

'Don't argue with me! *Move it!* CO's orders.'

Seeing the blaze in Keane's eyes, Elmore did not argue.

Pendrake had taken the Typhoon low, low down, a sleekly black hawk skimming the ground, closing in for the kill. He had positioned himself neatly in their blind spot, just beneath them. Had they been flying in a wider formation, the wingman might well have spotted him. But it was obvious they had wanted to bring as little attention to themselves as possible.

A wider formation or a wingman weaving to keep a good lookout would have quickly attracted attention, including among the non-vigilant. The poor rearward vision from even the 'Gustav' version of the 109 also counted against the enemy pilots. Pendrake found himself comparing it unfavourably, as he closed range, with the excellent vision afforded by the new canopy of the Typhoon he was now flying.

He selected the leading aircraft as the first target. The wingman, probably less experienced, would be shocked and slightly disorientated by the sudden demise of his leader. It would be a psychological advantage when the time came to attend to him.

Still unseen, Pendrake crept in nearer still. He couldn't afford to miss. He was not at all keen to take on a two-on-one engagement, in an aircraft he was still getting used to.

He was close enough. At that very moment the wingman spotted him. He could almost hear the shout as the pilot warned his leader. Both drop tanks went simultaneously, tumbling like silver pear drops. They were fast, but not fast enough.

Almost at the instant that the tanks went, Pendrake

fired. The Hispano cannons were devastating. Tracer streamed ahead of him as they thumped out their killer song at the target 109. They ripped it apart, tearing it to pieces in a violent explosion that seared outwards in an expanding, boiling fireball. Then suddenly there was nothing. Something trailing a black plume tumbled to the ground. There was no parachute.

The second Messerschmitt leapt skywards like a startled minnow darting from a predatory pike. Pendrake hauled on the stick and the Typhoon bellowed after it, eating up the distance. But whoever the wingman was, he was no slouch and Pendrake soon realized he was not dealing with an inexperienced pilot after all. Perhaps he had taken the wrong one first.

They tore upwards in their aerial ballet of death, the black avenging Typhoon gaining in the climb on the smaller, camouflaged Messerschmitt. Just as it was about to come into range of the cannons, it twinkled to the left and plunged earthwards. Pendrake half-rolled in the climb and hauled on the stick. The Typhoon described a tight curving dive as it went after the 109. He again had the enemy aircraft before him. But it was banking tightly low down, heading south.

Pendrake understood instantly what was happening. The enemy pilot's primary concern was escape. Getting lower on fuel by the second, on his own, deep into enemy territory and very far from base, he had little choice. He would obviously only fight to survive long enough to get away. Pendrake also saw that his current course was taking them both towards the airfield.

'Homebase, Homebase!' he called urgently. 'Cobra One calling. Am chasing single bandit, heading towards you. Fighter, *not* bomber. Repeat. Fighter, *not* bomber. Call off the guns! Repeat. Call off the guns!'

The last thing he needed was some overexcited gunner, short on good recognition, blasting him out of the sky in error.

'Roger, Cobra. One bandit, fighter. Will call off the guns.'

'Cobra One, out.'

At the airfield, the Tannoy was again doing its stuff. '*Gunners stand down! Gunners stand down! Single bandit, fighter, heading towards the airfield. All other personnel remain in shelters. I repeat. All other personnel remain in shelters!*'

In one of the shelters, Sean Kelly said to Mackenzie, 'Strange. Why stand down the gunners?'

'It must mean the CO's on the tail of that bandit and doesn't want to get shot down by itchy trigger fingers. It happens. I've been hit by our own ack-ack. Blew a damn great hole in the wing of my Spit before those jokers woke up. I was not a happy boy, believe me.'

'Hang on,' someone else said. 'I hear something!'

Everyone listened. Very faintly but growing perceptibly louder, they could hear the high scream of an engine, counterpointed by a familiar bellow.

'I'll be damned,' Kelly exclaimed softly. 'The CO's bringing him home! I've got to watch this.'

'You can't go out there,' another voice cautioned. 'Fighters carry bombs too, you know.'

'I know. I've done it. But I'm not going to miss this for the world.' Kelly hurried out of the shelter.

'Hell,' Mackenzie said. 'If the CO's going to button up a bandit right over our heads, I'm not staying in this hole.' He followed Kelly out.

Soon, everyone was following suit.

The Tannoy blared again. '*Get back into those shelters! Get back into those shelters!*'

The other shelters were emptying too, as the noise of the two aircraft grew louder. People stood to gape upwards.

The person on the public address system gave up. 'Oh, what's the bloody use,' came the unguarded comment before the Tannoy was switched off.

Pendrake could see the airfield in the distance. The Me-109 was still low down, still fleeing, but with little real hope of escape in a straight race. The Typhoon was gaining inexorably.

Suddenly the enemy aircraft shot upwards, wrenching on to its back almost immediately, then pulling down as if about to complete a tight loop. But it rolled swiftly upright and was bearing down upon Pendrake in a head-on pass.

Pendrake was ready as soon as he'd seen the roll commence. Knowing what was coming, he broke hard left to displace, but continued the roll through 180 degrees, and pulled the stick hard. The 109 tried to correct and fired, but was going too fast. Tracers lanced the air and missed. The enemy pilot overshot and immediately began to turn hard as the Typhoon sliced in behind him. He jinked violently, trying to locate his black nemesis.

Pendrake had climbed and was now on his back looking through the top of the canopy at the Messerschmitt below him. It was again heading south. For the first time since Megan's death, he actually felt sorry for an enemy pilot and sensed a peculiar solidarity with the man, as one aviator to another. It was a terrible situation to be in. No matter how good the pilot might be, the strain would be overwhelming.

But the solidarity did not extend to wanting the enemy's survival. Pendrake was totally implacable. He remembered Megan's terrible death. He remembered also what had happened to the relatively inexperienced Braddock. He had done something exceedingly rash and the ace who had got him had not been merciful. As far as Pendrake was now concerned, the enemy pilot's only chance was to bale out. It was either that, or certain death. There were no other options.

In the Messerschmitt, Major Hans Brillermann was not thinking about baling out. He was thinking of getting back to pass on the information about the black aeroplane, and the others he could now see on the airfield. *This was the special unit!*

Even as he kept an eye out for the special Typhoon that had so efficiently shot down Leutnant Forschmeister, he triggered the camera. At least he'd have some photographs. Then he had to break off to go into another defensive manoeuvre, as he spotted the Typhoon curving down on his tail.

The epic battle came inexorably towards the airfield.

The screaming Messerschmitt tore upwards, followed by the snarling Typhoon, the clear bright sky of the late afternoon marking them out sharply as they danced high above the mellow Cotswold hills. They were two deadly predators engaged in a territorial battle in which the victory of the one would mean the demise of the other.

Elmore stood with both hands shading his eyes as he followed their choreography.

'Will you just look at that,' he said, mainly to himself. 'Nothing that 109 can do seems able to shake off the CO.'

'Wouldn't want that to happen, would you?' Dodson asked.

'Hell, no. But you got to feel sorry for the poor Nazi bastard.'

'You can feel sorry if you like. I want the CO to turn him into a flamer. If *you* were up there with *him* on your tail, he wouldn't be feeling sorry.'

The Messerschmitt was not giving up. It had now gone so low over the airfield that it seemed about to hit one of the hangars. But it screamed between them, with the Typhoon hot on its tail.

Pendrake flew between the hangars, reluctant to shoot for fear of stray shells causing havoc on the ground. The enemy pilot must have known it, and had deliberately employed the ruse.

They shot across the airfield, seemingly about to crash into something. The noise of their engines, from ground level, was at once terrifying and exhilarating. The entire station, it seemed, was now watching the contest.

Karen Lewis was outside the squadron building with Montcarneau. He glanced at her surreptitiously, noticing her anxiety; but there was something else too. She looked excited, and full of pride. Her lips were swollen and moist. Once, her tongue inched out like a shy pink animal, to lick slowly at the lower lip before quickly disappearing once more. It was, he thought, a most sensual act. He wondered whether Pendrake was even aware of the furnace he was stoking within her.

Montcarneau smiled to himself. 'He will be all right,' he said gently. 'It is easy to see who is the master in this trial by combat.'

His voice startled her, and she blushed.

'I know he'll be all right,' she said firmly, then added uncertainly, 'I do hope so.'

Her eyes anxiously followed the twists and turns of the jousting aircraft, now leaping once more for the heavens. It all looked so beautiful, she thought. A graceful prelude to death. Totally oblivious of the man standing next to her, she forced herself not to think of Mike Pendrake dying in an explosion of fire up there.

Watching as she craned her neck upwards, Montcarneau saw a tiny pulse flutter intermittently in the gentle curve of her throat, and smiled again to himself.

The end, when it came, was sudden and almost an anticlimax.

Major Hans Brillermann made a slight error of judgement, the pressure having at last got to him. He had left the airfield perimeter, once again low down, and had been herded into making too tight a turn by Pendrake. The 109 simply went into a high-speed stall and slammed into some trees beyond the airfield. It exploded in a great gout of flame on impact.

Pendrake came low across the runway, pulled into a steep climb and rolled slowly, twice.

'I'll be damned,' Kelly said. 'There must have been two of them, and he got both.'

People around them were cheering loudly. It seemed the whole station was doing so.

'He's going to be a tough act to live up to,' Mackenzie said.

'Or to please,' Kelly added.

Keane, standing to one side, heard the exchange. He rubbed his right shoulder absently. He'd been told he had an appointment with the medical officer.

He watched as the Typhoon came in for a most stylish landing.

6

The Messerschmitt had burned fiercely and by twilight was still smouldering. Several people went to have a look at it, some to take souvenirs, until they were forbidden to do so. However, the pilots had grabbed themselves a piece of wing with the black cross on it as a first trophy for Cobra Squadron.

Pendrake did not visit the crash site.

The aircraft recovery team had found pieces of wreckage scattered over a wide area. Among those was the under-nose camera, virtually intact, its exposed film in perfect condition. There was not much left of Hans Brillermann. Rhys ordered that the remains be properly buried.

'They can collect him after the war,' he said. 'After we've won.'

Pendrake was in a darkened room in the Photographic Intelligence Section with Rhys. The retrieved film had been developed and was now in a projector.

'All right, Sergeant Pascoe,' Pendrake said. 'Let's see what's on this.'

The WAAF sergeant in charge of the section started the projector. They watched as the silent film began to roll. It was remarkably sharp, and very clearly they saw how the doomed 109, still hoping for escape, had corrected its course to make deliberately for the airfield. The buildings and the aircraft were sharply detailed. There was also a zoom function that allowed detailed close-ups of the new Typhoons. It was very evident that some of the film had been shot during the dogfight, as the Messerschmitt's flight between the hangars was clearly depicted.

'A very determined man,' Rhys commented as the film ended and the lights came back on.

'And brave,' Pendrake added, surprising himself.

The recovery team had so far found no documents by which to identify either Brillermann or his unit. Investigators were scraping away at such items of the wreckage that might yield identification numbers.

Then Pendrake voiced the thought that was in all their minds. 'Someone over there knows enough about us to have mounted this operation. The breach must have come from Halloran's people. There must be someone in his group in Normandy who's talking to the enemy. Perhaps even one of his much-vaunted infiltrators in the château.'

Rhys was looking steadily at him. 'Was that the reason you chose not to tell Montcarneau about this film?'

'I'm being careful until I see our good major again.'

'But Montcarneau has the local knowledge you need.'

'He can still do the job he was sent to do. If he, or someone close to him is responsible, it hardly matters now. He's not going anywhere. They never expected their recce aircraft to be shot down. Mounting the operation so soon after our deployment, they probably expected to catch us on the hop. And they would have, had I not gone up when I did.

'As for the 109s, they would have been keeping radio silence. When those at their base realize their aeroplanes are not returning, they'll assume they've simply been shot down; which could have occurred at any time during the flight.

'If it is Montcarneau,' Pendrake continued, 'we're actually quite secure. He can't risk further communication, now that we're alerted, even if he has no idea we've got the film. If the breach is in France, there may be more attempts, especially when we move to the forward airfield. From now on, those two Spitfires brought in by Kelly and Dodson will mount a standing patrol. I should have taken a leaf out of your book, sir,' he added ruefully. 'I'm thinking of my welcoming committee.'

'Oh, that,' Rhys said with an embarrassed smile. 'I assure you there was no tactical thinking behind it.'

'Even so, I've learned the lesson. The crews can rotate the duty. The younger pilots can get their hours in on the Spits, before I unleash the Tiffies upon them. The flight commanders can handle that when I've made my selections.'

'And meanwhile?' Rhys asked.

'Meanwhile, we treat Monsieur Montcarneau normally until we know one way or the other.' Pendrake turned to the sergeant. 'Sergeant Pascoe, as our most senior Photo Intelligence bod on the station, I leave it to you to ensure that this film remains secure until I ask for it, and that no one makes mention of it. This means *all* your personnel.'

'You may count on me, sir,' she vowed.

'I'm sure I can. One other thing – who knows about the camera having been found, apart from your people? Who actually found it?'

'Two members of my section saw one of the recovery team pick it up, sir. It was quite some distance from where the aircraft hit. They immediately took it from him and advised him to say nothing to the others unless otherwise instructed by you or the station CO, and brought it straight to me.'

'Good show. Well done. Then we'll leave it in your very capable hands.'

'Thank you, sir.'

Pendrake was on his way back to his office when he ran into Montcarneau.

'So, Squadron Leader,' the Frenchman began. 'I hear there were two of these Germans, and you got both of them.'

'Yes.'

'You are having quite a day. You are a formidable warrior.'

'Simply trying to stay alive, Monsieur Montcarneau.'

'Michel, please.'

'Michel.'

'And I shall call you Mike,' Montcarneau went on. 'We have the same name, so it is fitting. I think, Mike, you are too modest about your talents. I think what happened today is more than just trying to stay alive,' he observed shrewdly. 'We all saw what happened to the second aeroplane. He was outmatched.'

'I was lucky.'

'If that was only luck, then you know more than

most of us. You know how to make it. Will you soon be going to dinner in the mess? We can go together.'

'I shall be going to dinner, but there are a few things to attend to first.'

Montcarneau nodded sympathetically. 'Ah, the joys of command. The young lady is still awaiting your return,' he continued, as if divulging a great secret. 'Very loyal, that one. She will stay until the morning if you do not dismiss her.'

Pendrake glanced at his watch in concern. 'Good heavens. She should have gone to the mess by now.'

Montcarneau gave his private smile. 'You are an excellent fighter pilot, Squadron Leader, and from what I have so far seen, you are already becoming an equally good commander. But there are other things which I believe you do not see.' He gave an expressive shrug. 'But maybe you do see, and do not want to. Hmm? I will see you in the mess.'

He went on his way, leaving Pendrake to ponder upon his words.

Lewis came to her feet as Pendrake entered.

'You're still doing it,' he admonished her.

She sat down quickly. 'Sorry, sir. Habit.'

'Then lose it. I'm not running a square-bashing camp.'

'Yes, sir. That was a very good show up there . . .' she went on, excitement bringing a slight breathlessness to her voice, '. . . getting those Jerries. Especially that last one.'

'I was lucky,' he told her, repeating his words to Montcarneau.

'I don't believe anyone on the station looks upon it as just luck, especially the pilots. A few of them came up to me to sing your praises.' She smiled. 'They made me promise not to tell you what they actually said. You're winning, sir.'

Despite her adherence to service discipline in maintaining just the right amount of familiarity, her startling blue eyes were betraying her. Pupils dilated, they seemed to want to swallow him.

Pendrake appeared totally unmoved by this. 'So far,' he remarked portentously.

Privately, he was very pleased that they currently held him in high regard. The spectacular downing of the Messerschmitts, especially the last one as she'd said, had put the fire into them. But that would not prolong the honeymoon period indefinitely. Things would soon change. When the rigours of the training to come started taking their toll, it would be interesting to hear what they thought about him then.

'Oh . . .,' she began, interrupting his train of thought, 'we've heard from Flight Lieutenant Wilson.'

'Bingo Wilson? Why isn't he here? I need him.'

'Seems as if a huge bomb had been lying unnoticed in a ditch for days, along the back road he was taking. The ditch was grassed over and full of water. Then the bomb exploded, leaving a big crater, cutting the road itself in two.'

'Is Bingo all right?'

'Oh yes. He wasn't there when it happened, but he's had to detour and got caught up in a convoy of Americans.'

'That would have pleased him. And when does he expect to be with us?'

'As soon as he can, sir.'

'Not much we can do in that case,' Pendrake

admitted, adding lightly, 'After all, there is a war on, they tell me.' He studied her closely. 'And you, young lady, are quite tired. It's been a long day. By now, you should have been in the mess having dinner. I just saw Michel Montcarneau outside, on his way there. You ought to join him.'

'And you, sir?'

'What about me?'

'Are you off to the mess?'

'Not at this very moment, but I shall be along. I'm about to select the flight commanders . . .'

'Then you'll need all the information . . .'

'I can do that.'

'With my help, you'll get through it much more quickly, sir,' she said firmly. 'You've got to eat too.'

He looked at her steadily. 'Are you bullying me, Section Officer Lewis?'

'Just doing my job, sir.'

'I see. And you won't leave unless I make it a direct order.'

'No, sir. Although . . .'

'"Although"? You wouldn't be thinking of insubordination, would you?'

'Not quite, sir.'

'Not quite? One is either insubordinate, or one isn't. There are no half-measures.' A tiny smile came and went. 'I ought to know. And having no doubt heard of my . . . er, past exploits with the brass, so do you.'

'There you are, sir.'

'All right, Lewis. You win. Let's get cracking.'

'Yes, sir.' She beamed at him.

*   *   *

A string quartet was playing in the minstrels' gallery at the château. Its incongruity was heightened by the fact that the musicians were in the black dress uniform of the Totenkopf SS.

Glancing up at them from the dinner table, Ketelheim thought that the Gestapo who had organized it all were either totally oblivious of the irony or, as was perhaps most likely, playing another of their psychological games with the owners of the château. Meckler had informed him that this was a common occurrence, as though every so often the Gestapo needed to spice their days up a bit. It also sent an unmistakable message to the Resistance.

Before the dinner, Meckler had taken him on a guided tour of the defences within the grounds. All the patrolling guards were black-uniformed SS, but the anti-aircraft gunners were all Waffen-SS. Relations between the soldiers of the two branches of the organization were, at best, politely distant. The veterans looked upon the *die Toter*, as they offhandedly called them, as pampered brutes. While the 'brutes' looked upon the veterans as being too big for their boots and disrespectful, just because they had seen service on the Eastern Front and had a few Iron Crosses.

The fact was, the vets were secretly envied by guards of the Totenkopf, members of which sported their own Iron Crosses knowing they had been earned for activities that had required something rather less than valour. The veterans never let them forget it. Meckler made no attempt to rein in his men and on more than one occasion Ketelheim had urged him to be less blatant in his contempt.

As he now listened to the quartet's surprisingly

excellent playing, the whole dinner seemed to him to be quite a bizarre event. In addition to the two generals, there were other high-ranking individuals. An Obergruppenführer from another SS Panzer division, and who outranked Herrenbach by one, was clearly of the type that Meckler had been talking about. This SS lieutenant general, whose name was Schlierhof and who wore a monocle, had arrived with a motorcycle escort of four outriders, and was resplendent in black. Meckler had whispered that he was certain Schlierhof's Panzer troops all wore black as well. Excellent target practice for the Allies, he'd added.

There were also two senior Gestapo men, in civilian evening wear. The most senior outranked every military person in the room. The Abwehr general was accompanied by another Abwehr officer, a Colonel Eigen. The only women at the lavish table were those of the Malzey family, and the woman who accompanied Boucheron, claiming to be his wife.

Ketelheim could see that though they disguised it tolerably well, the baron and his family felt humiliated by being forced to attend. He was certain that was the reason the Gestapo had demanded their presence in the first place. The whole thing, the well-stocked table, the two highly polished, eight-branched candelabra, the SS musicians, the high-ranking guests – especially of the SS – all together in the gilded banqueting room, was an exercise in deliberate humiliation. For the true owners of the château, nothing could be clearer.

They did not behave like conquered people and bore the invasion of their home with quiet dignity. Ketelheim found within himself a grudging admiration for them, and knew why. In the not too distant future, he believed, if the forces of the Reich did not hold the line in France and elsewhere, the people of Germany would soon be facing a similar situation, from an implacable foe bent upon revenge. He wondered how his own family would fare. The thought made him even more determined to do fierce battle with the enemy.

Ketelheim was seated next to the baron's oldest daughter, Mariette, a big-boned handsomely curved woman, not yet thirty, with rich, dark-brown hair and pale-brown eyes. On his left was her younger sister, Odile. She had the same strong build but was fairer, with long blonde hair that gleamed in the candlelight. Meckler was sitting on the other side of her and she was conversing politely with him, unexpectedly brown eyes attentive every time she glanced in his direction. Opposite Ketelheim was the forbidding presence of Schlierhof.

The SS lieutenant general suddenly looked up from his plate. The main course for the evening was a wild boar that had been hunted by SS troops, cooked by an SS chef, and served by young French women.

'Well, Ketelheim?' Schlierhof began. 'How do you find the boar? To your Prussian taste?' It sounded like a challenge.

Momentarily caught out by being so directly addressed, Ketelheim said, 'It is excellent, Herr Obergruppenführer.'

Schlierhof nodded in agreement, before turning to Meckler. 'Our SS cooks can show the Luftwaffe a thing or two, eh, Meckler?'

'To judge by this, Herr Obergruppenführer,' Meckler began diplomatically, 'you are right.'

'Of course I am right.' Schlierhof now looked

along the table to where Waffen-SS Major-General Herrenbach was in conversation with the junior Gestapo man. 'Friedrich,' he went on expansively, generously mellowed by the Malzeys' excellent but ever-depleting wine stock, 'I like these two young officers. From what I've seen, they give me great confidence. I like the defensive set-up you've got here.'

Herrenbach gave a slight, courteous nod. 'Thank you. My confidence in them is equally strong.'

The monocle tracked round and fastened upon the baron himself. 'Now you tell me, Baron,' he said in tolerable French, 'despite your generosity with your home and your wines, you would like to see the back of us, eh? You must be hoping the Allies will come to your rescue.' There was the tiniest of smiles on his lips as if, having baited a trap, all he needed to do was wait.

'I do not want them to have this house either,' Malzey replied evenly.

The eye behind the monocle was unblinking, while the other seemed amused.

Schlierhof smiled. 'Well spoken.'

He continued eating, now and then glancing at the baron as if hoping to catch an expression that might betray Malzey's true feelings.

The higher-ranking Gestapo man, who had observed the exchange with some interest, now paused, fork in mid-air and turned to Schlierhof.

'Perhaps the Countess might be more forthcoming, Schlierhof,' he suggested, with just a hint of slyness as he glanced at Mariette. 'She lost her husband, you know.' He continued eating, as if losing all further desire to participate in the proceedings.

'Oh, I am sorry, madame,' Schlierhof said to her with a display of concern that Ketelheim thought was too heartfelt to be truly genuine. 'We were not responsible, I hope.'

'As a matter of fact,' she responded coldly, 'you were. Some of your SS.'

'Don't let her apparent disenchantment fool you, Schlierhof,' the Gestapo man said, concentrating on his plate. 'There is more.'

The SS lieutenant general looked at Mariette with a raised eyebrow, his monocle glinting in the candlelight. 'Madame?'

'The stupid Resistance,' she answered vehemently. 'They forced him to join. Now he's dead. I cannot forgive them.'

Schlierhof looked from her to the baron and back, as if trying to decide whether she really meant it. The baron was stony-faced. Schlierhof then glanced at Odile, who was now openly flirting with Meckler.

'It would seem, Herr Daggenau,' he said to the Gestapo chief, 'that there appears to be dissension between the generations.'

Daggenau shrugged.

Schlierhof smiled at Mariette in a way that Ketelheim thought bordered on the predatory.

She turned to Ketelheim. 'Tell me, Colonel,' she surprised him in English, 'do you believe the Allies will invade?'

Ketelheim glanced cautiously at the Abwehr general who nodded, just perceptibly, that he could answer.

'Well, madam,' he replied with ease in the same language, 'I believe they will. But we shall be ready for them.'

'But do you know where they intend to attack?'

'Wherever it may be, we shall be ready,' Ketelheim replied firmly. He noted that all the senior officers were pleased with his answer.

'Your English is very good, Colonel,' Mariette said, in an apparent change of subject. 'I am impressed.'

'I was an exchange student in England in the thirties.'

'And have you never thought that perhaps you might have killed some of your former friends? I do not mean to make a political point, you understand. I am, however, fascinated by the possibility.' Mariette, the Countess Malzey, gave a perfect impression of a woman who asked questions out of curiosity, but with no real interest in profound answers.

Aware of everyone's sudden, undivided attention, with the sole exception of the baron, who was locked away in a world of his own, Ketelheim said, 'Are there not Frenchmen currently killing former friends? And are they not of the same nationality?'

'Bravo!' Schlierhof exclaimed. 'I believe he has you there, Madame!' he finished in his passable French.

'I believe you are right, Herr Obergruppenführer,' she said to him in German.

The eyebrow raised itself once more. 'You are indeed someone of many linguistic talents,' he complimented her in his native tongue.

'One must have the skills of society, if one *is* society.' She made it sound as if this were quite distinct from being merely French, but encompassed all those who belonged to 'society' internationally. She gave the impression that Schlierhof was among this elite.

Schlierhof, clearly flattered, acknowledged the inclusion with a slight nod of the head. Daggenau looked on with an expression of smug disdain.

The dinner continued, the animated conversation among those at the table covering a wide range of subjects. Mariette played the slightly empty-headed aristo, while Odile flashed her eyes at Meckler. The baron, a slim, prematurely greying man, his countenance made pale by his repressed sense of outrage, ate in dignified silence, speaking only when spoken to and then only with the barest of civil replies. None of the baron's family exchanged a single word either with the collaborator Boucheron or with the woman who lived with him in the master's suite of the château as his 'wife'.

Strategically positioned about the table, the young French women who had served the dinner continued to do so on silent feet or waited patiently to be summoned. They listened in on the conversations while seemingly completely uninterested, their thoughts carefully hidden from all but themselves.

'That ought to do it.'

Pendrake straightened in his chair to survey his handiwork. Lewis, standing to one side, leaned forward slightly to have a better look. She was close enough for him to sense the warmth of her body. As she studied the four sheets of paper spread out on the desk, head to one side, a wing of her hair fell slightly forward, baring the neck and jawline. A hand moved absently to brush it back. It fell forward again almost immediately, so she left it alone.

Pendrake did not look at her, but kept his eyes

firmly on sheets of paper on which he had written the names of the pilots, dividing them into three flights. The fourth sheet contained the names of those to be held in reserve.

She nodded slowly as she read.

'Approve, do you?' he asked.

She turned her head to look at him. The deep blue eyes were dark and startlingly near. 'It's not for me to approve, sir . . .'

'Come on, Lewis. Don't be so pedantic. What do you really think?'

'I think the allocation works very well. If you're happy with this final draft, I can have it typed up and put a copy on the squadron notice board in the orderly room, and one in the crew room as well.'

'Tomorrow morning. Not tonight. You can't have it typed up right away as everyone's long gone. And I won't have you remaining here to do it. The morning will be soon enough. Now let's get to the mess before they stop serving dinner.'

She straightened, automatically smoothing the skirt of her uniform, her movements unconsciously sensual. Again, he chose not to look at her.

As they were walking through her office on the way out, Wilson barged in, looking very tired.

'Bingo,' Pendrake exclaimed. 'At last! I'd given up hope of seeing you before morning. You look absolutely brassed off.'

'I am, I am,' Wilson said with feeling. 'I got caught up in an armoured convoy that had lost its way. That wretched bomb had blown a great hole in the road I'd intended using. I kept thinking if raiders came over, they'd have found a nice fat target with me in the middle.' He removed his cap and plopped it on Lewis's desk. 'But I see you had a much better time,' he continued to Pendrake, while looking at her. 'I ran into the stationmaster. He says you bagged a couple of 109s today. Lucky sod.'

'They came for a sniff, but found me upstairs. I was on a test flight.'

'You bagged them in one of the new jobs?'

'Yes.'

'Good are they, these new Tiffies?'

'Better. Very powerful, and the bigger wing makes for good agility. And as for the view . . . Find out all about it for yourself tomorrow.'

Wilson was still looking at Lewis. 'Will there be an introduction? Or are we waiting for hell to freeze?'

Pendrake shook his head in mock despair. 'Section Officer Karen Lewis, Flight Lieutenant Bingo Wilson, my deputy.'

She held out her hand. 'Sir.'

'Forget the sir,' he said as he shook it. 'And what he really means is that I'm his stooge.' He grinned. 'I'll carry the can when he makes a mess of things, which, granted, is not very often, thank God.'

'I'd watch him if I were you, Lewis,' Pendrake cautioned. 'He can be dangerous.'

Wilson grinned once more. 'Only a little.'

She looked at him with amusement. 'I'll watch him.'

'Yes, please,' Bingo Wilson said.

'If you're hungry,' Pendrake told him, 'join us for dinner.'

'Will they still be serving?'

'We'd better find out. I'm starving.'

They left the office and went out of the building. Outside in the gloom a patrolling sentry armed with a rifle, bayonet fixed, challenged them.

'*Halt! Who goes there!*' the man barked.

'Squadron Leader Pendrake, Flight Lieutenant Wilson, Section Officer Lewis,' Pendrake replied.

The man came forward and snapped to attention. 'Oh it's you, sir. Ma'am. No lights left on?'

'No.'

He peered at Wilson. 'Ah. You just came in, sir.'

'Yes,' Wilson replied drily. 'You nearly punctured me.'

'Sorry, sir. Never seen you before. Can't be too careful.'

'Quite.'

'Good job you did with those Jerries today, sir,' the sentry went on to Pendrake. 'Bloody good job. We came out of the shelters to watch. We enjoyed seeing you get that bastard ... Oh, sorry, ma'am,' he said to Lewis.

'That's quite all right,' she assured him. 'I've heard worse. Goodnight.'

'Goodnight,' ma'am. Sirs.'

'Goodnight,' Pendrake said. 'Keep up the good work.'

'Sir!' The sentry cracked his boot down smartly, wheeled, and continued his patrol.

At the château, the dinner was over and the baron, as uncommunicative throughout as he'd been from the very start, had retired to his quarters as soon as he decently could. The musicians were still playing, but neither Ketelheim nor Meckler was at the table.

Mariette and Odile had offered a personal tour of the parts of the château that had been allowed by the Gestapo. Forbidden areas included the Malzeys' separate quarters.

Schlierhof was not pleased. 'The woman has snubbed me for that Luftwaffe matinée idol,' he growled to Daggenau. 'A mere lieutenan colonel!' he added in outrage.

'He's hardly a matinée idol,' the Gestapo man told him smoothly. 'Such women are fickle, Herr Obergruppenführer. Anyway, let her have her fun while she still can,' Daggenau continued ominously, in rapid German. He glanced up to survey the French serving girls coldly. 'Leave us!' he ordered in French. He waited until they had all gone, before speaking again.

Outside, two blank-eyed Totenkopf SS guards stood at the door.

'The situation here at the château will not go on for ever,' Daggenau resumed. 'Eventually we shall have no further use for them and then . . .' He let the sentence die, having no need to explain further.

Schlierhof understood. 'Before you do anything to her, I must have her first.'

'Of course,' Daggenau said, considering that a foregone conclusion.

The carnal desires of the Waffen-SS lieutenant general amused him, but would be of future use. The time would come when the dossier he already had on the man would be of great value. If the Allies won, it would be a bargaining chip. If they didn't, it would be an instrument of power over Schlierhof.

Herrenbach had changed position to sit with the

Abwehr general, and they discussed the possible options for countering the expected Allied invasion. If von Stahlenbüren already knew that his recce pilots Brillermann and Forschmeister had failed to return, he gave no indication.

Herrenbach noted Daggenau's conspiratorial expression as the Gestapo chief conversed with Schlierhof. Herrenbach did not trust Daggenau in the least. A man to watch constantly, he thought. A man who would be a very dangerous enemy indeed.

'So tell me, Mariette,' Ketelheim began in English as they strolled arm in arm along the wide corridor of the portrait gallery. Meckler and Odile trailed a short distance behind. 'Is your mother still alive?'

'Oh yes. It was not her night.'

'Not her night? What do you mean?'

'I must put this delicately. They would rather not attend these functions at all, but Herr Daggenau insisted. So they reached a compromise. My parents are adamant that if they must be forced to attend, only one should do so at any given time. Herr Daggenau agreed.'

'So your parents hate us strongly?'

'Do you want the truth? Or a diplomatic answer?'

'I always prefer the truth, no matter how harsh.'

She paused to look at him. 'You're an interesting German. My parents despise the Gestapo,' she added.

So do I, he told himself silently.

'She hates the SS – all kinds – almost as much,' Mariette went on, 'and the average German only less so. You allowed the Nazis to take power, you see. Her family originally came from Alsace, and she has a great love for the other Germany. This one is diseased, she says.'

He was silent for a long time.

'You did ask for the truth,' she reminded him as they walked on.

'I almost wish I hadn't. Any brothers?'

'Yes. Two.'

'And I take it they are in uniform?'

'Are you trying to find out whether my brothers are in the Resistance?'

'No. It was genuine curiosity.'

'They are both dead.'

This time it was Ketelheim who stopped. 'I am sorry. Believe me.'

She gave him a little tug, to move him on. 'But it is war. Is that what you were about to say?'

'It *is* war. What did they do?'

'My older brother died commanding his tank platoon in 1940. The other, younger than I am but older than Odile, was torpedoed in 1942. He was serving on a British warship.'

'I am not surprised your parents hate us. I am equally surprised you do not. After all, you have also lost your husband.'

'I am practical,' she said. She glanced back at Odile and Meckler. 'My sister seems to have taken to your friend. She has been attentive to him all evening.'

'And is she also . . . practical?'

'No. She's young, and I think follows a more basic urge.'

Mariette had paused once more, this time before a large portrait of a young woman.

'She's very beautiful,' Ketelheim said admiringly as he studied it.

'My mother.'

'Both you and Odile look like her, in different ways.'

'Are you saying we are beautiful?'

'Yes. Very.'

7

By 0700 hours the next morning, a new board in the station operations room carried the details of the new unit:

Cobra Squadron

Officer Commanding:	Sqn Ldr M. M. Pendrake, DSO, DFC, AFC.
2nd In Command:	Flt Lt D. G. Wilson, DFC.
Squadron Adjutant:	Section Officer K. Lewis.

There followed a list of all pilots by flight, and their current operational status, as well as that of all squadron aircraft.

On the squadron, some of the pilots were clustered round the orderly room notice board, while others studied the one in the crew room. The information on each was the same. The three flights were identified by number, instead of a phonetic or colour designation. Call-signs were also allocated identification numbers.

Pendrake, as CO, would always be Cobra One. Wilson was Cobra Two. The flight leaders were Cobra Double-One, Cobra Two-One, and Cobra

Three-One respectively, the first number denoting the flight in question. Their seconds in command were Cobra One-Two, Cobra Two-Two and Cobra Three-Two. The remaining pilots were identified in chronological order, according to flight. As CO and deputy, Pendrake and Wilson could assume command of any flight. There were six pilots per flight, with a reserve of two, which was currently filled by the youngest pair of the sergeant pilots.

Keane was both surprised and pleased to find he had been given command of One Flight. He was due to visit the medical officer for his check-up, and had not expected it. He knew Pendrake was worried about the stiffness in his right arm.

He noted that the Pole, Josef Wojdat, was his second in command.

'Looks like you got me in your flight,' a familiar voice said at his shoulder.

'I have indeed, Captain Elmore. You won't give me any trouble, will you?'

'Who? *Moi?*'

Keane looked at him balefully. 'Give me any, and I'll have your guts for a kangaroo jockstrap.'

'You say such nice things.'

Lewis, walking past the crew room door, overheard the exchange and smiled to herself. They did not notice her as she went by.

At each board, voices competed with each other as their owners commented upon their allocations.

'Hey, Kelly!' someone shouted. 'You've got Three Flight. Are you sure you know how to fly?'

'I was flying my pa's crop-duster when I was twelve, boy!'

'God. You Yanks tell such tall tales.'

Laughter followed this.

'Well, well,' came Dodson's voice. 'He's given me command of Two.' He was standing next to Kelly.

'Is that good?' Kelly demanded. 'Or bad?'

'Time will tell, old son. Time will tell.' Dodson turned as he sensed someone approach to stand just behind him. 'Ah. Flight Sergeant Charlton. I see you're my number two. And in brackets, next to your name, what do you see?'

Charlton came closer to look, and made a sound of astonishment. 'P/O designate. He's recommended me for a commission! I'm going to be a pilot officer?'

'There you are. Who says there isn't a God? You're well overdue, old son. About time that Distinguished Flying Medal was properly recognized. Congratulations.' Dodson grabbed Charlton's hand and shook it vigorously.

'Well, sir,' the flight sergeant pilot said hesitantly. 'I haven't got it yet.'

'Who cares?' Kelly said expansively. 'It's as good as done. Put 'em here.' He, too, shook the bewildered Charlton's hand. 'And you can buy the first round in the mess.'

'I knew there was something wrong about being an officer,' Charlton said ruefully.

Soon, the others were grabbing his hand, patting him on the back, congratulating him.

Kelly, searching the faces about him, spotted Mackenzie entering the room. 'Hey, Mac. Seen the roster, buddy? You're my number two.'

'God help me,' the Canadian said.

Laughter again erupted as they relieved the tension that had built up within them. They were all very much aware of the dangers they were bound to face, and none allowed himself the luxury of thinking how many names would still be on the board when the mission was over.

A WAAF approached the group in the orderly room. 'Please go and sign for your books at the desk, gentlemen.'

'Books?' someone asked. 'What books?'

'Flying manuals, pilot's notes. For the Typhoon S.'

There was a loud, collective groan.

'We're pilots,' another complained. 'Not students.'

'You'll be dead pilots if you don't learn how to fly those Tiffies out there,' a firm voice said.

They all turned to see where it had come from.

Bingo Wilson was standing there, legs planted solidly, fists on hips, facing them. 'I'm Wilson, deputy squadron commander. I got in late last night after you lambs had dinner. And lambs to the slaughter you will be, if you don't get those books and *study* them. They'll save your lives. Might even make decent pilots of some of you. After you've all got and signed for His Majesty's property, I'll see you in the briefing room. Holiday's over, gentlemen.'

In his office, Pendrake called, 'Enter!' in answer to a discreet knock.

Lewis came in, looking bright and fresh. She carried a thin folder, held against her bosom.

'Ah, Lewis. Bright and early. Good. Slept well?'

'Yes, sir.'

'Excellent. Big day, today. It begins.'

'Yes, sir. When did you get in?'

Pendrake stalled for a moment. 'Well . . . er, had an early breakfast.'

'When, sir?' she insisted.

'What is this, Section Officer? Are you nannying me?'

'No, sir. But you'll be no use to the squadron if you're overtired.'

'I only got here at six. The whole station had been long awake.'

'How early, sir?' The blue eyes were insistent.

'Well . . . perhaps 0530 hours.'

She waited.

'Perhaps it was . . . earlier than that. I have plenty to do. This is not easy, you know. Two days ago I was carefree and happy on my lone missions over France. Today I've got twenty-one souls to keep alive in the air, counting Bingo Wilson.'

'Twenty-two.'

'I beg your pardon?'

'Twenty-two, sir. You. A tired pilot is no use to himself or the squadron. It's what you'd say to them.'

'And now you know what I would say to my pilots?'

'Yes, sir,' she said. 'I think . . .'

'All right! All right, Lewis. I've got the message. Now, have the manuals been distributed?'

'Being done as we speak.'

Pendrake nodded. 'Good. And . . .'

'Flight Lieutenant Wilson's got them filing into the briefing room.'

He stared at her. 'You're even finishing my sentences.'

'May I go on, sir?'

'Be my guest.'

'The MO will see Messrs Keane and Mackenzie soon after, plus any of the other pilots on your list. And' – she opened the folder and took out a single sheet of paper – 'this just came in. Thought you might like to see it straight away.' She handed it over.

It was a signal. He stared at it, then broke into a grin of satisfaction as he read:

'SIX FURTHER UNITS AGREED. DESPATCH SOONEST. H.'

'We're in business, Lewis. We've got our aircraft.'

'Yes, sir.'

'We could do with two extra Spits as well,' he remarked thoughtfully, 'for the standing patrol. Two waiting to scramble while two are in the air. It would also allow them to alternate the flying. Save the wear and tear on the aircraft. An hour up, an hour down.'

'We might be giving our luck a bit of a push, sir, asking for more. But it does seem that at the moment they'll give you anything you want. Rather accommodating of them.'

'It certainly looks like it, Section Officer Lewis,' Pendrake agreed, then added, 'The trouble is, the devil always wants his due. Makes me wonder about the price we may have to pay eventually.'

'That's something I have a feeling we'll find out soon enough, sir.'

'I'm not sure I do want to find out,' Pendrake said with a grim smile. He stared at the signal, as if hoping to see the answer already there. 'Oh, hang the consequences. Acknowledge receipt of the information to the originator of the signal and ask for two extra thoroughbreds.'

'Thoroughbreds, sir?'

'Halloran will know. If they do send them, we'll also know we really are the blue-eyed boys.'

'And then?'

'And then, Lewis, we worry. Because it will be uncomfortably apparent that the condemned are eating a hearty breakfast.'

'Yes, sir,' she said quietly. She glanced at the wall behind him. 'That's new. I noticed it when I came in.'

Pendrake twisted briefly round to glance up at the large framed copy of an aviation cartoon he'd hung there. It was of a Typhoon in an aggressive climb, the big chin scoop of the radiator filled with bared teeth, a fierce eye set a short distance on the upper nose behind the propeller spinner, and a single scar running from beneath the eye.

'I'm not sure who added the scar,' he explained, 'but it's not in the original artwork. Bingo gave this to me to celebrate my DFC. He brought it with him last night, so I thought I'd put it up. What do you think? Not overdoing it?' He sounded genuinely concerned.

'Not at all, sir. I would even say put it in the briefing room. It would amuse the pilots. Put them more at ease.'

'I'm not so sure . . .'

She looked at him.

'I'll think about it,' he said.

'I'll remind you,' she warned.

'I know you will,' he said, resigning himself to the fact.

'Why do you call him Bingo, sir?'

'Oh that.' He gave a brief chuckle. 'When everybody was yelling "Tally-ho" as they mixed it with Jerry, he shouted "Bingo". God knows why. Inevitably, the nickname stuck.'

The pilots were all seated when Wilson entered and mounted the low dais.

'All right, gentlemen,' he began. 'I trust you have all got your school books?'

A few comedians waved theirs at him.

'Very good. Now I do hope you can all read, because I shall be asking questions when the time comes.'

A loud groan greeted this.

'I know, I know. You're hard done by. You thought you had left school for good. Bad luck, gentlemen. The learning never stops. For my sins, I have been designated your chief instructor. It is my job to see that you are able to get those Typhoons into the air and back down again without bending them, or yourselves.

'Those of you who have flown Tiffies, however minimal your time, will be pleased to know that this is a very different beast altogether. It is very powerful, as you now all know . . . and for those of you bred on nightmare stories of the vanishing tail fin, you will have observed the squadron leader's somewhat exciting little demonstration yesterday.'

Loud chuckles, tinged with relief, followed these words.

'Yes, yes. It was impressive and we're very happy the Tiffy's no longer the tailless wonder. But that was the CO, and none of you comes close. But by the time

I am finished, I would like to think that when any of you comes into contact with a 109, or, God help you, a 190, it will be Jerry who'll be hitting the silk as his aircraft disintegrates about him or, better yet, never lives to fly another day.'

He paused, eyes raking them.

'The thing is,' he went on softly, 'can you do it?'

'Yep,' someone said. 'We sure can.'

Wilson's eyes tracked and found Elmore. 'You are?'

'Elmore, sir. Captain, US Army Air Force, and south of the Mason–Dixon.' Elmore grinned.

'Well, Captain Elmore, you're the first.'

'Me, sir?'

'You, sir.'

'First what?'

For reply, Wilson barked, 'Flying Officer Kelly!'

'Sir!' Sean Kelly answered.

'You, Mr Kelly, will be taking Captain Elmore under your wing for the first of a new series of patrols. From today,' Wilson continued before Kelly could respond, 'the CO has ordered a regular patrol of Spitfires up top to watch out for surprise visitors, like those we had yesterday, for the duration of our stay here. We shall all be taking turns, so those of you looking for Spit time will get a fair amount. And Mr Elmore . . .'

'Yes, sir?'

'When you bring that Spit back to earth, do so very gently indeed. I don't know how you treat your girlfriends, but don't treat that aeroplane like one of them. If you are gentle with the ladies, be even gentler with the Spit. Bend her, and I'll bend you. Are you receiving me?'

151

'Loud and clear, sir. Very loud and clear.'

'Then I'm very glad your ears had a clean this morning. Mr Kelly, when we're through here, both of you pick up your gear and get aloft. Time on patrol, one hour.'

'Sir.'

'One other thing ... Messrs Keane, Mackenzie, Wojdat, Kelly and Dodson are to be my deputy instructors. With help from time to time from the CO, I shall convert each of you to the new Typhoon. Each in turn will teach those assigned to you. We've not got a lot of time, gentlemen, and there's a big job ahead. Flight Sergeant Charlton ...'

'Sir?'

'The CO wants a word with you afterwards.'

'Very good, sir.'

'All right, gentlemen. The Spitfire patrol roster will be on the notice board, as well as the training schedules for the day. Check that, and be ready for take-off at the appropriate times. In the meanwhile, I want you to study those manuals until you know the aircraft as well as you know yourselves and perhaps even better. All flight commanders not detailed for immediate take-off, make yourselves ready for a commanders' meeting with the CO. Mr Mackenzie, as deputy Three Flight, you'll stand in for Flying Officer Kelly while he's aloft and report to him afterwards. Thank you, gentlemen. That is all.'

Ketelheim and Meckler were on their way back to their respective units from the Château de St Sauveur. They had stayed the night at the invitation of the baron's daughters, but had not slept in the Malzey quarters.

The baron would certainly not have allowed it in any case, even if the Gestapo would not have objected. The major part of the building, having been commandeered by the Gestapo, contained several bedrooms for use by military and political guests.

Both Waffen-SS generals, Schlierhof and Herrenbach, had left during the night, Schlierhof in a foul mood because Mariette had chosen to snub him for Ketelheim. At least, that was how he had preferred to see it.

Ketelheim and Meckler had an early breakfast by themselves, and had not seen the sisters again.

'So, Karl-Heinz?' Meckler now began as the Mercedes boomed its way along the narrow forest road. 'Will you see her again? We have been invited, after all.'

'If I have the time. But remember, I'm a married man. And you?'

'Most certainly, I shall see the delightful Odile. She has the most desirable body and I believe she would like to put it to good use.' Meckler laughed aloud in anticipation. 'And I, I am not married.

'You have made a very bad enemy in the Obergruppenführer, Karl-Heinz,' he went on soberly. 'Schlierhof's a very nasty customer. I've told you about the things we have done on the Eastern Front. Schlierhof revelled in it. His arms should be red up to the armpits. He belongs in a slaughterhouse. Forget the surface niceties of last night. He hates the Luftwaffe with a passion. As far as he is concerned, the Luftwaffe failed to defeat the Tommies in the Eagle Battle – what *they* call the Battle of Britain – failed on the Eastern Front, and is not doing enough to stop the Allied bombers . . .'

'*What?*'

'Don't snap at me, Karl-Heinz. I'm telling you what he thinks, and there are many like him who blame the Luftwaffe for their own failings.'

'If people interfered less in operational decisions,' Ketelheim said in a hard voice, 'perhaps we would have had more success. We have lost a lot of good men because of stupidity by . . .'

'Uh-oh. What's this? Am I hearing dangerous criticism from you? Yesterday, you were warning *me* against indiscretions.'

Ketelheim smiled grimly. 'In 1940, we did ask Fat Hermann for Spitfires.'

Meckler grinned at him. 'You've really got the bit between your teeth this morning. Calling the great Reichsmarschall Göring "Fat Hermann".' Meckler gave him a sly look. 'You're sure it's not because of the delightful widow?'

'I'm . . .'

'Yes, yes. You're married. Tell me then . . . how is it with you and Trudi? Remember, this is your best man you'll be answering.'

There was a very long silence. The car rumbled its way through the forest, watched by the unseen eyes of Meckler's soldiers.

'Before I took over this command,' Ketelheim began at long last in a flat voice, 'I went home on leave. Just back from the Eastern Front, I was eager to see her, of course. I could hardly wait. She wasn't there. No one knew where she was. I was beginning to think she'd been killed in a bombing raid while she was out. Two days later, she turned up. There was a man with her. Someone with high Party connections.' His lips tightened and a muscle in his jaw throbbed visibly as he remembered. 'While I was out in the East freezing in a miserable tent and longing for her, he was . . . she was . . .'

Ketelheim stopped, unable to put into words what his wife had got up to during his absence, and took a deep breath. He fell silent again as a shocked Meckler continued driving, glancing at him from time to time.

'I haven't seen her since,' Ketelheim said at last harshly, 'nor have I contacted her.'

They drove on in another long silence.

'I'm very sorry,' Meckler ventured at last, glancing out of the corner of his eye at his friend, as if unsure of Ketelheim's mood. 'I know how much you . . .' He stopped, then continued brightly, 'Let's take up that invitation. I'm not saying you should do anything with the merry widow; but a man needs a woman's company. And I don't mean going to a whorehouse. I mean a good, sophisticated woman like our hostess.'

'You're sure you're not being influenced by your loins?'

'I won't deny it. Odile does things to me. Yes, I want to satisfy myself in her. I want to spend a whole night exploring that marvellous body. A fighting man needs to be able to do that. But I also think it would do you some good to at least spend a little time with Mariette. What you do then is entirely your business. Read poetry to her, smell the flowers . . . anything. At times like these, who knows where we may be tomorrow? So, Karl-Heinz . . . what do you say? Shall we see them next week?'

'What about the Gestapo? Won't they have something to say about it? And your Obergruppenführer Schlierhof? You just warned me about him.'

'He's not *my* lousy Obergruppenführer. Herrenbach's my commander. As for the Gestapo, I know we saw Daggenau and Schlierhof playing cosy-cosy; but let me tell you, Schlierhof would stab Daggenau in the back at the first opportunity, and Daggenau would return the favour.

'But Daggenau won't give us trouble; at least, not for the time being. He's too busy playing with his prisoners and hunting out the Resistance helpers in the district. His weasel of a deputy, Grüber, might sneak around a bit, but I don't think he'll do anything without Daggenau's say-so. And Daggenau would not want to lean on me and offend Herrenbach, who's a much tougher customer than Schlierhof, despite being the junior rank. Also, don't forget it's my troops guarding his little hell on earth. Well? Shall we accept the invitation?'

'I'll think about it.'

'Don't take too long.'

In the château, Odile and Mariette were having breakfast in Mariette's bedroom. Both women were still in their night clothes, with Odile wearing something under her dressing gown that would have driven Meckler insane with lust. When the gown came open, which was often, the short nightdress bared all of her long, strong legs and most of her thighs. There was no underwear beneath the exceptionally thin garment.

Despite the time of year, she possessed a light tan

that was clearly a legacy of many years' worship of the summer sun. Of a generally bigger frame and taller than her older sister, she exuded an uninhibited and powerful sexuality as she sat cross-legged on the bed. Mariette's own sensual attractiveness was more subtle, but still evident.

Odile bounced slightly on the bed as she made herself more comfortable, her blonde hair a gleaming slow-motion curtain about her face.

'Well, they're gone,' she said. 'Did you mean it when you asked them back?'

Mariette nodded. 'Yes. As the commanders of the ground and air forces in the area, they're just what we need. We must cultivate them. But be careful, Odile. That Waffen-SS colonel is dangerous. He is nice and pleasant to you, but only because he wants you in bed. Do not forget what he really stands for.'

'I can handle him,' Odile said lightly.

'I am not so sure. What will you do when he thinks it's time he started undressing you?'

'I'll cross that bridge when I get to it.'

Mariette looked at her, brow furrowed. 'You're not really attracted to him, are you? Odile! That would be . . .'

'Don't worry. I know what I'm doing. I've done more dangerous things than this.'

'Perhaps. But this man is no fool. He's not like the others. If we are to continue being of use to the Resistance, we cannot be compromised . . .'

Odile hummed a little to herself then bit enjoyably into half a crusty roll, dipped in honey. 'And what about you?' She wiped a small, golden tendril that had slid off the edge of the roll and on to her full lower lip with a finger, then licked the finger clean.

'*Me?*' Mariette looked at her as if she'd taken leave of her senses.

'Yes. What about your airman? He thinks, like all those other idiots, you're a widow.'

'*My* airman? Don't be ridiculous. And besides, he's married.'

'How do you know?'

'Because, Odile, dear sister, I'm a married woman. I understand these things.' Mariette looked thoughtful. 'Although . . . I think he may have problems.'

'You know all that from just the one evening?'

'You can discover plenty, if you know what to look for. I caught him looking at you and Franz. There was a longing . . . no, no, not for you . . .'

Odile pouted. 'I am insulted,' she said theatrically.

'He was longing for someone else,' Mariette went on, ignoring her sister's interruption. 'There was a sadness in his eyes. His wife is either dead, or she is playing around and he knows it. I believe she is playing around. The sadness is not for someone who is dead, but for something that was once valuable and is now lost. The more I think about it, the more I'm certain I am right.'

'You're pretending that Michel is dead, and they all believe it. What kind of sadness do you show in your eyes?'

'Ah but you see, we're much better at it than men. We are experts at hiding what we really feel. It's not the expression on the face but what is hidden in the eyes. You're very good at it. You always were, even as a child.'

Odile gave her sister a sideways look, a tiny smile playing briefly about her lips. 'If you say so.'

'Look,' Mariette began in a change of subject, 'let's go for a little walk today. See if they've brought in any more guns or tanks, or changed positions.'

'We can always ask that horrible Grüber to accompany us,' Odile said with a giggle, 'to protect us from the soldiers. Grüber thinks I like him.'

'Be careful of him too. A rat like that is even more dangerous, especially when rejected. Meckler is someone who will react openly. Grüber will sneak behind your back. Remember what they did to Jeanne-Anne.'

Then something very strange happened to Odile. The sexual animal vanished. The laughing eyes grew chillingly cold.

'I'll never forget,' she said.

Helmut Grüber had been aptly described by Meckler. The man was indeed a weasel. He fitted perfectly the job description Hitler had laid down for the species he dubbed the *Gauleiter*. Grüber was the quintessential odious deputy, right-hand man, *éminence grise*. He could be relied upon to carry out any dirty work with great enthusiasm. A nonentity before the ascent of Hitler opened up a whole new world to him, he was the epitome of an inadequate who had suddenly found himself granted virtually unlimited power, within his own jurisdiction. He did what such people in his position invariably do: he abused it.

He had once been little more than a subsistence farmer in a small mountain village in Bavaria. Full of anger and frustration about his lot in life, he had been forced to endure from boyhood the taunts of his male peers and unending rejection by the village girls. They called him a weasel even then.

He had joined the Party in its very early days and quickly gained favour with its leadership for his ruthless espousal of the National Socialist ethos. Soon he was given a local command, then a district. When the Nazis eventually took over the reins of government, Grüber became a very powerful man indeed. Before long, the very girls who used to reject him began to seek favours from him. He made them pay, the only way that would please him; even the wives of those who had once taunted him.

High rank as Daggenau's number two had not blunted his desire to revenge himself upon all women. It simply meant he now had a wider selection to choose from; but even he would not dare go against Daggenau's orders as far as the Malzey sisters were concerned. However, it did not mean this prevented him from carrying out his normal duties. In matters regarding Gestapo activities in Occupied France, *all* French citizens were suspect.

Grüber was feeling particularly good that morning. He rolled out of bed, stood up and stretched his pale, thin body. His vulpine face, with its head of black strands of short, lank hair, turned to look at the bed as he brought his arms down. One of the French serving girls was lying beneath the rumpled bedclothes, back towards him. She was huddled in a foetal position, as if protecting herself. His lovemaking had been brutal, lacking finesse or any real emotion. It had been a service. Nothing more.

'You had better get back to your work,' he

commanded harshly in bad, arrogant French. 'You will not forget our little arrangement, will you? *Will you?*'

'No . . . no, monsieur,' came an answering mumble.

'Good. As long as you remember that and you come to me when I require, your family will be safe. You will be replaced if you fail me, and you will all be transported. I know you miserable French are hoping for the invasion. Even if it does come, we will make them wish they never tried. They won't be able to save you, my lovely Agnès. Do you hear me?'

'Yes, monsieur.'

'Now get out. Put on your clothes. Hurry! I have work to do. You can wash somewhere else.'

Agnès Grappin got out of the bed, never once turning to face him and hurriedly dressed with trembling hands. She quickly left the room, her body hurting as a result of Grüber's sexual attentions and ashamed that for some time now she had been his spy in the château. On occasion, he had warned her that she was not the only one.

8

The soft knock made Pendrake look up from his desk. Lewis entered.

'Flight Sergeant Charlton, sir.'

'Ah yes. Send him in.'

She stood back and Charlton marched in, came to a halt and saluted.

'Flight Sergeant Charlton reporting as ordered, sir!'

'At ease, Flight.'

'Sir.' Charlton relaxed.

Pendrake nodded at Lewis and she backed into her office, closing the door softly. The two Spitfires, with Kelly and Elmore at the controls, roared overhead on their way to patrol altitude.

'How do you like the idea of being a pilot officer, Peter?' Pendrake began as the sounds of the Merlins faded.

'Very much indeed, sir. But it's taken me a bit by surprise. Very unexpected.'

'Fully deserved.'

'Did you put me up for it, sir?'

'Yes. No problem with confirmation. It will be made official very soon. You'll have to go away for a bit when our little show is over, but I hope you'll be coming back to us.'

162

'I'd like to, sir.'

Pendrake nodded. 'Pleased to hear it. I'd hate to lose you to some other unit. Until your scraper arrives, I've arranged for you to move to the officers' mess . . .'

'If I may interrupt, sir.'

'Go ahead.'

'Unless it's an order, sir, I wouldn't mind remaining with the other sergeant pilots until the rank does arrive . . .'

'Granted,' Pendrake said. 'In any case when we move from these salubrious surroundings to a forward airfield, we'll all be billeted together. There is something else I did want to mention. The other sergeant pilots are fairly green. I'd like you to take them under your wing, especially young Benson. Would you do that?'

'No trouble at all, sir. Leave it to me. I'll sort them out.'

'Thank you, Pilot Officer Charlton.'

Charlton grinned as Pendrake stood up to approach him. 'Sounds strange, hearing it.'

Pendrake held out a hand. 'Get used to it. Congratulations, Peter.'

'Thank you, sir.'

As Charlton went out, the phone rang. Pendrake reached over to the desk and picked it up.

'Squadron Leader Pendrake.'

'Ah . . . Mike.' It was Rhys.

'Yes, sir?'

'We've got a bit of a problem. Your aircraft.'

Pendrake waited.

'The Typhoon 1B you brought in,' Rhys explained. 'I'm afraid the mods are rather more complicated than at first thought. You see, the "S" versions you've got out there are actually all-new aircraft. Now that we've done a partial strip-down, it appears that bringing yours to an equivalent standard requires a major rebuild. That means a return to the factory.'

Pendrake, hiding his disappointment, said, 'That would take more time than we've got.'

'Precisely what I thought. Knowing one of the reasons you wish to keep the aircraft, we've come up with an idea – or rather Sergeant Ransome has – which we hope you'll approve of.'

'May I have a word with him?'

'He's on his way to you right now. I think you'll like the suggestion. Listen to what he has to say.'

'Very well, sir. I'll wait to hear.'

'You won't be disappointed. Are you settling in all right?'

'Yes, sir. Those two 109s are continuing to do me some good.'

Rhys gave a chuckle. 'Can't deny it was a rather spectacular way to begin your command. The mess for lunch?'

'If I can get away.'

'The joys of command.'

'Just what someone said to me yesterday.'

Rhys chuckled once more. 'Never a truer word, old boy.'

The ground-crew sergeant was ushered into the office five minutes later.

'I hear you've got a solution to our problem, Sergeant Ransome,' Pendrake began.

'It's just an idea, sir . . . but it's a way out, if you'll agree.'

'The wing commander's already explained about

the difficulty of doing the job on site, so I'm open to any ideas you've got.'

'A little cannibalization, sir,' Ransome said, 'is what I'm thinking about. If we cut a panel about a foot square from your old aeroplane with the er . . .' He stopped, uncertain how to describe what he was thinking about.

'The hand,' Pendrake finished for him.

'Er . . . yes, sir. If we cut the panel, we can then cut a similar panel – an exact match – from the new aircraft. The panel with the . . . um . . . hand can then be flush-riveted to the new aeroplane, painted over and you'd never be able to tell the difference. The part that's been clear-doped will be exactly as before. There will be no structural penalty. We've already checked where it would go. We also thought the Typhoon you used yesterday to get those 109s would be the perfect choice. It could be your new personal kite, sir. We'll transfer all your kills to it.' Ransome ended his words in a rush and waited for a reaction from Pendrake.

Pendrake turned, then stood perfectly still by his desk, to stare at the cartoon Wilson had given him. But he wasn't seeing the drawing. His eyes were looking into the past and seeing Megan's intestine on the scorched tree. His face paled and the scar on his cheek felt hot for a brief moment.

At last he turned towards Ransome once more. 'That old Tiffy and I have been through a lot together. All right, Sergeant. Do it. How long will it take?'

Clearly relieved, Ransome replied, 'It will be done in no time at all, sir. She'll be ready for flight this afternoon, if you need her.'

Pendrake nodded. 'That will be fine. Thank you.'

'Oh, and how would you like the aircraft kills put on, sir? Swastikas, like on the old Tiffy? Or black crosses on a faded white background?'

'Keep the swastikas, but not as bright as they currently are. In fact, make all the kills low-key. We don't want them to stand out in the air against our new black paintwork, do we?'

Ransome smiled. 'We certainly don't, sir. The blokes are quite excited by the number of kills you've got. They say it looks as if you've been wiping out the Jerries all by yourself, and it'll take hours to stencil them all on. They're exaggerating about the time, sir.'

'Exaggeration or not, just don't let Flying Officer Wojdat hear you say that. He might get upset if he thinks I'm leaving nothing for him. All right, Sergeant Ransome. Thank you for coming. I like your idea.'

'Sir.'

Ransome saluted smartly and went out.

Pendrake went through to Lewis's office. 'When are the flight commanders due?' he asked her.

'After the medical, sir. I thought it would be better to wait until then. Medicals began an hour and a half ago.'

'Which gives us . . .?'

'About forty minutes.'

Pendrake glanced at his watch. 'I've got just enough time to get to Dispersal, have a look around to see how things are progressing, then get back here. I'm going to see how Bingo Wilson's doing with the fledglings. Leave you to hold the fort?'

'Of course, sir.'

'Thank you, Karen.' It was the first time he had addressed her with anything approaching familiarity.

'Sir.'

At Dispersal, Wilson had four of the Typhoons occupied. None had been started and he was going from aircraft to aircraft, pointing out salient features to the pilots in the respective cockpits. By a fifth aircraft, Charlton was talking to Benson, the youngest of the sergeant pilots. Pendrake noted that one of the aircraft had been moved to a hangar and he could see two of Ransome's men working away at the left rear fuselage.

He caught up with Wilson as his deputy was stepping off one of the Typhoons. The day was mildly chilly, but with no wind to speak of and with a high but cool sun, was crisp and pleasant.

'How's it going, Bingo?'

Wilson glanced up at the cockpit where Wojdat was busy familiarizing himself with the layout. 'Old Josef's very quick. I'm thinking of authorizing his first flight.'

'And the others?'

'They're coming along ... especially our New Zealander, Knowles. Amazing, really. For a man who's never flown single-seaters, he seems in his element.' Wilson smiled. 'Must have been a frustrated fighter pilot.'

'Aren't we all? Need me for anything?'

Wilson shook his head. 'No. But I'll yell if I do. Don't worry, Mike. I can handle it. You're the commander.' Wilson grinned. 'You've got serfs to do the dirty work now.'

Pendrake stuck his hands in his pockets and looked irresolute for some moments. 'What I want to do is get up there and fly.'

'Can't just do that any more, old son. You've got responsibilities now. Tell you what,' Wilson continued, relenting slightly, 'when I think they're good enough, you can take them flying. That should scare the pants off them.'

'I'd rather have them scared now than later. Flight commanders' meeting in . . . thirty minutes. If you've got any with you by then, send them on. You don't have to be there. No point interrupting the training. We'll talk later.'

'Right,' Wilson said as they walked towards another aircraft. 'Now push along, Mike, sir, and let me do my stuff.' He climbed on to the Typhoon and made his way up to the side of the cockpit. 'That, old son,' he said to the nervous pilot, 'is the supercharger lever. You don't want to mistake it for the throttle and grab at it in error. You might get a very nasty surprise. On the other hand, used judiciously, it will get you out of trouble . . . or should. Got it?'

The pilot nodded wordlessly, peering anxiously at the lever as if expecting it to jump up and bite him on the nose.

Pendrake gave a rueful smile and glanced upwards. There were high clouds in the otherwise clear sky. He could see a couple of specks describing a wide, slow circle. The Spitfire patrol.

'See you later, Bingo,' he called.

Wilson waved at him without turning round.

As he walked slowly back towards the staff car, the explosive start of one of the 2400-horsepower engines made him pause to look. Wojdat was getting ready for his flight. Pendrake decided to wait for the take-off.

The Typhoon began to taxi smoothly. Wojdat had clearly got a grip on things very quickly indeed. Pendrake watched keenly as the aircraft made its way towards the runway threshold, stopped, and Wojdat opened the throttle. The Typhoon bellow filled the air.

Then it was surging forward. Pendrake watched as the tail rose slightly as the Typhoon's great wing began to generate lift. Now the entire aircraft was off the ground, maintaining an infinitesimal raising of the nose. There was barely any swing to the right. The wheels came up. Wojdat continued to hold the aircraft low as the speed increased in a great rush.

Then the nose snapped up and the Typhoon hurled itself skywards.

'Not bad,' Pendrake said to himself approvingly. 'In fact, bloody good.'

'Not much I can teach him,' a distant voice said.

Pendrake turned to see that Wilson had paused in his tutorial to judge Wojdat's take-off. The pilot under instruction had a look of apprehensive envy as he turned his head to follow the Typhoon's flight.

Then Wojdat began to throw the Typhoon about.

'Show-off!' Wilson shouted at the cavorting aeroplane. He turned to his pupil. 'If you want to fly this thing like that nice man up there,' Pendrake heard him say loudly over the noise of Wojdat's exuberance, 'treat what I say to you like the Ten Commandments.'

Again, the pilot nodded wordlessly.

Pendrake smiled to himself as he entered the car. Bingo was doing all right. Wojdat too.

He checked the other aircraft, but forced himself not to visit the hangar to see how the work on his own Typhoon was progressing. He returned to the squadron offices with ten minutes to spare, just as the Spitfire patrol came in to land.

'Was that a Typhoon I heard a short while ago, sir?' Lewis asked as he entered.

'Yes. Wojdat. Barely needed any instruction. If the others are half as quick I'll be a very happy man. Any news on the medicals?'

She handed him a folder. 'The flight commanders are in your office.'

'And any response to the Spitfire request?'

'Nothing as yet. No news . . .'.

'Is not always good news.'

He opened the folder and quickly read through the sheets of paper. Everyone was cleared except for Keane, whose stiff right arm and shoulder needed more time.

He shut the folder and handed it back. 'Keane's not going to be too pleased.'

'He isn't,' she confirmed. 'You might have to calm him down.'

He nodded. 'I'll handle it. Kelly's just landed. I take it Mackenzie's deputizing?'

'Yes, sir.'

'No matter. I'll start immediately. They can liaise afterwards.'

'Very good, sir.'

'At ease, gentlemen,' Pendrake said as he entered his office. 'Let's make this informal. Grab seats wherever you can.' He went to his desk and sat down.

'Right,' he went on. 'This is as new to me as it is to you, so we're all going to have to help each other. You'll have realized by the almighty din a short while ago that we've got someone up already. That was our friendly Pole, Wojdat. Took to it like a veritable duck to water. I'm not expecting everyone else to be as quick, but I do expect fairly rapid progress. We do not have the luxury of time.'

'That puts me at a disadvantage, sir,' Keane said. 'The doc's *grounded* me,' he added, outraged by the medical officer's audacity.

'We'll dispense with the "sir" in here. I do appreciate your problem, Dominic. It's mine too. You're a bloody good pilot and as far as I'm concerned, a valuable flight commander. I do not intend to risk losing you, by forcing you into an aircraft while your arm and shoulder stand the slightest chance of inhibiting your flying ability. My reponsibility ensures that I take the doc's diagnosis seriously. I'd like to think that in my place, you'd do the same for me.' Pendrake's eyes held Keane's in their gaze.

Eventually, Keane took a deep breath and nodded slowly. 'You're right, I reckon. Only it's bloody frustrating. I've got to ask the boys to go up and do their best while I'm stuck on the ground. A flight commander who doesn't fly. Hell of a way to lead by example.'

'I do appreciate the difficulty. Your priority, therefore, is to get that wing working properly again. I'm going to need you for the show.' Pendrake grinned at him. 'Don't think you're going to sit it out.'

The Australian gave a reluctant, barely visible smile. 'As long as you mean that.'

'Oh, I do, even if it means I've got to get you up to scratch myself.'

'I'll hold you to that. So . . . what's the mission?'

Pendrake stood up. 'Come with me.'

They followed him through to Lewis's office.

'Any idea of the whereabouts of our French guest?' he asked her.

'With the wing commander, sir. He's being shown around. Shall I contact them?'

'No need. But if he makes contact, let me know immediately. We'll be in the model room.'

'Very good, sir.' There was a question in her eyes, but she did not voice it, and he ignored it.

'Gentlemen,' he said to the others, and walked out.

They trooped after him to the guarded room where the model of the château and its environs was installed. He switched the lights on as they followed him in. They stared at the display before them, each trying to work out what part it would eventually play in their lives.

'Find yourselves a good position from which to study this,' he told them and when they had, went on, 'This, gentlemen, is our target. Take a good, long look.'

There was a light wooden rod like an elongated swagger stick, leaning against the edge of the platform. Pendrake picked it up and began to indicate.

'Château. Primary target . . . but of virtually equal importance from a survival point of view – ours – are the defences . . . here, and here, and here, the château itself . . . Airfield with Focke-Wulf Fw-190s, and in and around the woods of the château, anti-aircraft emplacements, manned by the Waffen-SS. Within the grounds, more guns with these two multi-barrelled flak jobs just here, by the roof. There will be more of these nasties in the woods. Very, very dangerous and must be destroyed at the earliest opportunity. Take good note of their positions. Additionally, there are tanks and armoured vehicles, virtually all having some anti-aircraft capability.

'At the height at which we shall be operating, you can assume that light weapons will also be a threat to be considered. I intend to carry out a simultaneous, three-pronged attack.' The pointer was moving once more. 'The airfield, to neutralize the fighters; the woods, to engage the guns and tanks; and the château itself. We will be over the target area while it's still dark, but just before dawn. By the time dawn arrives, the attack should be long over and we'll be on the way home. One very important point: this red section of the château is not to be attacked . . . under *any* circumstances.

'I know we shall be attacking in poor light. However, any of you finding yourselves over the château must take note of your point of entry, which will then enable you to know exactly the position of the red zone. Memorize its relative position from any angle of entry. You'll have the opportunity to study this model as often as you like. On the day of the mission briefing, we'll have a detailed map on display.

'Timing will be vital. I shall cover that at a later date.' Pendrake straightened, holding the pointer in both hands across his lower body. 'You will all have seen from the model that I do not have to tell you how dangerous an undertaking this will be. Our best hope of success is to train rigorously, so as to carry out our attack with absolute precision and, hopefully, minimal or no casualties. If we do encounter fighters, we must also be able to take them on and *win*. We all know what happens to those who do not. They die.'

Pendrake stopped and studied their expressions. They were all staring at the model as if mesmerized, and were silent for a long while.

'Mother of God,' Mackenzie uttered at last, softly. 'The SS are growing like daisies in there.'

'Then we'll make sure they remain where they are. Permanently.'

'And those 190s,' Keane said. 'We've got to make sure they stay on the ground. Otherwise . . .'

Pendrake looked at him. 'That's your job, Dominic. I told you I needed you.'

Keane's eyes stared into his. 'Yes, sir.'

Keane had a reputation for very steady eyes, especially when first introducing himself. Don't call me 'Cobber' he would say, while those eyes zeroed in on the unfortunate victim. The eyes did not waver as they now looked at Pendrake.

'Can you do it?'

'Yes, sir,' Keane repeated.

Pendrake nodded, placed the pointer back against the platform, then leaned forward, resting his hands on the edge. He looked at each man, searching out their individual faces with probing eyes. The scar on his cheek glistened faintly in the hooded lighting.

'It's not going to be easy,' he told them, 'but it can be done. I cannot at this stage tell you the purpose of the mission. However, I can tell that our efforts will make a major contribution to the war effort in this theatre. There will also be ground forces in the area to mop up anything we leave standing.

'You'll be pleased to know that I have asked for, and we shall be receiving, six further Typhoons. This will give us a healthy margin with which to absorb any aircraft attrition. I intend to have three flights of at least six aircraft each, over the target area. If we keep the attrition rate down, we could have seven to each flight, plus myself. I shall be leading the attack on the château.

'Assume that we'll meet with ferocious resistance, so attack with your own ferocity to overwhelm the enemy. Don't give him time to think, and thus to react. If resistance is less than expected, then so much the better. Irrespective of enemy response, there will be no let-up in the aggressiveness of the attack. Remember, our business is killing Jerries, and there'll be plenty to go round. Originally, I was not going to inform you so soon. However, I've decided that since the available time is three weeks . . .'

'*Three weeks!*' It was Dodson.

'As I thought,' Pendrake said. 'Concentrates the mind wonderfully. Three weeks, gentlemen. That's all we've got.'

A short while after lunch, Pendrake got a call from Ransome.

'Can you come over to have a look, sir?' the ground-crew sergeant asked. 'We're nearly done.'

'On my way,' Pendrake said.

When he got to the hangar, the two aircraft were wing to wing. The difference between them was marked, the Typhoon S looking perceptibly bigger and meaner.

Ransome came up to him. 'Come and have a look, sir.'

Pendrake noted that the other members of the ground crew were eyeing him warily. It was obvious they weren't sure how to take the man who had downed the two Messerschmitts with such skill, but who also flew with the mangled hand of a dead enemy plastered to his aircraft.

Pendrake followed Ransome. The sergeant stopped by the left rear fuselage of the black Typhoon and pointed. It was a remarkable job. There was no indication whatsoever that the clear-doped remains had not been on the aircraft from the very beginning. It was only when Pendrake went over to look at his old 1B that the black panel on that aeroplane betrayed the change. They had done a straight swap.

'Fair exchange, sir,' Ransome explained.

'Indeed. A quite marvellous job, Sarge. My compliments.'

'Thank you, sir. We haven't done the change of kills as yet, but we've already put your two 109s on the blackbird.'

'I've decided to leave them where they are,' Pendrake said, looking at the markings beneath the cockpit rim. He gave the older Typhoon a gentle pat. 'She deserves her laurels. The blackbird can notch up her own tally,' he added, borrowing Ransome's nickname for the Typhoon S. 'And as you can see, she's already started.'

'Righto, sir. We'll leave the old kills on the 1B.' The sergeant peered up at the cockpit. The kills practically covered the side. 'Quite a score, sir.'

The first line of ten small swastikas denoted ten

aircraft downed. Beneath that were the silhouettes of twenty steam engines in double rows of ten. Next came tanks. There were twenty-five of those. The bottom line carried three rockets to show the sites destroyed, three patrol boats, and a radar antenna. Then on a line all by itself, was a silhouette that looked like part of a submarine.

'Did you really get a sub, sir?' Ransome enquired, staring at the marking.

'Just a third,' Pendrake replied. 'Three of us caught it just before dawn, limping along on the surface. It was heading towards the Cherbourg peninsula. It had either been hit in a battle somewhere and couldn't dive, or something had gone wrong and it was hoping to make it somewhere safe before daylight, from where it could later sneak down to the pens at St Nazaire. It would have managed it too except the dawn beat it, with the added bad luck that we happened to be there. We hit it with rockets before they could man their gun. Went down like a stone.'

'Well, sir, I agree with you. It would be a shame to rob the old girl of her glory.'

Pendrake gave the aircraft another pat before turning to Ransome. 'I'll leave you to it, Sarge. Thank you all,' he added to the ground crew. 'Excellent work.'

As he left, a Typhoon started up, while in the circuit another two were coming in to land.

Three days later all the squadron pilots, with two exceptions, had made at least two flights each in the new Typhoons. The exceptions were Keane, who waited in frustration for his arm and shoulder to get better, and Benson. Though he had flown a Spitfire patrol, Benson seemed to be having problems with the Typhoon. It was as if the aircraft intimidated him.

Even Elmore, who had no problems with the Spitfire and who on one occasion took off diagonally across the airfield, managed to land again with reasonable – by his standards – gentleness. The landing-gear was still in one piece after two of his landings.

But the time had come for Benson to make his debut. It was a grey sort of day and a light rain had fallen earlier, leaving the grass sparkling as if with a mild frost. Charlton was standing outside the cockpit, giving last-minute words of encouragement.

'Now remember . . . move the throttle smoothly. Don't rush it, and you'll be all right. Watch out for the swing. It's gentle so *don't* over-correct. OK?'

Benson, helmet on, stared at him and nodded.

'Good man.' Charlton patted him once on the shoulder, then climbed down.

Wilson approached as Charlton moved a safe distance away from the aircraft. 'Is he all right?'

'As right as he'll ever be,' Charlton replied. 'Either he'll do it, or he won't.'

They watched as the Typhoon was started. No problem there. Benson used the throttle as he'd been instructed. The powerful engine settled down to a steady idle. Benson left the canopy open as he taxied towards the runway. The aircraft was handled perfectly.

'So far, so good,' Charlton murmured, following the Typhoon with his eyes as it made its way to the threshold. 'Now just remember what I said,' he went on, speaking to the distant Benson. 'Easy does it.'

The Typhoon stopped. The canopy was slid shut.

The engine roared as Benson opened up the throttle. It began to roll forward. The tail came up. An incipient swing was corrected; but then it went too far the other way. Opposite correction was made as the speed built. Another swing, this time more pronounced, followed by another correction. The swing was reversed, quite violently.

Charlton watched in mounting horror. 'He's over-correcting! I told him to watch out. He's going to lose it!'

By now, the speeding Typhoon was swinging this way and that. It left the ground briefly, to touch down again in mid-swing. It gave a sharp pivot and began to head off the runway. The engine rose to a screaming bellow before suddenly dying, then it roared again, fitfully. The aircraft was now off the runway and heading straight for a fuel bowser. The driver saw it coming and tried to move out of its way.

As if now with a mind of its own, the Typhoon seemed to correct itself and again headed for the speeding truck. The aircraft tried to take off, actually leaving the ground completely. Had it continued upwards, it would have vaulted the truck. Instead, in sank back to earth.

Charlton and Wilson watched in helpless despair as the inevitable occurred in what seemed to them like slow motion. The Typhoon collided explosively with the fuel truck. A great fireball expanded from the point of impact then began to fold in on itself before expanding rapidly once more. They felt the heat of the blast on their shocked faces.

Then they began to run towards the blaze, already knowing it was a pointless effort.

In the control tower, just before the impact, they'd heard Benson screaming in terror and frustration.

'*I don't want to die! I don't want to die!*' he'd repeated over and over.

Pendrake heard the explosion, rushed out of his office, through Lewis's, and outside. She was hot on his heels. They made it in time to see the blaze and the rising pall of smoke in the distance.

'Oh dear God!' she exclaimed softly.

'I'm going out there,' he told her sharply. 'Stay by the phone. If anyone rings, tell them where I've gone.'

She was staring at the fire.

'*Section Officer Lewis!* Did you hear me?'

She brought herself back with a start. 'Yes, sir!'

'Better get back inside,' he said in a gentler tone. 'Not much you can do.'

'No, sir. Who . . . who do you think it is?'

'That's what I'm about to find out. Now off you go.'

He ran to the car without waiting to see if she'd done as he'd ordered.

He brought the car to a skidding halt, got out and ran to where Wilson and Charlton were standing. The crash crews were already at the wreckage, but the fierceness of the flames was beating them back. Even if anyone had survived the initial impact, there would have been no chance of effecting a rescue.

'Who was it?' Pendrake demanded.

'Young Benson,' Wilson replied flatly, not looking round. 'I hope he died when it happened. There was a driver in that bowser as well. Couldn't have felt anything though.'

'Damn it!' Pendrake muttered tightly. 'Damn it! What happened?'

'Over-corrected, sir,' Charlton answered. 'I warned him about that. I warned him . . .'

'Steady on, Peter. Not your fault.'

'Perhaps if I hadn't mentioned it, he wouldn't have been so preoccupied with correcting the swing that he forgot everything else.'

'You can't take the blame for that. Everyone gets a warning about the swing first time out. Afterwards it becomes instinctive. Now push off, you two. Talk to the others. I'll hang on here. Bingo, see that there isn't too much gloom and despondency around.'

'Yes, of course.'

They went off while Pendrake remained, staring at the fire as it continued to defeat the efforts of the crash crew to put it out, though it did not spread.

'The first letter,' he said to himself softly.

The scar on his cheek seemed to glow as it was reflected by the fire.

9

Pendrake went through to his office without saying a word to Lewis, only vaguely aware of her troubled eyes following him as he passed. He went up to his desk and stood there staring at the cartoon Wilson had given him, hands at his sides, fingers bunched tightly into fists. A soft knock sounded on the door behind him, but he did not respond.

Lewis slowly pushed it open and stood in the doorway, watching his rigid stance. She looked down and saw the tightly closed fists, which after a while came reluctantly open.

She entered, closing the door softly behind her, and went up to him. Tentatively, a hand reached out, intending to touch his shoulder, offering comfort. Then she hesitated, changed her mind and brought the hand back down.

'He was so young,' she said.

'We were all young, once,' he retorted with a harshness that surprised her. He whirled suddenly and the cold fire in his eyes startled and frightened her at the same time. 'And people die.' He turned from her once more. 'Now I must write my first letter as a commander. Was there something you wanted?'

The coldness of his tone struck at her and she blinked uncertainly.

'I . . . I just thought you might want someone to talk to . . .'

He walked round to his chair and sat down, the cold eyes looking up at her. 'About what, precisely? About death? This is wartime. People die singly, in their hundreds, their thousands, every day. Pilots are going down all over the place. What makes this so special?'

His words shocked her. 'You know you don't believe that, sir!'

'What I do or do not believe is not up for discussion. I've got a job to do. More of these men are going to die before it's over, and it's up to me to get as many of them over the target as possible. And that's what I'm going to do. I want all of them in the briefing room within twenty minutes. Pull them off whatever they're currently doing. If the Spitfire patrol is down, I want those pilots to attend. Thank you, Section Officer Lewis. Now please see that it's done.'

She was staring at him, the blue eyes suspiciously moist.

There was no warmth in his own eyes. 'I trust you have not lost the use of your limbs?'

'No. No, sir.' She tightened her lips, turned, and went out.

He waited until the door had closed behind her, then put his head in his hands.

Mackenzie was leading the Spitfires back to the airfield.

'Smoke!' he called to Wojdat in the second machine. 'How come we missed an attack?'

'We do not know it is an attack,' Wojdat said, eagerly checking that the two 20mm cannons and four .303 machine-guns of his Spitfire XIV were ready to fire, just in case. Wojdat didn't need an excuse for a scrap.

'Check us out,' Mackenzie ordered. Homebase would have warned of an impending attack, but you never know. It could have been a sneak approach that might have caught them by surprise and all communications could be down.

'Roger. Checking.' Wojdat pulled slightly behind and did a complete circle, scanning the sky about them for hostile aircraft. 'No bandits,' he eventually called regretfully.

It had been a source of constant disappointment to him that since the downing of the 109s by Pendrake, no other enemy aircraft had seen fit to come calling. He would have been quite happy for such an event to occur every day . . . as long as he was part of the welcoming committee.

'Roger,' Mackenzie responded. 'Rejoin formation.'

'Roger. Rejoining formation.'

As Wojdat formatted on his wing, Mackenzie called the airfield. 'Homeguard to Homebase. Returning from patrol. Are you under attack? Over.'

'Not under attack, Homeguard. Repeat. *Not* under attack. You are cleared to land. Over and out.'

'What the . . . Did you hear that?'

'Yes,' Wojdat replied.

'Then what the hell happened?'

'We will find out soon, I think.'

Wilson was waiting for them when they landed, their faces registering profound shock when he told them what had taken place.

'Such a young boy,' Wojdat remarked softly, himself just twenty-two. He stared in the direction of the still-rising smoke, though the fire had by now been put out. 'He was not even nineteen.' He shook his head. 'This shit war. It takes all the innocents.'

'God damn it,' Mackenzie muttered.

'We'd better get along,' Wilson urged them. 'The CO wants to see everyone in the briefing room. He has a few strong words to say, I fancy.'

Pendrake stood before them grim-faced.

'I will not mince words,' he began. 'Benson is dead because he behaved foolishly.' He looked at the shocked expressions brought on by his comments and continued unrepentantly, 'Yes. You heard correctly. Benson was given clear instructions. He was particularly warned to remain calm. In short, he panicked and now he is *dead*. But I blame myself. Despite the fact that he handled the Spitfire adequately and, given time, would have become a fine pilot, we do not have the time, and he was not yet ready for the Typhoon. I should have obeyed my instincts and rejected him as soon as I felt uneasy.

'I therefore give you fair warning – your first mistake, if you survive it, will be your last with this unit. I do not care what rank you are, how many hours you've got, how many kills, or how many aircraft you've flown. From now on, training will be intensified. If you're going to die, the enemy will be responsible. You will not be allowed the luxury of either ignorance or inattention. I will be absolutely ruthless with anyone who does not measure up. The manuals you were given were not doorstops. They're there for you to read, digest and understand. *Use them.* Flight Lieutenant Wilson!'

'Sir!'

'Carry on.'

'Sir.'

Pendrake stepped off the dais and went out.

'Jeez!' Elmore said to no one in particular. 'Some horsefly bit him in the butt? Why did he have to be so hard on Benson? The poor kid's dead, for Chrissakes. Fried to a . . .'

'Captain Elmore!' Wilson snapped.

'Yeah.'

'Shut it. Now everybody, back to work. I want each of you to make at least one Typhoon flight before nightfall.'

As they went out, Elmore found himself next to Kelly.

'What's with the CO, Sean? Doesn't he care about what happened to Benson?'

Kelly sighed. 'Sometimes I wonder if we come from the same country. Use your brains, Elmore. Of course he cares.'

'Got a helluva way of showing it.'

'If you live long enough to get a command, you might understand. Just.' Kelly walked on ahead.

'I only asked a simple question,' Elmore muttered to himself.

'Perhaps you are a simple man,' commented Wojdat, who was passing by.

'Great,' Elmore retorted. 'Now I've got a darned Polack on my back.'

But Wojdat was already out of earshot.

Back in his office, Pendrake laboured over the best way to compose the letter he needed to write to Benson's parents. Was there ever a best way? he wondered. How do you tell doting parents that their only son, barely nineteen, has burned to death in his aircraft?

'You don't,' he said aloud.

You tell them about a young boy, eager to do his bit, but frightened too. No. Don't tell them about being frightened, in case your own fears and your own hatred of the enemy permeate the letter. Don't spoil their picture of their son.

He paused, temporarily defeated, and suddenly began to appreciate the difficulties of Foxy the Viscount, his former CO, in similar circumstances.

'You knew what you were doing, you old schemer,' he said, 'when you recommended me for this command. I wish you could take it back.'

But Pendrake knew there would be no respite for him. The joys of command, as Montcarneau had so perceptively remarked.

He started on the letter for the third time.

Wilson and his fellow instructors took Pendrake's words to heart. For the next three days, the airfield echoed with the continuing bellow of Napier engines. It seemed there was never a moment when a Typhoon or two was not in the air.

Wilson pushed the pilots hard and from time to time Pendrake turned up at Dispersal to check progress.

On each occasion, he went away feeling pleased, but giving nothing away. Keane was at last passed fit to fly, and the Australian put in as many hours as he possibly could until he caught up and then surpassed many of those who had started before him.

There were no other accidents. Elmore learned to take off in a straight line, and to land the aircraft smoothly. The time was fast approaching when they would all be taught to use the Typhoon in the role it was designed for: as a formidable fighting weapon, in all weathers, and at any time of the day or night.

Pendrake was so satisfied with progress that he gave them a day of rest, but they were still required to continue their study of the manuals.

The morning of that day dawned brightly and the tired pilots were so relieved that after the three days of virtually non-stop intensive flying they could enjoy a lie-in, most of them missed breakfast. Wojdat, who never seemed to get tired, had volunteered to fly the Spitfire patrol. And Elmore, who never missed breakfast no matter what, was another of the exceptions. He was detailed to be Wojdat's wingman.

The noise, when it came, startled the dozing pilots awake and they rushed to their respective windows to check, primed to head to the nearest shelters, expecting an attack. The multiple sound of powerful engines approaching seemed to fill the world.

'Who's on patrol?' someone yelled.

'Must be Elmore and Wojdat,' came an answer. 'They're not here. Mason-Dixon never passes up a chance to eat, and Wojdat won't stop flying until he gets every Jerry, or they get him.'

'An attack?'

'We'd better get out of here if it is.'

But when they rushed outside, an astonishing sight greeted them.

Six black Typhoons, in perfect echelon starboard formation and trailed by two Spitfires, were approaching the airfield. When the first aircraft reached a point roughly halfway along the runway, it broke smartly left and up into a crisp ninety-degree bank to curve across on to a reciprocal heading. The mighty Napier was throttled back, the aircraft banked once more, wheels coming down. With exact precision, each following aircraft performed the same manoeuvre, including the Spitfires, giving the impression of a vast fan spreading in the air across the airfield.

'Wow!' exclaimed Kelly. 'They look beautiful. Those guys handle those planes like aces. Somebody must like us. The CO's got his extra Tiffies.'

'Those Spits are extra too,' a voice said. 'That's not Wojdat and Elmore.'

'You're right,' Mackenzie said. He was staring upwards at two small shapes. 'They're up top.'

'So now we've gotten *four* Spits as well.' Kelly sounded pleased. 'Great! Wonder who's bringing them in. Did you see those peel-offs? Beautiful, beautiful.'

'For an air show,' a cautionary voice put in. 'But can they fight?'

The first Typhoon landed. It was a classic three-point touchdown. The remaining aircraft followed precisely in its wake.

'God,' Kelly said. 'Don't those landings make you feel sick with envy? Hey, you don't think the CO's so cheesed with us,' he went on to them all, expressing a sudden worry, 'he's asked for new pilots, do you? I mean, after what he said when Benson . . .'

'He gave us a day off. He wouldn't do that unless he felt we were getting things right,' Keane said from a doorway. Instinctively, he rubbed at his right shoulder.

'One way to find out,' Mackenzie said. 'Let's get dressed and see who they are.'

'Now why didn't you think of that, Kelly?' a new voice, the New Zealander, Knowles, demanded.

They all laughed and hurried back inside, but Kelly's words had sounded ominous.

A second surprise awaited the Cobra Squadron pilots when they'd made it to Dispersal. The new aircraft were being marshalled to a stop, and one by one the engines were cut. The abrupt, relative silence appeared to leave the echo of their arrival hanging in the March air.

Kelly, Dodson and Mackenzie were the first to reach the lead aircraft. As they did so, the patrol Spitfires swept low along the runway then broke into their own rather spectacular peel-off, to come curving in to land. Wojdat had always been a superb practitioner of the art, but Elmore was catching up. Both made excellent landings.

However, not many people were watching. Nearly all attention was focused on the new Typhoons and Spitfires.

Kelly, Dodson and Mackenzie watched agape as the pilot of the lead Typhoon, goggles still on, slid back the hood, then picked up something from within the cockpit and began applying it carefully.

'What the hell?' Kelly began softly, astonished. '*Lipstick?*'

The helmet came off, and a mass of blonde hair tumbled down.

'Oh . . . my . . . God,' Dodson whispered in reverence. 'A blonde job. How . . . how . . .?'

'How are you?' Mackenzie called, stealing a march and hurrying up to the cockpit. 'Here, let me help you out of there.'

'Why thank you,' she said, smiling prettily at him. Her green eyes sparkled with amusement.

Male consternation was repeated at each of the other aircraft, including the Spitfires. All were 'blonde jobs', though they were not all blonde. They came in different heights, sizes, and hair colours. All were astonishingly attractive. The pilots, having witnessed the women's professional flying abilities, found themselves trying to balance their damaged egos with their desire to entertain their female guests. One of the female pilots was so small that they wondered how she managed to see over the nose of the huge Typhoon at all. Yet her flying had been impeccable.

'Kind of makes us look pretty silly, don't it?' Kelly murmured to Dodson as Mackenzie helped the blonde pilot out.

It was obvious she was quite capable of climbing out of cockpits, but chose to humour the Canadian. At the other aircraft, the rest of the squadron were also rediscovering the pleasures of chivalry.

'I have a feeling,' Dodson said, 'the CO's going to have a few stinging comments to make to us.'

'Funny. I've got the same feeling.'

Mackenzie dropped to the ground and helped his charge off the aircraft. 'Flying Officers Kelly and Dodson, Miss Amanda Treven of the Air Transport Auxiliary.'

She shook hands with each man, her green eyes amused by their confusion. 'Don't looked so shocked. I've been doing this for some time, you know.' Her voice was full of warm laughter. 'I've delivered many different aircraft, including Lancaster bombers. Mike Pendrake's the CO here, isn't he?'

'You know the CO?' Mackenzie asked.

'Oh yes. We're old friends,' she added mysteriously.

'Wouldn't you just know it?' a disappointed Mackenzie began. 'Just my luck.'

The ATA pilot gave him one of her best smiles. 'We're just good friends.'

'I've heard that one before.'

'Come on. Take me to him. I've got to deliver these aeroplanes officially.'

'Yes, ma'am,' he said, giving in gracefully. He turned to see Kelly and Dodson hurrying towards the other aircraft. 'Hey. Where are you two going?'

'Pastures new!' they called back.

Pendrake's car, on the way to Dispersal, pulled up when they were halfway to the squadron buildings. He got out, eyes full of surprise. '*Amanda?*'

She gave him a great hug, while Mackenzie looked on ruefully. 'Hullo, Mike,' she greeted him warmly. 'Nice new rank, I see. How does it feel.'

'That would take hours to tell.' Pendrake looked at Mackenzie. 'Thank you, Mac. I'll take it from here.'

'Yes, sir,' Mackenzie said with his wistful smile. 'Oh to be a CO.' He turned and hurried back to where the new aircraft were parked. 'Leave some for me!' he shouted at the others.

Pendrake looked at Amanda Treven. 'What's this? You're here for a few seconds and you're already breaking my pilots' hearts?'

'I'm the one with the broken heart.'

'Amanda . . . you know that's not true.'

'Megan and I were best friends, Mike. It hurt me too when she was killed. And I'll even admit I was jealous when you married her instead of me. But you can't grieve for ever . . .'

'Let's do the hand-over,' he interrupted tersely.

She gave him a world-weary smile. 'I'll let you change the subject. For now.' She kissed him quickly where the scar marked his cheek.

'I'd heard you had taken up flying,' he began as they got into the car and headed back to the squadron, 'with the intention of getting into the ATA. But it never occurred to me you'd one day wind up on a station where I'd be, *and* flying a monster like the Tiffie, of all things. You were so . . .'

'Ladylike?'

'Not quite that . . . but you know what I'm getting at.'

She nodded. 'People used to think I was just an empty-headed blonde, waiting for the right moment to snare an indolent young man with inherited wealth . . . but war changes many things.'

'I never believed that about you.'

'I know,' she told him fondly. 'That was why I thought Megan was so lucky . . .' She stopped suddenly. 'Oh my God, Mike. I'm . . . I'm so sorry. That was quite stupid of me.'

'Not to worry,' he assured her; but his eyes had briefly lost their welcoming warmth as the memory of Megan's death once more assailed him. 'And here we are. My first squadron.'

Lewis was standing outside, near the entrance. She looked interestedly at the car as it drew up.

'And who's that pretty thing waiting so patiently for you?' Amanda Treven enquired pointedly, eyes sharpening. 'My word. She's even wearing nylons.'

'Section Officer Karen Lewis, my adjutant. And I haven't noticed the nylons.'

'Your adjutant, in nylons, and you haven't noticed. She looks frightfully possessive. Should be an interesting evening.'

He glanced at her as he parked in his slot. 'Evening? You're staying the night?'

'But of course. All of us. The Ansons will be picking us up tomorrow, to take us back to HQ at WW.'

'This will make the boys happy. I gave them the day off.'

'And you? Will you be happy? Will I see you in the mess later?'

'You will.'

'And Section Officer Lewis?'

'What of her?'

She gave a private smile of mystery. 'We shall see what we shall see.'

'Behave yourself, Amanda.'

'I always behave myself . . . according to my own lights.'

Pendrake's own tiny smile betrayed memories of times that seemed centuries ago. How innocent we all were, he thought.

'I know how you behave,' he told her.

'Forewarned is forearmed,' she said unrepentantly.

As they climbed out, she saw that Karen Lewis's blue eyes were riveted on her.

'If that isn't a challenge,' she murmured to herself, 'I don't know what is.'

They were having a rare old time in the mess that evening. Outside, a light flurry of snow eddied about. It didn't settle. The ATA pilots, some of whom had not seen each other for several days and even weeks before the ferry flight, were catching up on horror stories about particular aeroplanes they'd previously delivered to other units. The squadron pilots, meanwhile, danced attendance on them. For the evening, Pendrake had invited the sergeant pilots as guests of the mess.

Wojdat was in his element, having discovered to his joy that not only was one of the ATA pilots a Pole, but her family happened to come from a small town close to his own home. They were conversing with each other in a torrent of animated Polish, each glad to have someone with whom to share the language. Roza Licyzyk was so petite that she looked tiny by comparison with all the other women pilots. Yet she had brought in a hulking Typhoon.

Over in a cosy corner, Michel Montcarneau was holding court to an attentive statuesque, black-haired beauty and three squadron pilots who dearly wished he would go away and leave her to them.

The barman had turned on the speakers that were part of the station's radio diffusion system. Glenn Miller's *Moonlight Serenade* was softly playing.

Observing Wojdat talking to little Roza at one end of the room, Elmore said, 'I can hear the old man tomorrow. "If a slip of a girl like that can fly the Typhoon",' he continued in an atrocious imitation of an English accent, '"you should be ashamed if you cannot".'

'He'll never say that, Mason-Dixon,' Dodson said, going past with two beers. 'And that was a wretched accent.' He handed one to an elegant redhead at a nearby table, and sat down.

They'd brought two tables together. Four of them had managed to secure the company of two of the ATA pilots, of whom the redhead was one. The other was a sultry but very self-contained brunette with eyes that looked out upon the world with clinical detachment as she swayed very slightly to the music. Her husband, a lieutenant commander on a destroyer, had been torpedoed in the Atlantic two years before. His body was never found.

'You wait,' Elmore said with baleful promise. 'Where is he, anyway?'

'Entertaining our leader,' the redhead, Marcia Torrance, informed him. 'They know each other from way back.'

'Oh ho!' Elmore said.

'Leave it,' Mackenzie said to him sternly.

The brunette, Eileen Taft, gave him one of her less detached looks. 'You're always quick to defend him. Your CO, I mean.' It was a question as well as a statement.

'He has a tough job,' Mackenzie told her. 'He needs all the breaks he can get.'

'Well, he's sure got a break tonight,' the irrepressible

Elmore announced brightly. 'Not one, but two. Take a look, guys.'

They all looked and saw Pendrake enter with both Amanda Treven and Karen Lewis.

'Who is she?' Eileen asked in a voice heavy with meaning.

'That is Section Officer Lewis,' the fourth squadron pilot in the group replied. He was a sergeant named Williams, who came from Newport in Wales. 'Our adjutant.'

'She's very pretty and despite that pleasant smile trapped on her face, I'd say she's not happy to have our Amanda hovering around your CO. Not happy at all. Wouldn't you say so, Marcia?'

'Oh, I would. I would. To a woman, it's very obvious. Mind you, he's rather nice. That scar suits him. The battle-hardened warrior. Sends a woman weak at the knees.'

'Hey,' Elmore began in an aggrieved tone. 'Hold it. We're nice too. We're warriors as well. I was with an Eagle Squadron. Gotten me a couple of 109s and a 110. And Dodson, Mac and Taff Williams have . . .'

She patted him on the knee. 'Of course you're all warriors.' She glanced in Pendrake's direction. 'Strange, though, he doesn't seem really interested in either of them.'

'His wife died,' a voice said evenly from above.

They looked up, startled, and saw Bingo Wilson.

'Two days after they were married,' he continued in the same calm voice. 'Blown to bits by a bomb. He was there at the time. Not a scratch on him.'

Both women paled.

'How terrible!' Marcia said.

'He's handling it,' Wilson said in the same unruffled voice. 'He can take care of himself. Go easy on the liquids, gentlemen,' he went on to the pilots. 'You fly tomorrow. You will not be allowed to fly if, in the MO's opinion, your blood's changed places with alcohol. Not being able to fly will count very badly against you indeed. Within those parameters, enjoy yourselves.' He moved on.

Watching as Wilson stopped at another table to pass on his warning, Elmore said, 'He must have been a nice guy, once. I remember when . . .'

'Oh come on,' Mackenzie said. 'You know he's right.'

In the silence that descended, the music came to an end. The voice on the radio said, 'And here is another popular number.'

The upbeat of *Tuxedo Junction* flowed from the speakers.

Eileen, tapping a finger lightly to the rhythm, was looking in Pendrake's direction.

'He's still in love with his wife,' she observed quietly.

'A challenge to any woman, something like that,' Marcia remarked shrewdly. 'And irresistible.'

'Hey,' Elmore pleaded. 'Ladies. We're still here.'

'Of course you are, darling,' she said. She lit a cigarette and looked at him through the smoke that she blew. She smiled at them all, a little sadly. 'Isn't war hell?'

They had found a quiet table. As the women sat down, Pendrake said, 'What's it to be?' He looked at each of them in turn.

'Can your mess barman run to mixing a Martini, if you've got the stocks?'

'I think he can manage. As you can see by the unit badges, the Americans were here and they left quite a few things. And we've got a shaker.'

'You remembered.'

'I've not been on another planet, Amanda. Karen?'

She'd been listening to their banter, feeling a little out of it. 'Er . . . a beer, please, sir.'

'Let's dispense with the "sir", shall we?'

'Yes, s . . .' She stopped, and gave a quick nod.

'Share a Martini with me,' Amanda said to her unexpectedly.

'But I . . .'

'Get her a Martini, Mike.'

Pendrake looked at Karen. 'Is that all right?'

After a pause, she gave another quick nod.

'A little protective of you, isn't he?' Amanda said as Pendrake went up to the bar. 'Nice to see. But take my advice. Don't fall in love with him.'

A bright flush appeared briefly along Karen's jawline and upper neck. 'I . . . I don't know what you mean,' she said quickly.

'My dear, you've just betrayed yourself with those simple words. And I won't mention your blushes. He's still in mourning. Believe me. I know. She was my best friend and after it happened I tried to snap him out of it. I confess to having a personal interest. But it didn't work. We lost touch for nearly two years. It's the first time I've seen him since.'

Amanda paused, then went on reflectively, 'I wanted him to choose me instead of Megan. Of course, there was not the slightest chance. He was absolutely mad about her. And yet, if he had chosen me, I'd be the one who was dead. I wouldn't have flown that aircraft in today; and I wouldn't be here, trying to talk you out of falling for him. Bit of a thought, isn't it?' She gave a slight shiver.

Karen glanced to where Pendrake was waiting as the barman mixed the drinks. Amanda studied her expression closely.

'God,' the ATA pilot said softly, resignation in her voice. 'You have got it bad. Does he know? And please don't deny it – not to a . . . veteran like me, anyway.'

Karen shook her head, not trusting herself to speak.

'Just as well,' Amanda said. 'But please bear in mind what I said. When he does come out of it, you may not like the man that emerges.'

'And you?'

'If I loved him, I wouldn't care what he was like.'

'And do you love him?'

Amanda looked sideways at Karen, her head tilted slightly, glanced to where Pendrake was collecting the drinks and putting them on a small tray, then back to Karen again.

'Who knows?' she said.

10

There was no snow on the ground the next day.

Two Ansons arrived an hour after breakfast for the ATA pilots, who gave addresses and telephone numbers to the squadron aircrew who were in turn forbidden to make contact until after the mission. Bingo Wilson's warning had been taken very seriously and the medical officer had passed everyone fit to fly.

Pendrake accompanied Amanda to the waiting aircraft.

'Let's not allow another two years to pass,' she said to him, her green eyes searching his face. 'In fact, let's not even wait two months. How about dinner in town?'

'Don't say the Ritz,' he said. 'Everyone planning to meet in London always says the Ritz, or the Savoy.'

'Did you plan to take Megan to either?'

'Both,' he admitted reluctantly.

'All right. Not the Ritz, or the Savoy. I know a nice little place. Guaranteed not to be crowded by every uniform in the country.' She kissed him quickly on the mouth. 'Do look after yourself, Mike.' She glanced about her and saw the rest of her pilots saying their goodbyes. 'Most of your young men appear to have come to see my girls off. A few budding romances, perhaps?'

'Does that happen everywhere they go?'

'Not always. We don't often go to one destination in such a large group. Roza seems to have taken to your Polish friend.' She smiled at him. 'I like Karen. She's nice.'

He looked at her questioningly. 'I thought I detected a slight ... edginess between the two of you last night.'

'I wouldn't pay much attention to that. Woman's stuff.'

'Don't quite know what I'd have done without her,' he said. 'I'm fortunate she was assigned to me. She's rather a find. A treasure, really.'

'A treasure,' she repeated. 'I suppose so.' She turned and walked towards the waiting Anson. She didn't tell him she thought Karen reminded her very strongly of Megan.

The Ansons began to taxi towards the runway.

'That was some lady.'

Pendrake whirled to see Halloran standing behind him.

'Jack Halloran!' he exclaimed. 'No one warned us you were coming. Where did you spring from? I didn't see you come off the aircraft.'

Halloran, carrying the familiar briefcase, grinned at him. 'That's because you were so busy saying goodbye. I got told the Ansons were coming from White Waltham to pick up your ferry pilots, so I got there fast and hitched a ride. Very, very nice,' he added, looking at the aircraft Amanda Treven had boarded.

'An old friend.'

'Very, very nice,' Halloran repeated. He held out a hand.

'How do, Mike?' They shook hands.

'Doing all right.'

'Like your new airplanes?' Halloran continued as they paused to watch the Ansons line up for take-off. 'Got your Spitfires too, I see.'

'Thanks for getting that through.'

'Anything to help.'

'Well, yes. The price might be a bit steep.'

'I'm sorry. I . . . heard about young Benson.'

The Ansons revved up for take-off then began their sedate run. As the squadron pilots, already kitted out, waved furiously, Pendrake could see answering waves coming from both aircraft.

Halloran said, 'Your boys made new friends?'

'Perhaps. But you never can tell, with a war on, how long that might last.'

'I guess.'

The Ansons drifted primly into the air and Pendrake headed back to his car, followed by Halloran.

As they got in, Halloran saw the pilots hurrying towards their Typhoons. 'Keeping them busy.'

Pendrake started the car and moved off. 'They're coming along. Benson's accident taught them a harsh lesson.'

'I hear you got two Messerschmitts.'

Pendrake glanced at him. 'So you know.'

'You made a report. Anything to do with this outfit gets passed on to me.'

'I want to talk to you about that.'

'Oh?'

'Those 109s weren't just wandering around looking for trouble. They were on a definite mission. They were looking for this place . . . for us.'

Halloran stared at Pendrake. 'What do you mean?'

'What I did not mention in the report I sent in, was the fact that they were armed PR jobs with long-range tanks. I decided to wait until I'd spoken to you. We retrieved one of their cameras. The pilot had already taken some shots . . . of the airfield, and even very detailed close-ups of the new Typhoons. How was it, I asked myself, that the enemy seemed able to mount a photo-recce so soon after our own arrival here?'

'You tell me,' Halloran said quietly.

'Someone's been talking.'

'Are you suggesting *my* people . . .'

'I'm suggesting nothing. Bend your mind to it and see what you come up with. Because they were able to penetrate so deeply, I've assumed they maintained strict radio silence. This means, I hope, their base has no idea of the circumstances under which they were shot down. So we're still unknown, for the moment.

'The pilot who took the photographs would only fight long enough in order to gain sufficient breathing space, to enable him to carry out his mission: taking the photos. That was such a priority, he was prepared to risk being shot down. He was a pretty good pilot too. Every time I went into the attack, he evaded, and would only counter when hard-pressed. In the end, I boxed him into a corner. He overcooked it, and went in. Just over there, beyond the perimeter.'

'Where's the camera?'

'Safe.'

'May I see the film?'

'Of course.'

'Has Michel seen it?'

'No. He knows nothing of the camera.'

Halloran was staring at him again. '*What?* You didn't tell Michel? Why?' Halloran paused. 'Oh come *on*. You can't suspect *him*. Do you know how long I've worked with that guy on the other side of the water? When I first started, he kept me alive and prevented me from making an asshole of myself. I could have gotten killed lots of times if Michel hadn't been there to see I didn't get my fool butt shot off. I was the original eager American who thinks he knows it all. Michel was very patient with me. Not him, Mike. He's got his wife inside that goddam place, for Pete's sake!'

'He could be under pressure. The Gestapo are past masters at emotional blackmail. They know how to turn the screw. If anyone knows about that, you do.'

'You're wrong about Michel.'

'I hope so. I like the man. But you've got to accept we've got a problem. I do not expect another intrusion up here. But when we move to the forward airfield, we'll be within easy range for a night bomber assault. If that happens, our aircraft may be destroyed and your mission sunk without trace. I'd suggest you get your people to seal off all potential sources of leaks; and do it quickly. Time's running out, if you want to keep to the original schedule.'

Halloran was silent as they drove on to the squadron.

'I'll see what I can do.'

'That's all I ask. My pilots have a dangerous enough task as it is.'

By the time Pendrake had pulled into his parking slot, four Typhoons were up in the air.

Halloran watched the short film in silence. Michel Montcarneau had not been asked to attend.

When it had flickered to the end of its run, he gave a deep sigh. 'No doubt about it. They came hunting for you. I'll get word to my people about it. Damn it!' He sounded very upset.

'Thank you, Sergeant,' Pendrake called to the Photo Intelligence WAAF NCO at the projector. 'Seal both the film and the camera, and keep them handy for the major for when he's ready to leave the station.'

'Yes, sir.'

'Well?' Pendrake said to Halloran as they left the small room. 'What now?'

Halloran tapped his briefcase. 'It so happens that I've gotten some new information from the château. New gun emplacements and troop positions.'

'*New* emplacements . . .'

'Not really new. Just ones that were always there but we haven't put on the model, and new positioning. Better get Michel to handle that.'

'What will you tell him about the camera and the film?'

Halloran gave a tight smile. 'Nothing. See? You've got me at it.'

'I am sorry. I don't want you to fall out with the man who's looked after you since this madness began.'

'Hell, there must be things he hasn't told me about . . . in case I got caught one day. If he ever gets to know of this, I'll use that excuse.'

'Would he accept that?'

Halloran shrugged.

At the Château de St Sauveur, Mariette went for one of her restricted strolls in the grounds, under the stony gaze of the SS guards. There were wisps of cloud high in the otherwise clear sky. She heard a faint sound and looked up. Two fast-moving specks traversed the air directly above. She wondered whether one of them was piloted by Karl-Heinz Ketelheim.

'The Luftwaffe maintaining its constant patrol, madame.'

The suddenness of the voice made her jump and she turned to look into the vulpine features of Grüber. His smart turnout, his hair slicked to his scalp, only served to increase her feeling of revulsion. She gave no outward sign of this.

'I do apologize for startling you,' he told her smoothly. But there was no contrition upon the hated face. 'Not harbouring a guilty conscience, I hope?'

'What have I got to be guilty about?' she snapped.

'Now, now, madame. No hostility, please. You've always been so . . . cooperative. I would not like to have to revise my opinion of you.' Though he was softly spoken, there was an undisguised promise of the menace to come, should such a change of opinion actually take place. 'That would indeed be so unfortunate.'

'You . . . you startled me, Herr Grüber.'

'Again, I apologize most humbly.'

Having deposited his poison, Grüber walked silently away.

She looked about her and noticed a couple of the SS guards smirking openly. She decided to go back inside, her walk in the gardens now completely ruined.

Ketelheim was indeed piloting one of the pair of highly manoeuvrable and powerful late-model Focke-Wulf Fw-190Ds – specially designated Ta152Cs to honour the aircraft's designer, Kurt Tank – that Mariette had spotted flying high above her. He had deliberately altered his course so that his patrol track would cross directly over the château. He wondered what she was doing.

On the left side of the nose of the 190, he sported an emblem that had, from his early career as a fighter pilot, earned him the name 'Goldener Ritter' – Golden Knight. It was of a golden armoured knight mounted upon a golden charger at full gallop, lance held ready, surrounded by a black border. The pilots of his new unit had copied it and inevitably, they were known as the Golden Knights. He was quite touched by this mark of respect.

His thoughts lingered upon Mariette as the day for the invited return approached. He knew that Franz Meckler was virtually pawing the ground in his eagerness to get Odile into bed. But his own feelings about Mariette were ambivalent. After the shock of Trudi, he was not sure that he could feel any real warmth for a woman any more. A visit to a knocking shop seemed to him a far more honest form of distraction.

Yet, in a country where the invaders were heartily despised by a vast section of the populace, it was a welcome relief to be able to spend some time in the company of someone as pleasant and as sophisticated as Mariette.

'Black Two,' he called.

'Black Two,' came the crisp acknowledgement.

'Come in closer.'

'Coming in.'

He watched approvingly as Oberfeldwebel Jürgen Prinz tucked smoothly in. The boy was a good pilot.

Strange how life changed in so many confusing ways. Jürgen Prinz, son of a local chemist, came from his own home town and had lived only a few streets away. He wondered if the old chemist's shop was still standing.

Before I was sent to the Eastern Front, he reminisced, *he was just a child. Now he's a senior sergeant, flying on my wing.*

Prinz was a recent addition to his forces and had not yet been blooded, having not had a kill. The boy was eager to put that right. Ketelheim had taken responsibility for introducing him into the complexities of aerial warfare, and had made him his personal wingman.

He spotted a column of smoke in the distance. It was a good thirty kilometres away, and outside his patrol area. Other units would be engaged.

Prinz had also seen it. 'Black One! Some action?'

'I feel as you do, Jürgen,' Ketelheim said. In the air, he sometimes used the familiar '*du*' with the younger pilot. 'But we will not stray outside the patrol area. Some Tommies and Amis will come into our net. Have patience.'

He was as frustrated as Prinz felt. He, too, wanted action. But it did not come that day.

*   *   *

They were lucky with the weather and although the forecast was for rain the next day, it was as if spring had arrived. Meckler picked Ketelheim up in the Mercedes 540K. Each was in a spotless uniform and wearing a side-arm.

As he climbed in, Ketelheim was amused to see a bunch of flowers behind the seats. He had also brought one. Meckler watched as he placed it next to the other.

'So. I persuaded you.'

'Don't read too much into it,' Ketelheim said as the Mercedes roared off. 'I'm going for a restful afternoon.'

'You might be,' Meckler remarked. He wasn't smirking, but there was no disguising his intentions.

'Do you really believe a French noblewoman, admittedly very . . . er . . . physical, is going to let you sleep with her, in her invaded country, and in her own invaded home? Especially a member of the Waffen-SS, no matter how apparently cultured?'

'"Apparently"?' Meckler pretended to be insulted. 'Smile when you say that. I am not wrong about her, Karl-Heinz,' Meckler continued more seriously. 'There's a spark.'

'Don't get burned. That's all I'm saying.'

Meckler sniffed loudly at the air. 'Away with gloomy thoughts, my Golden Knight! Enjoy that air. My blood tingles.'

'I'd check lower down,' Ketelheim suggested with a smile.

'Even though spring's not here yet,' Meckler continued, undeterred, 'summer's soon coming.'

Ketelheim looked up at the sky. No movement interrupted the cool blue of its canopy.

'And something else too.'

At the château, Mariette said, 'I don't like that look in your eye, Odile. This is not just some man you have taken a fancy to. Remember what I told you before. This is Waffen-SS. Play him for all you're worth to help the Resistance, but please don't get too close. I don't want anything to happen to you.'

'You fret too much,' Odile told her nonchalantly. 'As I've also said before, I can take care of it.' She had put on a dress that showed plenty of bare leg. She performed a brief pirouette that caused the light material of the skirt to flare and rise well above her buttocks. 'What do you think? Will this do?'

'It will certainly make him want to take it off. It may be a nice day, but you'll freeze.'

'Oh Mariette! Be serious! I'll put a light coat over it.'

Mariette sighed. 'It will have to do, I suppose. Nothing I say will make you change it.'

'That's true enough.'

Agnès Grappin was hurrying along a corridor towards the baron's quarters when Grüber caught up with her on silent feet.

'Hello, Fräulein.'

She jumped and gave a frightened little squeal at the same time. 'Monsieur!'

For the moment, there was no one else in the corridor.

Grüber gave a wolfish smile. 'I seem to be startling all the women in this place lately. I'm beginning to get worried. You must all be hiding guilty secrets of one kind or another.' He raised a hand briefly to stifle her protests. 'Calm yourself. I am not trying to trap you. I am more interested in the . . . nobility.' His mouth turned down at the corners as he spoke the word. 'Have you heard anything of interest?'

She gave a nervous shake of the head. 'No, monsieur.'

'No matter. Keep at it. I have a policy of believing that no one is ever what he – or she – seems, no matter how outwardly convincing. Take you, for instance. You would like to kill me, wouldn't you?'

'Oh no, monsieur! No!'

'Oh yes, monsieur! Yes!' he mimicked contemptuously. 'It is what I would expect.' He reached for one of her full breasts. She flinched, but he held on to it and squeezed.

She gasped in pain. 'You're hurting me!'

He let go of her and she hunched herself against the lingering throb of his grip, half-expecting him to reach for her once more.

'Just remember,' he snarled softly at her. 'I can *really* hurt you, and your family . . . not forgetting your brother, for whom we can devise some very special treatment. Today the Malzey sisters are entertaining two German officers. See to it that you serve them, and listen to everything they say. *Everything*. No matter how frivolous. I will decide what is, or what is not, important. Understood?'

She nodded wordlessly. She knew just how much he could really hurt her and all her family. Everyone knew what went on in the cellars. Everyone knew what had happened to Jeanne-Anne from the Resistance.

Her eyes were filming over, but she did not break into tears.

Despite the rigours of the Occupation, her body still carried the remains of teenage puppy-fat – a ripeness that excited Grüber. His eyes roved lingeringly over her.

'Now on your way,' he ordered curtly, as if her presence had suddenly begun to disturb him. 'Come and see me tonight. I need to relax.'

Again she nodded, and hurried away. It was only when she'd locked herself in her small room that she allowed the terrible fear to overwhelm her, and at last let the tears flow.

Meckler did not slow down as they approached the barrier, and Ketelheim knew exactly why.

'Don't goad them,' he cautioned. 'They'd be quite happy to shoot us and hang the consequences.'

Meckler appeared not to have heard.

Ketelheim could see the Totenkopf guards beginning to ready their Schmeisser sub-machine-guns, despite the fact that they must have recognized the car.

'Franz!' he said, drawing out the name warningly.

Meckler still said nothing, then at the last moment, it seemed, slowed down and stamped on the brakes. The big sports car squealed to a halt, almost touching the barrier.

He grinned cheerfully. 'I can almost smell spring in the air,' he said to the guards.

For reply, they scowled at the two officers and clicked to attention. Their right arms shot out.

'*Heil Hitler!*' they barked in unison.

'The Oberstleutnant should not drive so quickly on

this road,' one remonstrated as the other went to raise the barrier. 'There could be . . . accidents.' It was a barely veiled warning.

Ketelheim gave the usual Luftwaffe salute, while Meckler waved a vague hand as they drove through.

''Hitler!' he said in his deliberate mumble.

'One day, Franz,' Ketelheim muttered at him. 'One day.'

But Meckler was about to let nothing spoil his mood. 'Forget those humourless fanatics. Let us instead look forward to a most pleasant few hours.'

From an upper window that overlooked the front garden, Odile saw the Mercedes arrive and smiled to herself.

Pendrake was leading a flight of four Typhoons on a low-level training mission. Every pilot had come up to standard and despite a few rough edges, there had been no further accidents. All in all, he now thought, it hadn't been bad going. The schedule was being maintained.

'This is Cobra One,' he said to them. 'Remember what I said before take-off. I don't want to see anyone above me.'

He took a quick look round and was pleased to note that not a single aircraft was flying higher than he was. They looked good.

'All right,' he continued. 'Line astern. Now!'

They manoeuvred smoothly into the new formation, forming a neat line behind him. In the other three aircraft were Keane, Elmore and Williams. Keane's arm no longer appeared to give him trouble.

Pendrake looked ahead and saw the deep Cotswold

valley he'd chosen for the exercise. He brought his goggles down.

'Follow me!'

He flipped the big aircraft on to its back and plunged downwards into the valley. He rolled upright, pulled the stick gently and was hurtling along at barely a hundred feet. One by one, with exquisite precision, the others followed him down. Their multiple bellow, amplified by the natural depression, echoed around it and pummelled the air.

Pendrake stood the Typhoon on a wingtip and hauled round a bend in the valley. A quick rearward glance showed the next aircraft right there, hanging on to his tail. Then the valley was coming to an end, a tree-lined slope fast approaching. There was space between the trees. He headed for the slot and rocketed up the hill through the screen of trees.

That ought to sort the men out from the boys, he thought as he breasted the rise and pulled into a steep climb.

He glanced back once more. No. There they were, slicing their way through the trees and pulling up in his wake.

He felt a smile of satisfaction stretching his lips in his oxygen mask. The fire was in their bellies.

But there was more to come. They would have to learn to use the aircraft as a weapon in all weathers, day or night. They would have to learn to attack in coordinated pairs, with split-second timing. And they would have to get it right in a very short space of time.

He took them through a punishing routine, forcing them to remain low throughout. There were times when he led them through spaces among the trees that would not allow passage of an aircraft unless it was tilted over on a wing. On one occasion it was like a slalom course where one mistake would result in a terminal collision with an unyielding tree trunk, or an embrace of branches. But they had to learn to use the trees. The trees were protection. A flitting dip behind a screen of them could mean the only difference between being hit and getting away.

Nobody panicked. Nobody made a mistake.

On their way back to the airfield, Pendrake saw another four Typhoons in the distance, low down, heading in the opposite direction. It was Bingo Wilson leading his bunch out.

Pendrake led the flight into an impressive peel-off for landing. Each aircraft landed perfectly.

'Keep this up,' he said to them afterwards, 'and you might be able to hit the target. Well done.'

He walked away, not letting them see the look of satisfaction on his face.

Elmore, feeling as if he'd just come from a gruelling session with a malevolent boxer, watched the receding form and said to no one in particular, 'I'm wrecked, but pinch me, somebody. I think I just heard a compliment.' Then he yelled, 'Hey!' And looked round.

Williams, the imprint of his oxygen mask etched on his face, was grinning at him. 'You said pinch you.'

'Well . . . well . . . not literally! And not so hard!'

'Oh. Sorry.' Williams kept grinning.

'You Limeys are crazy. You know that?'

'I'm Welsh.'

* * *

At the Château de St Sauveur, Agnès Grappin followed the Malzey sisters out of the building with a large picnic basket. Accompanying her, and carrying another basket and a couple of light rugs, was a young man who worked with her.

Meckler and Ketelheim were on either side of Mariette and Odile. As the party moved some distance from the château and were about to turn a corner past the family wing, they were confronted by a pair of Totenkopf guards.

Everyone came to an uncertain halt.

'We are your escort,' one of the guards said flatly. He was a Scharführer with exceedingly cold eyes.

The other carried a man-pack radio, the headphones pressed down over his peaked cap. He stared at them blankly. Both carried Schmeissers, with Luger automatics in black holsters at their hips.

Meckler immediately decided to take the initiative.

'Thank you for your concern,' he said to the guards, 'but the Oberstleutnant and I can offer the ladies every protection necessary. In fact, I was about to suggest that he and I carry the baskets and rugs, so that these good people can return to their duties in the house.'

The Scharführer, whose equivalent rank was that of sergeant, looked at the two officers as if they were the subordinates.

'That is not allowed, Herr Oberstleutnant. German officers should not carry baskets and . . .things for these people.'

Meckler ignored him and turned to Agnès. 'Can you understand German?' And when she had looked at him uncomprehendingly, said in French, 'We'll take

the baskets and the rugs. You two can go back inside.'
He reached for the one she carried.

But she would not let him have it. 'I must stay.'

He smiled disbelievingly at her. 'What's this? A chaperone? Surely not.'

Uncertain of what to say to that and fearful of Grüber's reaction if she did not remain, she stayed silent.

The Scharführer smirked. 'We'll accompany you,' he said in his native language.

'You will not!' Meckler countered. 'This is unnecessary.'

'Herr Oberstleutnant, I have my orders.'

'And *I'm* giving you an order, *Sergeant*,' Meckler snapped. 'I will tolerate no insubordination from you! You are not to accompany us. Do you understand?'

The SS NCO did not back down. 'I have my orders, sir!'

'Who gave them?'

The man did not reply.

'I see,' Meckler said stiffly. He turned to his companions. 'Please wait here,' he said in French, and strode back to the building.

His heels cracked rhythmically along the corridor as he went in search of one of the senior Gestapo men. He caught up with Grüber as the man was about to enter an office.

'*Herr Grüber!*'

The Gestapo deputy district chief paused. He did not appear surprised to see the furious Meckler.

'Did you order those men to watch us?' Meckler demanded sharply.

'Not to watch you, my dear Meckler. To escort . . .'

'To escort? Here? The entire area is saturated with

my Panzer troops. Are you mad? Do you expect the Resistance to suddenly attack us while we're having a picnic in the grounds?'

'One can never be certain where an attack may come from.'

Meckler stared at him. 'You are now a combat strategist?'

Grüber stared pointedly at Meckler's decorations. 'I am aware of your prowess in battle, Meckler. I am also aware that your troops provide the area's security. However, within the bounds of this château, the Gestapo takes precedence over *all* considerations. Do not make an enemy of me, Herr Oberstleutnant.'

'You are threatening *me*? Who wants to make an enemy of anyone? I am asking for privacy, man! As a senior officer of the Waffen-SS, I will not stand for insubordinate behaviour by one of your sergeants. Would you like me to make a report of this lack of cooperation *and* insolence by one of your guards, to Gruppenführer Herrenbach?'

Grüber blinked slyly, and appeared to back down. 'Let us not make this something more than it is. I shall return the men to their other duties. Will that do?'

'Yes,' Meckler snapped. 'Thank you.' He turned brusquely, and walked away.

Grüber's eyes were venomous as they watched Meckler leave.

Meckler strode up to the waiting Totenkopf guards. 'You are relieved of this duty,' he said to the Scharführer.

The man hesitated, his expression giving no hint of what he was actually thinking. Then the radio crackled. The radioman stiffened as he listened.

'*Jawohl, Oberscharführer!*' he acknowledged. He glanced at his superior NCO who gave an almost imperceptible nod. 'The Oberscharführer has been ordered to tell us it is no longer necessary to escort your party, Herr Oberstleutnant,' he announced to Meckler. He didn't look annoyed, but his voice betrayed him.

'Very well. You are dismissed.'

They stood there just long enough to register the fact that they did not consider they had lost the encounter, then clicked their heels, gave a 'Heil Hitler' and marched off without a backwards glance.

Both Mariette and Odile had watched the entire incident with apparent indifference, but in reality were most interested in this display of latent antipathy between these two branches of the SS. It was something that might well be of use later.

'Come,' Meckler said cheerfully in French. 'After this minor unpleasantness, let us continue with our afternoon.' He turned to Agnès's male colleague. 'I'll take that basket and your rugs. No need for you to come and sit around. We can manage.'

The man looked uncertain.

'Do not be afraid. Those guards are gone. I have had them dismissed. Here. Give me the basket. Karl-Heinz, you take one of the rugs and Agnès's basket.'

After further hesitation and a look at Mariette, the man handed it over. Agnès, however, refused when Ketelheim reached for hers.

'No, monsieur,' she insisted. 'I will accompany madame and . . .'

'All right, Agnès,' Mariette said. 'You can come. You can go back in, Philippe,' she went on to the young man. 'No need for both of you to wait on us. Thank you.'

Philippe gave a courteous nod. 'Thank you, madame.' He left them and returned to the château.

Odile gave Meckler a surreptitious look of resignation; but he was still cheered by the prospect of being with her. Perhaps Agnès would leave them after a while.

'Shall we speak German?' he asked. 'English? Or French?'

'Ladies' choice,' Mariette said, joining the spirit of his game. 'German, in honour of you two gentlemen and for bringing us such beautiful flowers.'

'We're most flattered,' he said to her, adding, 'Are we not, Karl-Heinz?'

'We are,' Ketelheim replied gallantly, 'and the flowers were a pleasure.'

Odile gave one of her more girlish giggles.

11

Each couple was lying on a rug, with Agnès sitting on the edge of the bigger of the two, upon which Mariette and Ketelheim lay.

'It's so peaceful here,' Mariette remarked in a lazy voice, 'it's hard to believe people are fighting a war.' She was leaning on an elbow as she looked about her. 'I cannot even see your soldiers, Franz,' she added to Meckler. 'Apart from those by the château.'

This was not strictly true, for she had spotted several in other places, and had noted their positions. Yet the silence was uncanny. There was none of the expected clanking of tank tracks, nor the surreptitious roar of an engine being tested; no practice firing of guns; no distant and disembodied shouting of orders. It was as if their part of the world were inhabited by ghosts of field-grey.

Perhaps we are ghosts too, she found herself thinking in the gentle warmth of the March sunshine.

Then Meckler's voice broke the momentary spell.

'They are there,' he assured her. 'Among the trees, on the slopes, in the vineyards, at the sides of the roads. All the way out for at least thirty kilometres from the château, in all directions. And with Karl-Heinz's aeroplanes up above, you should feel very safe.'

'I do,' she said. She looked at Ketelheim, who was lying on his back, eyes closed, cap partially obscuring his face. 'You've eaten too much and had more than your fair share of wine, Karl-Heinz. Are you asleep?'

'No,' he replied. 'I may have eaten well, but only sparingly taken wine. It's because it is so peaceful here, as you have said, that I feel so relaxed. I also have wonderful company. It's a beautiful pause in the dirty business of war.'

She smiled at his words. 'Then you are glad you came?'

'Yes.'

They had picnicked near a small stream that ran at the back of the château, some distance from it. In the strange silence, even the low murmur of the water seemed to make their own voices sound louder. Near the château, the flak guns on their special platforms could be clearly seen. These were manned constantly.

Odile and Meckler were lying close together — although because of the presence of Agnès, she restricted herself to tracing a finger lightly along his cheek and jawline. Her light coat had fallen open and the dress had ridden up, showing plenty of glorious leg and thigh.

'It's strange that we can't even hear the sounds of war,' she said.

'War, my dear,' he told her, 'is ninety-nine per cent waiting around for something to happen, and one per cent wishing it hadn't. Others may put it differently, but essentially it's the same thing.'

'It feels like the calm . . .'

'Before the storm,' Ketelheim finished for her. 'And the storm *is* coming.'

'You are certain?' Mariette asked.

'It must,' he replied. 'This whole thing must be resolved, one way or the other.' He moved his cap so he could look up at her. 'Either we win, or we lose – but it must be resolved.'

'And will you?'

'Will I what?'

'Will you win? How about you, Franz? What do you think?'

There was a long silence. Odile looked at Meckler keenly, while Mariette alternated her glances between him and Ketelheim. Agnès, not understanding a word that was being spoken, watched them all, knowing that something important was being discussed.

'If I were Daggenau, or Grüber,' Meckler at last replied, 'I would say we are bound to win. But I'm a realist. If we do win, it will be at such cost that I do not believe Germany can survive as a viable state. If we lose, the price will still be high, but not as much. But Germany *will* survive.'

'And Hitler?'

'He won't survive.'

Ketelheim had now turned his head briefly to glance at Meckler, astonished that his friend had spoken so openly to non-Germans.

'I am surprised to hear a member of the Waffen-SS say that,' Mariette said.

'I am a soldier and, I repeat, a realist. Do not believe this means my Panzer troops will not fight. They will fight, and very, very hard for every centimetre of ground. The Allies will also pay dearly for their victory, if they do eventually achieve it.'

'Karl-Heinz?'

'I agree. My pilots will also fight hard. The Tommies and Amis will not find it easy.'

'Oh, do let's stop talking about the war,' Odile put in brightly. 'Let us enjoy the afternoon.'

'I agree,' Meckler said.

'So do I,' Ketelheim concurred.

Odile looked at Agnès and switched to French. 'You don't have to stay, Agnès. You've been very helpful. You can go back to the château. I'm sure Philippe would like that.'

'Philippe?' Agnes said uncertainly.

'Why yes. I thought you two were . . .?'

'No. No. There is nothing between us.'

'But Agnès,' Mariette began. 'Everyone knows he is very attracted to you. He is also a very handsome young man.'

'There . . . there is nothing, madame. I do not find him . . . attractive.'

'Oh,' Mariette said, as if she had made a dreadful mistake. 'It just goes to show how mistaken one can be about certain things.'

But Odile was looking at Agnès, a slight frown creasing her forehead.

On the other side of the Channel, Pendrake was continuing to push his pilots hard. Immediately after breakfast, he'd hauled them into the briefing room to give them their tasks for the day. In pairs, they were to carry out simulated attacks on a target building in wooded country at precise times, and from different directions. Gun cameras would record the action, and no one would be able to talk their way out of a mistake.

'Timing is of paramount importance,' he'd told them, 'if you are not to collide with each other. In the real thing, you'll have plenty to worry about, without wondering whether an aircraft coming in from another direction is going to keep you company in the cockpit. Only thing, you won't have much to say about it.'

It was now 1500 hours, and Pendrake was leading his second sortie of the day. Tucked in close was Williams, as Cobra One-Two. Over to the right was another pair, Wilson and Knowles, who would be attacking within twenty seconds of the first. The third pair of the black Typhoons, flown by Elmore and Wojdat, would attack from the left twenty seconds later. Simulated release of all eight rockets in a single burst was to be carried out by each of the six aircraft.

In the attack on the château, the concentrated barrage of forty-eight ultra-high-explosive warheads delivered by six aircraft would virtually reduce to rubble the section of building attacked. However, Pendrake had decided to split the flight so that at least two aircraft would attack the gun emplacements, first with rockets, then with cannon fire. When the attack on the château was complete, all aircraft would concentrate on the ground forces.

Pendrake reached forward to turn on the gun-sight reflector switch. Next was the weapons selector box against the left cockpit wall just aft of the supercharger lever, and rockets selected. He then swiftly reached to his right to flick on the camera master switch. It was all done within a fleeting moment with practised, instinctive skill.

'All Cobra One aircraft,' he now called. 'Target in sight. Take positions. Going down. Follow me, One-Two.'

'Roger.'

Pendrake rolled the aircraft steeply and plunged towards the woods. Williams followed close behind.

Pendrake took his Typhoon to fifty feet, below the treetops, as he hurtled towards the ruined manor house that was serving as the target. He had his gun-sight lined up on the gaping maw of a long-vanished window. The building rushed towards him. He pressed the gun button. The camera recorded his 'release' and he was hauling on the stick just long enough to clear the building before going back down again, hugging a slope as he made his escape. He glanced behind to see Williams right there with him.

He climbed for height, better to observe the progress of the other aircraft. They came in bang on time, from different directions. None came close to hitting the other.

He waited for them to format on his aircraft.

'Well done,' he said to them. 'Now, to see how well you *did* do, all film will be viewed on our return to base. The camera cannot lie.'

Says who? thought Elmore. He had a feeling he'd messed up his attack.

The next daylight attack would be done with practice rockets which had concrete rather than high-explosive heads.

When the films were studied, everyone had scored including Elmore, much to his relief.

'Sir,' he said, when they'd seen Pendrake's film, 'that pile of stone looks like it was *in* your cockpit!'

'Just an illusion, Captain,' Pendrake told him. 'Take comfort. On the night, the target will be shooting back and you'll have neither the time nor the inclination to see it like this.'

'Thank you, sir. That sure cheers me up.'

On the next trip out, Pendrake was again leading the same pilots, and again repeating the heart-stopping manoeuvre as he dived towards the derelict manor house. After the attack, target-range personnel – who were positioned well out of danger – went to check the results. The concrete rockets, even without their explosive charges, had knocked huge chunks out of the ruined building with the sheer kinetic energy of the impact. Pendrake's window had become larger. All rockets from each subsequent aircraft had landed inside.

The intensive training for Cobra Squadron continued throughout the afternoon. They would also be flying an attack sortie for the first time that night, with weak lights placed in the ruins, to give them an aiming point.

'That ought to be fun,' Mackenzie said when he heard.

While Cobra Squadron was continuing its work-up for the mission, the picnickers at the Château de St Sauveur had decided that the day was at last no longer warm and were reluctantly making their way back. As they approached the main entrance, a big black saloon, preceded by two motorcycle outriders in black SS uniforms, powered up the drive. The motorcade swept past them in a crunch of gravel and came to a halt at the entrance.

They paused to watch.

Boucheron, accompanied by his wife, climbed out self-importantly. Daggenau was with him. Two guards at the tall, ornate doors snapped to attention as the party went inside. The saloon and the outriders pulled away to park near the pool of staff cars and other military transport. Boucheron had studiously ignored Mariette's waiting group.

Then Daggenau reappeared, and approached them. 'Ladies,' he greeted them politely in French, before switching to German, 'Gentlemen. Ah . . . Meckler, may I have a quick word with you?'

'Certainly,' Meckler said, wondering what it was all about. 'Please excuse me,' he said to the others and followed Daggenau a short distance.

Daggenau stopped. 'There is to be a meeting here,' he began, 'of some high-ranking officers of both the Wehrmacht and the Waffen-SS, to discuss tactical responses to the possible Allied invasion. As commander of the château defence area, you are required to attend.'

'When is this to be?'

'One week from today. The meeting is at 1600 hours. Be on time. You may consider that a direct order from Gruppenführer Herrenbach who will not be attending, though Obergruppenführer Schlierhof will be. You may also, therefore, consider yourself Herrenbach's deputy in this instance. Feather in your cap, Meckler. You are being groomed. It will be a long session, and you may have to stay the night.' Daggenau glanced in the direction of Odile. 'However, I do not expect you will find that too great a hardship.' He did not smile.

'And what about Ketelheim? He's in command of the Luftwaffe element here.'

'He is not required for this. We will not be discussing air combat.'

'I see. If this is a direct order from my commander, I shall of course be there. When I return to my command, I shall check with him.'

Daggenau's eyes were hooded. 'I expect you to.'

'Thank you, Herr Daggenau.'

'Thank *you*, Herr Oberstleutnant.'

Daggenau then went back inside.

Meckler returned to the others.

'What did he want?' Ketelheim asked in German.

'It appears I must attend a meeting here next week.'

'Just you?'

Meckler nodded. 'It's a meeting of all ground forces. Senior staff officers. Schlierhof's coming.' He glanced at Mariette. 'It's not a dinner.'

She looked relieved.

'I'll be staying the night,' he went on to Odile, 'so perhaps we can share a coffee afterwards.'

The disappointment he'd felt at not being able to have her to himself for even a short while had evaporated as soon as Daggenau had told him about the meeting. He now eagerly anticipated returning.

Her smile warmed him. 'I shall look forward to it.'

In Mariette's room later that evening, after Ketelheim and Meckler had gone, Odile said, 'We must send news about the meeting. Our people will know what to do.'

Mariette nodded. 'Some new gun positions too. They're always changing around. It's becoming difficult to keep up.'

There was a slight pause, then Odile said, 'Did you notice anything strange about Agnès today?'

'What do you mean exactly?'

'I thought she looked very nervous. I'd even go as far as to say terrified of something. She was afraid to leave us this afternoon. And that story about Philippe sounded unbelievable. She actually told *me* once how much she liked him. She seemed to have forgotten all about that today. I'm going to her room tonight to find out what's going on.'

Mariette looked at her in alarm. 'Grüber's pigs patrol the entire house. You know what they'll do – what *he'll* do to you – if you're caught. He just wants an excuse.'

'Mariette,' Odile began dismissively, 'I know every secret passage and hiding-place in this old pile of bricks, stone and mortar. Have you forgotten how we used to play tricks on our brothers?'

Mention of her brothers brought a shadow of sadness to Mariette's features. 'I haven't forgotten. I also have not forgotten that of the four of us you were the best at finding hiding-places.' Her eyes now looked at her sister fixedly. 'You've being going out during the night, haven't you? You've been taking some of those messages to the Resistance. Odile . . . do you realize what those troops out there would do to you if you were caught?'

'We ask those who work for us to take risks,' Odile

said unrepentantly. 'Why shouldn't we? What you're doing is very dangerous. I can't just play the man-eater all the time.'

'It protects you! We've lost our brothers. I don't want to lose you too. I know you've been going on raids.'

'What? Don't be ridiculous!'

'I've found your gun.'

Odile stared at her and said nothing.

'I followed you one night,' Mariette said. 'I came to talk to you and you were not in your room. I know the passage you used. It's the same one you used to go into when hiding from us when we were children. I found the gun in one of the places you used to hide your treasure when we played pirates. It's an American automatic. Where did that come from?'

After these revelations, Odile decided there was little point in useless denials.

'I found it near one of the tracks. It was in tall grass. I was hiding from a patrol one night, when I felt this thing hurting my elbow. At first, I thought it was a mine and I was terrified that if I moved I would blow myself up. Then I worked up the courage to feel for it. There was ammunition too. I think it's Jeanne-Anne's gun. It was near there that they caught her. She threw it away when she saw the patrol, hoping perhaps that would be enough to save her. But of course, as we now know, she had those papers on her. So she might as well have kept the gun. I'll use it on one of those pigs one day.'

'Even on Franz Meckler?'

The question brought Odile up short. She had not considered that. 'If he tries to kill me,' she said at last, 'yes.'

*   *   *

Agnès was making her way to her room when the silent feet caught up with her and a firm hand grasped the soft flesh of her upper arm. As before, she jumped with a squeal of fear.

'You are very, very nervous, *Fraulein*,' Grüber said in his revoltingly silky voice. 'I am sorry I have not been able to see you sooner, my dear Agnès, but I have had a busy day. So many people to . . . interrogate. Come with me to my room. You can tell me what happened this afternoon.'

'But . . . but, monsieur. Not much! I . . .'

'Come with me!'

There was no choice.

The room was far more luxurious and elegant than any in which Grüber had ever slept in his life. It was also one in which he would have been most unlikely to, but for the war. He pushed Agnès in before him and shut the door, locking it. The force of his shove caused her to stumble forward, so that she fell untidily against the large bed. The heavy curtains were drawn, sealing in the soft lighting in the room. He began to remove his clothes.

'Get undressed,' he ordered.

'Please, monsieur!' she pleaded.

'Oh, do stop whining. Take off your clothes and talk. What happened out there today?'

Miserably, she began to undress.

'Talk!' he snapped at her. 'What did you hear.'

'I don't know, monsieur. I did . . . not understand. They spoke your tongue.'

He stared at her. 'You mean *German*?'

She nodded.

'Strange. Did they suspect you might have had an

interest in what they would be saying and spoke German to prevent you?'

The implications of what he was saying served to terrify her even more. '*No, no*, monsieur. They just began to talk like that from the very start.'

'I see. Did you recognize anything? Names perhaps?'

'They did mention names.'

'Ah! Tell me.'

'Your . . . your name . . .'

'*My name?*'

She nodded, staring at him fearfully.

'And whose else? Speak!'

'Monsieur Daggenau . . .'

'And? Come on, girl! Are there more?'

She was practically speechless with fear now, dreading to say the hated name. 'Hi . . . Hitler . . .' She cringed, expecting him to strike at her.

His reaction was totally the opposite. 'They mentioned my name alongside the Führer's?' He spoke reverently, totally ignoring the fact that Daggenau's had also been mentioned. Then he looked at her suspiciously. 'Were they respectful? Or were they laughing?'

'Their . . . their voices were ordinary, monsieur.' She was so relieved that he hadn't struck her, she initially missed the fact that her naked body was now beginning to excite him.

'All right,' he said. 'We shall leave the subject for now. You have not really brought me anything. This means you will now have to please me.'

He reached for the cringing girl and turned her roughly over on to her stomach. He licked his lips as the hint of plumpness about the back of her thighs sent him into a compelling arousal.

'Oh please!' she begged, her voice now muffled. 'No! *No!*' But she did not struggle, fearing he might hit her.

He grabbed her at the hips and entered her savagely, pulling at her yet pushing her down at the same time. She screamed into the bedclothes. Ignoring her cries of pain, he reached beneath her to grab at her breasts and continued to abuse her until he was finally satisfied, straining and shuddering against her with a loud groan of release. At long last, he collapsed upon her violated young body.

The subdued lighting of the elegant room bathed them in a gentle glow; but there was no love in this brutal place. Her muted whimperings, punctuated by the harsh breathing of a spent Grüber, were those of a small wounded and trapped animal. He lay on her naked back exhausted, a thin stream of saliva leaking out of his open mouth and on to her skin.

Odile, her dressing gown over her nightdress, made her way along a dark passageway that was unknown to any others but the Malzey family. She reached its end and paused to listen. All was quiet. She waited, remaining absolutely silent and after a while, let herself out and into a cupboard beneath a small staircase. She waited again. Nothing.

Slowly, she shut the entrance to the passage, then pushed at the false panel within the cupboard. The panel effectively hid the hatch that sealed the entrance. Once she had manoeuvred herself past the panel and into the cupboard properly, she pushed the panel back into place, then opened the cupboard door slightly. Through the crack, she could see the dimly lit length of a short corridor. She cautiously stuck her head out to look the other way. Empty. The distance to Agnès's door was a mere four metres.

Odile got out quickly and hurried to the door on bare feet. She knocked softly.

'Agnès!' she whispered. 'Agnès! It's Odile. Let me in before I'm seen out here!'

There was a pause, then hesitant shuffling.

'Agnès! *Hurry!*'

There was the sound of a key turning and at last the door opened. Odile slipped in quickly.

'Close it and lock it!' she hissed. 'Then put on a light.'

Agnès did as she was told, then as the bedside lamp came on, Odile looked at her in shock. Agnès was naked, her body drenched in sweat, her face marked by continuing tears. She stood there, slightly hunched, knees and thighs locked tightly together, feet turned in, with the toes touching, arms hugging herself so fiercely it was as if she thought letting go would allow her body to fall apart.

'My God!' Odile said softly. 'What's happened to you?'

Agnès remained as she was and wept silent tears, body shaking, but no sounds came out of her. Odile went close and put out a hand gently. Agnès flinched away. Odile persisted until at last Agnès allowed herself to be embraced. She continued to hug herself and wept for a full ten minutes before haltingly, then in a torrent of words spoken in hushed tones, told Odile all about Grüber.

'I'll kill him,' Odile snarled.

'Please! No! Do nothing!' Agnès said frantically, pulling away in fright.

'It's all right. I didn't mean I was going out there right now to do it.'

'I'm so sorry I spied on your family. You have been so good to me . . . but my family . . .'

'It's all right, Agnès,' Odile repeated. 'You haven't told him anything as yet. But one thing I don't understand. You say he's threatened to arrest your brother?'

Agnès nodded.

'But, according to you, your brother Armand's in the Resistance and Grüber already knows this.'

Again, Agnès nodded.

'And Grüber claims he knows what he looks like.'

Agnès nodded for a third time. 'Yes.'

'I see. All right,' Odile said gently. 'Put something on and try and get some sleep. Come. I'll help you.'

After she'd helped Agnès to get ready, she said, 'You must not let Grüber suspect that you have spoken about this to *anyone*. He'd certainly arrest your family, and you with them. Continue as before and take courage. He won't touch you again. We'll look after you. I'll say my mother needs you constantly. Now lock your door after I've gone, and try to sleep.'

Agnès, looking like a lost child, eyes mirroring the hurt that had been done to her, nodded wordlessly.

Odile slipped out and made her way back to the cupboard. She was none too soon, for as she pulled the door shut booted feet echoed at one end of the corridor, where they paused.

Odile remained perfectly still.

After what seemed like years, the footsteps continued but did not get closer, and after a while they faded.

Odile went through the connecting door to Mariette's bedroom and gently woke her sister.

'Odile!' Mariette said in a sharp whisper, staring at her in the weak light she'd turned on. 'What are you doing?'

Odile told her about Agnès and Grüber. 'I know his little game,' she continued in distaste. 'I think Grüber's managed to get Armand to work for him, but hasn't told Agnès. He's using his threat of arrest to blackmail Agnès into having sex with him. *The bastard!* When the time comes . . .'

'Don't do anything foolish, Odile.'

'I'm not going to use the automatic on him . . . yet. In better times, I would have asked Dr Norbert to examine her. God knows what damage that Nazi bastard has done. But if we have her examined, he'll know she talked.'

'His time will come,' Mariette said in a hard voice.

'Do you think I'm right about Armand?' Odile asked. 'Is he working for Grüber, do you think?'

'We can't know for certain, but we can find out. We'll send someone out . . .'

'I'll go.'

'Odile . . . no. There are others . . .'

'I'm the best person, and you know it. If Armand is being run by Grüber, he mustn't be alerted. You know I won't do that. And don't worry, I'll get back all right.'

Mariette hated the idea, but gave in reluctantly. Odile would still go, irrespective of her objections. 'When were you thinking of going?'

'Now, if I'm to be back by morning. And don't try to make me put it off. We've got to make sure Armand doesn't find out who's really in the cellars, in case he passes the information on to Grüber. I'll use the passage that comes out in the south vineyard.'

'That's two kilometres long! There could be all sorts of things in there. Rats, snakes . . .'

Odile smiled. 'They know me, I know them. We keep out of each other's way.'

Mariette gave a sigh of resignation. 'You've used it before.'

'But of course.' Odile kissed her elder sister quickly on the forehead. 'I'd better be going.'

She left before Mariette could say anything in protest.

Odile crawled out of the dark hole and into more darkness. A huge, half-buried boulder on a slope that had for centuries formed a perfect barrier, hid the overgrown entrance from the world. Her eyes had already adjusted themselves to the gloom within the secret passage so that to her the darkness outside was relatively light.

As she made her way past the boulder she heard the drone of aircraft engines. She wondered what they were and hoped they would not drop any bombs near where she was. The thick clothes she wore could not have been more different from those with which she normally attired herself for the likes of Franz Meckler, and for those who saw her in the persona she liked to flaunt.

It took her an hour of careful progress, avoiding the

SS patrols, to reach the point where she normally made contact with the Resistance. What she subsequently learned sent her hurrying back to the château.

Two and a half hours later, she was back in Mariette's bedroom, having first hidden the clothes she'd worn and quietly washed the dirt off herself. She'd made sure she used only just enough water, turning on the tap slowly so as to minimize the sounds of it going through the pipes.

'Are you awake?' she called softly in the dark.

'I haven't been asleep since you left,' came the reply.

'Well? Did you find out anything?'

They did not put on a light.

'News from England. Someone *has* been talking. The Germans sent two planes to look for the base, but they were shot down. If it's Armand, the Resistance will kill him later. We are to be ready for the attack in one week. I've given them the new information about the guns. I have also told them about the meeting of all those officers here next week, so they'll get word to England to make the attack on that night.'

'Then we must be ready for when it comes,' Mariette said.

'This poor old place will be destroyed.'

'It will be deloused,' Mariette corrected her. 'We'll build it again. Now you'd better get some sleep. You must be tired and I feel worn out, waiting for you to get back safely. Imagine what would have happened if your body had been found out there.'

'But it wasn't,' Odile said and went back in the dark to her own room.

12

The morning weather at the airfield was gloomy. Cloud cover began at a thousand feet and seemed to go up for ever. The Spitfire patrol had returned to report that clear air was at 25,000 feet.

The weather matched Pendrake's mood as he sat at his desk, staring at a blank sheet of paper. It was to be his second letter of condolence.

The night-time training had been a limited success. For though there would be no lights showing during the attack on the château itself, he had allowed navigation lights as an aid to the maintenance of formation during the first night-attack practice.

All had gone well until the time had come for the final pair. The last man in, a pilot officer named Farrand, perhaps excessively worried about hitting his companion, had moved out of the approach line. He became disorientated and misjudged his angle of bank.

Had he kept his nerve, he would have made it. But he over-corrected and his wingtip brushed some branches. Again, the speed of the aircraft would normally have caused the tough Typhoon wing to slice away at the relatively thin branches of the upper foliage, enabling Farrand to haul the lightly damaged aircraft out. Such incidents had occurred several times during combat. Lancasters had returned with sprouts of leaves on their wings, Mosquitoes with foliage in their cockpits, and so on.

Unfortunately for Farrand, among the branches was a particularly sturdy one that had survived just long enough to jerk at the wing. The Typhoon had pivoted into the trees and exploded in a night-searing ball of fire.

Dear Mr & Mrs Farrand

It is with great regret that I must inform you that your son . . .

Pendrake stopped with a sigh. He laid down the pen. This one was going to be no easier than with Benson. It would never get easier, no matter how many times he might have to do it. There would be more after the attack on the château. If he didn't return, it would be Bingo Wilson's job. At least they were all unmarried. Small mercies.

The sharp bark of engines starting, followed by a multiple bellow, told him that six Typhoons were getting ready for a sortie. He had not called a halt to the flying. The thousand-foot cloud base meant that if they remained below that altitude they would have a clear run to the target range. They would be into cloud at the pull-up, but could easily limit the gain in height and be back out of cloud for the return to base. Besides, flying in cloud held no terrors for them.

He knew they would see the spot where Farrand had gone in; but they'd be witnessing far worse over the Channel. They would simply have to get used to it.

He listened as the aircraft took off, all engines running smoothly. He listened until the sounds faded.

A soft knock preceded Lewis's entry into the room. Her eyes, full of sympathy, seemed extra large and dark as she looked at him. She had brought a thin folder, which she placed gently on the desk.

'Pilot Officer Farrand's particulars, sir.'

Pendrake looked at it. 'Is this what we all come down to in the end, Lewis? A few sheets of paper? Surely we're more than that?'

Unable to give him the answer he needed, she could only look on, wishing she could put her arms about him.

He looked up at her. 'No clever words for me today?'

'It's . . . it's not an easy one, sir. There are many answers to . . .'

There was another knock.

'In!' Pendrake called.

An aircraftwoman came through with an envelope. 'Sir . . . ma'am.' She handed the envelope to Lewis, who opened it, took out a single sheet and read swiftly. 'Thank you, Hilary.'

'Ma'am.' The WAAF left the room.

Lewis passed the signal to Pendrake. He began to read.

ATTACK ONE WEEK FROM TODAY. TIME OVER TARGET 0330 HOURS. TAKE-OFF 0300 HOURS. MOVE TO FORWARD BASE ABLE THREE 19 HOURS PRIOR. LEAK FOUND. H.

So they had discovered the leak. Pendrake was glad it was someone on the other side and not Montcarneau. He returned the signal to her.

'No turning back now,' he said.

'No, sir.' She folded the signal with exaggerated care and placed it back in the envelope. She looked paler. 'Sir.'

'Yes?'

'I'd like to move to the forward airfield . . .'

'Out of the question. You've got to hold the fort until we return. I have a feeling this will be our permanent home.'

'But sir . . .'

'We'll be there for twenty-four hours, perhaps forty-eight. Besides, we'll be within reach of hit-and-run night bombers, and the accommodation will be rather less salubrious. Hardly worth your being there.'

He didn't tell her he also harboured a nightmare vision of seeing her blown up by a bomb, just like Megan.

'Now don't force me to make that an order,' he said to her kindly.

'No, sir,' she said and went out quickly.

He sighed, and swiftly read through the thin file on Farrand before going back to his letter-writing, starting afresh.

Dear Mr & Mrs Farrand
It is with the deepest regret . . .

Ably supported by Wilson, Pendrake continued to push his pilots hard, not giving them time to dwell upon Farrand's death. Taking turns with Wilson and the flight leaders, he led various attacks into the target-range area, pressing them to surpass their own best performance. His methods achieved results, and two days after the signal from Halloran he began to feel they were at last turning into the precision-honed killers he wanted.

As for the pilots themselves, they discovered that their daily routines were split between flying, eating and sleeping. Even Elmore had developed into a finely tuned fighting machine. He hadn't lost his crazy sense of humour, but he had reined in many of the less-endearing aspects of his bravado.

Pendrake was again at his desk on the morning of the third day after the signal, when he heard the unmistakable sound of an Anson flying overhead. He picked up his cap and went into Lewis's office.

'Where's Montcarneau?' he asked as she looked up.

'Making a few last-minute changes to the target model.'

'I'll get him. I think his flight out just came in. If you need me in a hurry I'll either be in there, or at Dispersal.'

'Very well, sir.' Her eyes followed him out.

In the model room, Montcarneau was standing to one side looking at his handiwork, when Pendrake entered.

'Hullo, Michel. Finished?'

'Ah, Mike. My plane?' he said, and when Pendrake had nodded, 'Well, I am as finished with this as it is possible to be under the circumstances. Take a look here. Do you see those tracks which lead to the château?'

Pendrake looked, then nodded. The tracks, three of them, radiated in different directions.

'I suggest they are your best points of entry. You can get between the trees, and very low. Mark them on your maps. If you look here, here and here, you will see that you can be relatively free from the guns until you are near the château. Perhaps by then your rockets will be doing some damage before the gunners wake up. Two of the tracks are across vineyards, and the one in the south goes up that slope here, before flattening out to the château. That route is OK, I think.'

Pendrake studied the model closely. 'It was a possibility I had considered. Now you've recommended it, you've confirmed my hunch.'

Montcarneau looked pleased. 'I am glad I have been of help to you. And we are grateful for what you and your brave men are doing for us.'

'I'd rather be up in the air, Michel, than taking my chances with the Waffen-SS in those woods.'

'Ah well, see how different we are. I like to know I am on the ground. I can hide. In the air . . .' Montcarneau gave an eloquent shrug.

Pendrake grinned. 'I can hide too. But each to his own. Are you packed?'

'I didn't bring much. May I say my goodbye to the charming Miss Lewis?'

'Certainly. I'll wait outside by the car.'

'Thank you.'

In Lewis's office, Montcarneau said, 'He needs you, but does not realize it. Look after him, my dear.'

'I will,' she promised. 'And you, Michel, don't take any chances. Good people like you must survive this.'

'Thank you, my dear. I shall do my very best. Perhaps we shall meet again and if not before, then certainly after the end of the war, when we have won. You must both come to the château . . . you and the brave squadron leader. It will be rebuilt after this. You must come,' he repeated.

'I will, and I'll make sure he's with me. It's a promise.'

Pendrake had a surprise as he approached the Anson with Montcarneau. Halloran climbed out, holding on to his cap against the propwash, and came towards them. For once, he did not have the briefcase. The aircraft's engines continued running, in preparation for take-off. This was clearly a very short stay.

'Thought I'd come over to say goodbye,' Halloran said over the noise of the Anson, holding out his hand, 'and to wish you and the guys luck. A Lysander's taking us over tonight. Got to be with my people when they go in.'

They shook hands firmly.

'You take care out there, Mike,' Halloran said.

'And you, Jack. As I said to Michel, I don't envy your mixing it in those woods with the SS.'

'Unfinished business.'

Pendrake nodded. 'I understand.'

Halloran gave a tight-lipped smile. 'Some heavy-duty brass are going to be in the château when you hit. Give 'em hell.'

'You too.'

A final handshake from Montcarneau, and Pendrake stood back as both men hurried to the Anson.

Soon, the aircraft was taxiing back to the runway, and in a short while it was lifting into the air, taking Halloran and Montcarneau on their way to whatever destiny awaited them on the other side of the Channel.

The day before the move to the forward airfield, Pendrake called all his pilots to the model room.

'Arrange yourselves as best as you can around the platform,' he said to them, 'and take a long, hard look. You won't be seeing it again before the mission. At the forward airfield, you will receive a full briefing, prior to take-off. Your flight commanders are already well versed on the target. However, the briefing will cover in detail the purpose of our task.

'There are now twenty of us instead of our original twenty-two, and as a result there will be a slight reassignment of pilots for the attack. We shall have two flights of seven aircraft each, and one of six. One Flight, led by Keane, will go for the airfield. Two Flight, Dodson, the guns and tanks in the immediate area of the château are yours. Begin inwards and work your way outwards. I will lead Three Flight, comprising Wilson, Kelly, Mackenzie, Williams and Hargreaves, to attack the château itself.

'Your respective flight commanders will furnish you with the necessary information for the move to the forward airfield. Remain in here as long as you need to, for a maximum of two hours. Study the layout well. If you do get separated, you'll not want to waste time wondering where you are. Nothing gunners like more than a lost pilot stooging around trying to get his bearings.

'The flying programme continues today. There will be at least one sortie for each pilot to the target range, then you may all stand down. Prepare only your essential kit for the move. We won't be setting up home there and shall be returning after the mission, once we have landed at the forward airfield and rearmed and refuelled. Flight commanders' meeting at 1700 hours. Thank you, gentlemen.'

No one made any mistakes. Every pilot put his practice warheads right on target, and cannon firing at board targets placed near the ruined manor to simulate gun positions were shredded. By the time 1700 hours came round and the flight commanders filed into Pendrake's office, Wilson was looking pleased with himself.

'By the look on your face, Bingo,' Pendrake said, 'I take it we've still got all our remaining pilots.'

'Alive and kicking and ready to go, and the targets pulverized.'

Pendrake looked at them in turn. 'Well, we do seem to have managed it. Thank you all.' He waved a hand at them as he sat on the edge of his desk. 'Perch anywhere . . .'

Lewis knocked and entered. 'Just wondering if any one would like some tea. It's good stuff.'

All hands went up.

She smiled at them. 'Hilary will bring it in.'

'Take-off will be at 0800 tomorrow,' Pendrake said to his flight commanders as she went out. 'You've already got the route details. From now on you fly in pairs, the same leaders and wingmen as for the attack itself. We'll take off by flight, One Flight leading. Bingo and I will go on ahead, so your flight will seem a little undermanned, Mr Kelly.'

Kelly gave a quick grin. 'Undermanned, but just as mean, sir.'

'Be as mean as you like over the target and you shan't hear any complaints from me. For some time now,' Pendrake continued, 'various attacks have been mounted all along the coast of occupied Europe from Denmark to France. Tiffy 1Bs have been doing pretty much what I was, hitting at everything in sight. There has been an escalation of these attacks, to keep Jerry guessing. He'll not be expecting us at the château when we come knocking. We were nearly compromised . . .'

He paused as the WAAF aircraftwoman came in with the mugs of tea on a tray.

Kelly sprang to his feet to take it off her.

'Thank you, sir,' she said with a shy smile at him.

'My pleasure.'

She hurried out, after giving him a glance that was certainly daring.

'All right, Sean,' Pendrake said. 'You can stop fraternizing with my staff and pass the tea around. Thank you,' he continued as Kelly handed him the mug upon which an anonymous artist had stencilled 'COBRA ONE'. 'We were very nearly compromised,' he went on. 'Hence those two 109s. They were searching us out. That particular leak, I've been assured, has now been plugged. But this does not mean we should take any chances at the forward airfield.

'The aircraft will be dispersed, with their pilots close by. Sleeping arrangements will no doubt be quite primitive, when compared with our current luxurious situation. As I've never been to Able Three, I can't tell you what to expect. So make the most of your time and have a good long sleep tonight. Tell your pilots.'

Pendrake stopped. They were all looking at him

solemnly and he wondered if each was thinking the same thing.

How many would be coming back?

After they'd gone, he stood reflectively before his desk and looked at the aviation cartoon Wilson had given him. It was then that he sensed Lewis had entered the room.

He turned slowly to face her.

'Karen . . .' he began.

'No. Don't ask me to.' Her eyes, wide and dark, looked at him for the first time without deference for rank. 'Don't ask me to make arrangements for you. You're coming back.'

'It's a simple request.'

'No! You're coming back!' she repeated vehemently.

He tried again. 'No one knows what might happen. I want you to have the cartoon . . .'

'I won't listen!' She had stopped about three feet from him, her eyes never leaving his face. 'You can't make me.'

'Look, Karen . . .'

'No!' She turned away, to quickly leave the room.

He stared helplessly at the closing door.

In her own office, she tried to hold back her tears. It wouldn't do to be seen to be crying. She'd handled it all wrongly. That was not how she'd wanted to say goodbye to him. What if something did happen and he did not return? His last memory of her would be her refusal of his request.

There was a vivid picture of him in her mind: the scar suddenly glowing in a face made pale by the thought of what was to come and of the men he might lose. He'd looked so alone.

How could she do that to him?

Her entire body ached. What she really wanted was to have him deep and safe within her. She carefully dabbed at her eyes, composed herself and went back in.

He watched as she re-entered. He thought she looked a little strained, but that was to be expected. The great blue eyes were unnaturally luminous.

'I'll do it,' she said.

'Thank you. I've written a few letters. Send them off for me if . . .'

She nodded. 'I know.'

'I meant it about the cartoon.'

'I know you did, and it . . . it's very good of you to think of me.' A slight tremor had entered her voice. 'But I shan't have to take it because you'll be back.'

'Thank you for the vote of confidence.'

'Yes.' She seemed to be trembling just perceptibly, as if on the edge of control.

'Thank you, Karen.' he said again.

'Sir.' She turned, and went out once more.

Again he found himself staring at the closing door. Why hadn't he told her about the changes that had begun to occur within him? It was the first time since Megan's death that he'd started to . . .

He halted in mid-thought. He hadn't yet finished taking his revenge for what they had done. The scorched wood was still there in his mind, with bits of her all over the place. The nightmare was alive within him. There was still plenty to do.

That night, he slept soundly.

* * *

Punctually at 0800 the next morning, Pendrake lifted the black Typhoon cleanly and tucked in the wheels. Over to his right and a little to the rear, Bingo Wilson kept perfect station.

They banked sharply while still at only a hundred feet and curved round the airfield to head south for Able Three. As they turned, he saw that One Flight was moving on to the runway for take-off. The other aircraft were also all on the move. Soon, One Flight was taking to the air.

As he settled into a shallow climb with Cobra Two fixed in place on his wing as if glued there, he glanced behind to see the rest of his brood climbing in a series of pairs spread out over a great expanse of sky. It was, he thought, an impressive sight.

He felt proud of them.

Lewis heard the multitudinous bellow of the twenty aircraft and remained at her desk. She did not want to see them leave. The aching she'd felt the day before had pursued her into the night and was still with her. If anything, it was stronger.

I need him inside of me, she found herself thinking. But now he was gone, and might not come back.

She caressed the mug with 'COBRA ONE' on it. One of the ground crew had originally brought it to her, saying it was for the CO. She refused to allow herself to contemplate the possibility that Mike Pendrake would not return.

Karl-Heinz Ketelheim walked out to his Focke-Wulf 190 with a jaunty Jürgen Prinz at his side.

'Think we'll have some more action today, sir?' Prinz asked. He'd been blooded, had got his first kill, and was eager for more.

'Hoping for a repeat of our little sortie the other day, eh?' They had caught two Typhoons 1Bs that had strayed into their area.

'Yes, sir!'

'We might, Jürgen. Then again, we might not. Have patience. More will come. Believe me. Now let's see if today the Tommies or Amis might decide to wander our way again.'

But although they patrolled extensively and even saw smoke rising at several points in the distance, nothing came within their area.

Frustrated, they returned to base.

At the château, Odile had accosted Grüber. She was wearing a long, body-hugging dress with a split on either side that reached the upper thigh. As she walked, her legs were displayed in fleeting, sensuous flashes.

Grüber had observed her approach with undisguised longing.

'Good morning, Herr Grüber,' she began in French.

'Good morning, Mademoiselle Malzey,' he replied, his bad French making him sound even more unctuous than usual. 'To what do I owe the pleasure?'

'It's Agnès.'

'Oh?' His expression gave absolutely nothing away. 'And what about her?'

'You may have noticed that she's been on our side of the château for the past days.'

'I haven't,' he lied smoothly. 'Are you having a problem with her?'

'Oh no. It's just that my mother, as you know, is not too well and she wanted Agnès to tend to her. I felt that as Herr Daggenau and yourself are in charge here, you should know if we've changed any of the staffing arrangements. As Agnès will be spending this extra time with us, I felt it would be best to let you know. If you have any objections . . .'

'No objections at all. Of course, you do realize that if the Reich has need of her, we do have the right to demand her presence.'

'Of course.'

'However, I am certain the new arrangements will be perfectly in order.'

Odile gave him a melting smile she did not feel. 'Thank you, Herr Grüber.'

'My absolute pleasure.'

Talking to Mariette later in the family wing, Odile looked as if she wanted to vomit.

'"If the Reich has need of her",' she repeated his words with contempt. 'For "Reich" substitute Grüber. All the time I was talking to him, he was undressing me. It's what I was playing for, but even so . . .' She paused; the idea nauseated her.

Mariette waited silently for her to continue giving vent to her feelings.

'Horrible little man!' Odile went on. 'He showed no emotion when I mentioned Agnès. It was as if nothing at all had happened, but I could sense he was wondering whether she'd talked. I'm certain he thinks she didn't. The way his mind works, he can't believe I would know and say nothing. I didn't look as if I was hiding his dirty secret. I also think he feels he's done me a favour which he hopes to be able to call in later. Ugh!'

'Don't be complacent,' Mariette cautioned, 'even if he seems to believe it. That kind always suspects everyone. It's the trademark of the Gestapo, which is why he's part of it. If he even thinks she might have talked . . .'

'Soon it won't matter if he does know,' Odile said coldly. 'His time is coming. We must make sure,' she continued, the warmth returning to her voice, 'that the parents are safe before the raid begins.'

Mariette nodded. 'They're getting ready to go underground with us tonight. I'm glad we managed to get Agnès here in time. It's a pity about her brother. We'll never really know why he did it.'

'When this war is finally over,' Odile said, 'there will be a lot of this kind of pain for many families.' She looked about her, as if saying goodbye to the room. There was no telling how much of the building would be left standing. 'The Resistance know which passages to use to get in and they'll be in place by the time the air raid begins. To think we could have all got out a long time ago.'

'You know why we couldn't. We couldn't leave our St Sauveur to those pigs and we're of far greater help to the Resistance, even as prisoners in our own home.'

But they knew there was an added, harsher and more horrific reason. Their compliance had been secured with the lives of the people of the district. Both Daggenau and Grüber had let the family know in no uncertain terms that an escape attempt, successful or otherwise, would have had dire consequences for the populace.

The decision to remain had not been difficult after

that, despite the horrors being perpetrated in the cellars.

Franz Meckler was greatly anticipating his return to the château. Once the tedious business of the tactical conference was over, it would be a private coffee in his room with Odile. Who knew where the rest of the evening might lead?

He walked out of the small hotel that served as his headquarters, with his second in command, Major Udo Sonnenberg.

'Well, Udo, I'll leave it all in your capable hands when I go to see the big chiefs this afternoon.'

Sonnenberg gave him a sideways look. 'And the beauteous Odile, no doubt.'

'Aah, my good friend. There's a body! Magnificent. A true goddess.'

Sonnenberg smiled briefly. 'After the hell of the Eastern Front, you need something to bring a little cheer into your life. It's the first time I've seen you so worked up about a woman since . . . oh, let me see . . . Leni, Ludmila, Magda . . . Shall I go on?'

Meckler took no offence. 'This is very different. Leni was a boyhood crush back home. Magda . . . well, Magda was Magda. I hear she's now got a general in tow. In Russia, I helped Ludmila bury her child. She couldn't believe there was any humanity in a Waffen-SS soldier and perhaps got a little too grateful, then that bastard Major Kramer shot her when she wouldn't service him. Being a captain under the command of that Nazi shit was no joke.'

'I remember,' Sonnenberg said with feeling. 'It was even worse being a very scared lieutenant.'

'Well, the Russkis got him in the end. And very good riddance. I can still see the people we butchered in the name of warfare and ideology.' Meckler gave his colleague a brief pat on the shoulder. 'They took a piece of you too.'

Sonnenberg, a married man in his early thirties, had lost an arm. He hadn't seen his wife and boy for years. The last time, the child had been an infant. At least they were still alive.

'But you saved my life,' he now said. 'To this day, I cannot understand why you weren't killed. I'll always remember lying there looking up at you through a red haze while you stood over me firing that heavy machine-gun like some kind of Aryan hero from a bad opera. I hate to make your head even bigger, but you were magnificent.' Then Sonnenberg grinned. 'Especially as it meant I was going to live, after all.'

'Just stay alive, Udo. Just stay alive till this whole nasty business is all over. Germany will need men like you.'

Cobra Squadron swept in to land at Able Three near the south coast of England, in an impressive display of ultra-sharp flying. On approach to the well-camouflaged forward airfield, Pendrake had instructed all three flights to join up in line astern. Like a great black tail, the twenty aircraft roared in at minimum height to sweep into the break and peel off in a continuing, shifting ballet as Typhoon after Typhoon stood on its wingtip to curve round for the landing. The pattern spread itself over a great area of sky. Those on the ground watched with awe and a surge of pride.

They landed one after another, with a regularity that the spectators would later claim was at precise intervals that could be measured to the nanosecond.

The first person Pendrake saw as he climbed down from his aircraft brought a huge grin to his face.

'Spy!' he exclaimed happily. 'How the devil did you get here? What did they have to bribe Foxy with to let you go?'

The Intelligence officer from his old unit looked at him gravely. 'So you don't know.'

Pendrake felt a knot in his stomach. 'Know what?' And as Stanley's silence confirmed his worst fears, he continued, 'Oh no. Not Foxy. It's some mistake, Spy. It must be!'

Stanley shook his head slowly. 'I'm afraid not, old boy. It's been confirmed. Foxy took a new boy out on a rhubarb. You know what he's . . . was . . . like. Hated not being up in the air. So he took this new chappie out to show him the works.

'They got bounced just south-east of Caen, by two Me-109s. There was a heavy flak battery nearby and it put up a ferocious barrage. The Jerry gunners didn't seem to care if they hit their own aircraft. The new boy caught a packet from the flak, but was only damaged. Foxy sorted out the two 109s and got them both. But his wingman, a kid named Patterson, had suffered mild engine damage and had lost some speed. Naturally, Foxy began to shepherd him out of the area and headed for home.

'The battle had taken them away from the flak, but they were not out of the woods yet. As they made their way back, two Fw-190s came flashing down from up high. Patterson went down on that first pass. The poor blighter never knew what hit him. And Foxy himself got peppered, but he was still able to fight. The Tiffy's a tough old bird, as you well know. But something strange was happening. One of the 190s seemed to take little part in the proceedings, except to herd poor Foxy into the guns of the other. There were Golden Knight emblems on the 190s.

'The Resistance saw those when the fight came low enough. Said it reminded them of a hunt where the skilled hunter would initiate the recruit, helping him with his first kill. It was murder, Mike. According to the people on the ground, Foxy outwitted the unskilled pilot every time, but each time he went in for the kill, the ace came down to chase him off. It went on like that for ages. I think they just wore old Foxy down, and he must have been distracted by his diminishing fuel by then.'

Pendrake, listening to the tale with a simmering anger, took time to reflect how he himself had driven the pilot of the photo-recce Messerschmitt 109 to distraction over the home airfield. The pilot had been very good, and he'd simply used all his own skill to eventually gain the upper hand. It was war. But this had been a cold-blooded game.

'In the end,' Stanley was saying, 'the ace virtually set it up for his comrade, who took the shot. And that was it. Foxy never got out. There was no chute.'

Pendrake had listened to the harrowing tale benumbed, his fury growing by the second. He felt a powerful heat behind his eyes.

'I'll bet he's the same one who got Braddock,' he said tightly. 'I hope I meet that bastard one day.'

'You well might,' Stanley told him. 'The area where

Foxy went down is right in your target area. That 190 may well come from the airfield.'

'It's Keane's job to attack the field. But I hope he misses that sod. I want him up in the air.' Pendrake removed his helmet and gripped at it, as if squeezing the life out of the unknown Focke-Wulf pilot. '*I want him!*'

13

While Able Three could not be described as a luxurious airfield, it was not as bad as the pilots had feared. The runway was steel matting on a bed of hard-packed earth. There was no mess, and sleeping accommodation was a series of four-man wooden huts with basic metal beds, not far from each group of dispersed aircraft. This arrangement suited Pendrake, for it meant the pilots of the Typhoon pairs could be reasonably close to their aeroplanes if they needed to take off in a hurry.

Everyone ate in the same building, another wooden hut, long and low-lying. Ops and Briefing were in a similar structure. The control tower was hidden among tall trees and was virtually invisible from the air. All other airfield services were similarly concealed. Even the dispersal areas were beneath camouflaged canopies. It was obvious to the Cobra Squadron pilots that Able Three had not been set up just for them and that the forward airfield had many other, clandestine uses.

The briefing began at 1700 hours. At the end of the briefing room was a huge map, with coloured tracks leading to and from the various sections of the target area.

First to speak was Stanley. As the Spy launched into a very detailed briefing of the mission, it dawned on an astonished Pendrake that the Intelligence officer had known far more about the matter than he had previously disclosed. By the time Stanley was drawing his brief to its conclusion, every pilot was fully conversant with the detailed aspects of the target area, and the true purpose of the mission.

'One other thing to watch for,' Stanley now said. 'There is the possibility that a specialized night fighter *Staffel* or squadron, using the twin-engined Junkers Ju-88, may be in your area. This is not hard information, but you'd be wise to keep a sharp lookout. If they are there, it's because of the damage that has been done to the coastal radars. These aircraft are obviously gap-pluggers.

'As you do not carry radar warning for them to home in on, they must rely on visual identification and other radar acquisition. Your black finish will make it more difficult for visual ID. And I happen to know that some of the Fw-190s have also been modified as single-seat night fighters. The pilots of these are fighter aces who were previously on bombers. At first, this sounds crazy; but when you consider that a bomber pilot spends long hours flying on instruments, it begins to make sense. A pilot with such high skill at night flying who is also an ace in fighter combat . . . Well, you don't need me to elaborate. So watch your backs. Squadron Leader Pendrake will now take over.'

Pendrake nodded to Stanley and went straight in. 'First thing I want to say is that I am proud to lead you all on this mission. When we began, with the short time allowed, I must confess I didn't think we'd make it this far. But you've proved me wrong and that's one instance when I'm glad to be. I was even wrong about you, Captain Elmore.'

'Well, sir, don't count your chickens.'

The room exploded into laughter that was at once relief and genuine enjoyment of Elmore's remark. Even the Spy smiled appreciatively.

Pendrake waited patiently for the laughter to die down. 'We'll cross the water,' he continued, 'as low as we dare, to avoid any coastal radars that may be operational, and any of those night fighters that the Spy has just mentioned. Try and remember that the windmill in front of your nose is not an outboard motor. A Tiffy can do many things, but she won't swim. Hit that water, and you're fish food. So it's instruments, instruments, *instruments*.

'Time over the target is 0330 hours, which equates with 0430 local and is thirty minutes before sunrise over there, at 0500. We shall therefore be arriving with the dawn, but in sufficient gloom to catch them by surprise. It also means you should have enough light to see what you're doing. Turn your instrument lighting as far down as is necessary for you to still be able to read them. You will experience less out-of-cockpit momentary blindness.

'A cruise at 380mph will give us twenty-five minutes to target. This will leave us with plenty of fuel, plus a wide power margin to our top speed of 460. At low to medium levels, we can eat 190s for breakfast, so we keep them there. Your aircraft will be equipped with special armament for both rockets and cannon. The rounds for both carry greater explosive force than is normal. I'm not sure whether we can dent any Tiger Panzers we may see, with the cannon; but Panthers, and armoured vehicles and anything else will die, especially 190s.' He paused for the resultant chuckles, then carried on, 'The rockets will take care of the rest. Choose how you wish to fire them . . . in a full salvo of eight, or in pairs. Prime rule, don't hang about.

'That's it, gentlemen. Make all the final checks you need, then have yourselves a good rest. Take-off is at 0300 hours. You will be called half an hour before. Good luck, and let's see you all back here when it's over. Met will give you the weather. Thank you.'

Pendrake was standing by his aircraft in the twilight, when Bingo Wilson came up to him.

'Terrible thing about Foxy,' Wilson began.

Pendrake nodded. 'I never expected it. Foxy seemed indestructible. I owed him a lot.'

'Yes.' Wilson paused to take a deep breath of the cool evening air. 'Do you really think it was the same 190 that got Braddock?'

'From what Spy has said, it sounds suspiciously like it.'

'I'd like to get the sod.'

'I have first claim,' Pendrake said.

'If you miss him, he's mine.'

'I won't miss.'

There was another pause as both men, deep within their own private thoughts, watched the sky grow dark.

'Look, Mike, if . . .'

'Don't say it, Bingo. You're coming back.'

* * *

In the Château de St Sauveur, Meckler smiled with pleasure as he saw Odile walking towards him. She was dressed in a flowing black dress that came sharply in at the waist, then curved snugly down the hips to fall in soft folds to her ankles. The top showed a discreet but teasing roundness of breasts which promised a fullness he found intoxicating. He hardly dared believe his luck that she had come to him. As she walked, he saw that there were multiple slits in the folds of the dress and every so often, her bare, unstockinged legs gleamed at him. On her feet were golden sandals, and her golden hair shone past her shoulders like an extra piece of raiment, matching perfectly the dark texture of her dress.

'So you kept your word,' he said to her in French as she stopped before him.

'I kept my word.'

'I did order the coffee . . . the real thing. It's . . . it's in my room.' He smiled sheepishly. 'Look at me. I'm like a schoolboy on his first date. Is that any way for a Waffen-SS lieutenant colonel to behave?'

'I don't know,' she said, smiling at him. 'How do Waffen-SS lieutenant colonels behave?'

'Some,' he began seriously, 'you would not like to know. My God, you are beautiful. Come. We should not be standing here like a pair of statues. Please come in.'

He stood back for her to enter, then shut the door. The smell of the coffee pervaded the room.

'Lock it,' she said. 'We would not like to be disturbed, would we?'

'No . . . No,' he replied quickly and did as she had requested.

She looked about her, eyes lingering upon the big bed that was the centrepiece of all the furnishings. 'So they gave you this room. It was one of my favourites.'

'Was it? Oh, I'm sorry,' he said sympathetically. 'Of course. You'll know every room in this place.'

'Yes.'

'The . . . the bed is very big.'

'All our beds are very big.' Her eyes wandered to where the coffee waited. There was a small, unopened bottle of Asbach brandy with it. 'Are you trying to get me drunk?'

'What?' He seemed genuinely startled. 'Oh. No. That bottle has travelled with me throughout the war. I promised myself I would only open it if something very special happened to me. I have seen many things . . . done many . . . but until tonight, nothing was worth opening it for.'

Despite her reasons for being there, she was touched and almost hated herself for the deceitful role she was playing. Then she remembered the cellars, and Agnès, and all the things that had happened to France, and all doubts vanished. Keeping him here, no matter how accomplished whoever was second in command might be, would slow down the response time of the Waffen-SS units. That might just be enough to make the difference between success and failure. At least, she thought, what she was about to do was with someone she did honestly find attractive.

Outside, a pair of silent feet walked past Meckler's door. Grüber continued walking, a foul look of jealousy on his pinched features.

'They didn't mind you leaving?' Odile asked.

'No. I had served my function as the most junior

officer there. They're still talking … Schlierhof, Daggenau, the revolting Grüber and a few others, including a couple of Wehrmacht brigadier generals.

They were sitting at the table and Meckler had poured the coffee. He now poured the Asbach into two small glasses he'd brought with him.

'Don't tell me the glasses travelled too.'

'Oh yes. They're my father's.'

She gave her familiar giggle. 'You carried that all through your battles?'

'Yes. You think it is strange?' He put a cup and a glass before her. 'Let me tell you something even more strange. On the Eastern Front, we once captured a Russian general. He had a complete samovar with him, all highly polished.'

She giggled again. 'What happened to him?'

'He tried to escape of course and was shot.'

The giggles went. 'That sounds familiar.'

'No, no. It was a genuine escape. He killed ten of our troops. I was almost sorry he was killed. A very brave man.'

'Who killed him. You?'

'No. A one-armed friend of mine.'

'I see.'

'Well,' Meckler said brightly, raising his glass. 'To you, a goddess.'

'I'm no goddess, Franz.'

'To me, you are. Raise your glass. Please.'

She raised the glass.

'Now you must drink at one go. That's how I would like to do it tonight.'

'All right.'

'To you,' he said.

'To the end of the war,' she said.

He looked at her steadily. 'Yes. I would like that.' They drank together.

'Wooo!' she said, as the Asbach went down.

He grinned. 'Good?'

She nodded, not yet ready to speak, a hand against her chest.

'Coffee, perhaps?' he suggested.

She nodded quickly and took a swallow.

'You own vineyards,' he said. 'You must have drunk a variety of . . .'

'This . . . this one was something special,' she interrupted.

He picked up the bottle, studied it, then put it back down.

'Yes. It was, wasn't it?'

She did something to her dress and stood up suddenly. The dress tumbled away from her like a slow waterfall. She had nothing on underneath.

He stared at her, his eyes nearly popping. 'My drink has done this to you?'

She shook her head slowly, her own eyes fastened upon him. She said nothing.

'You are a goddess,' he said hoarsely as she walked slowly over to the bed and sat upon it, her legs slightly apart.

She still said nothing.

Meckler stood up and slowly unbuttoned his tunic. 'Are you sure of this?'

She nodded silently.

'For days and days I have been dreaming of being able to . . .'

He stopped as he threw the tunic to the floor. He

sat down again and hauled off his jackboots while she continued to watch him. Then, rapidly, he removed the rest of his clothing. He came towards the bed and stood before her.

No words passed between them.

He got to his knees and began to kiss her on the ankle, moving slowly up her inner leg all the way to the top of her thigh. A *frisson* of pleasure caused her body to tremble slightly, and a sharp intake of breath came from her.

He continued to work upwards until he reached her breasts, his body sliding itself over her. She lowered herself slowly as he did so until her entire upper body, propped by her buttocks on the edge of the bed, lay upon the large duvet.

He kissed her body in adoration for several minutes, until she felt she must squeal for release. And still he continued to kiss her. When at last he came into her, it was a powerful entry that made her gasp out loud as she brought her legs about him, trapping him within her.

And yet, for all his vigour, he was strangely gentle.

'I shall have to go back,' she said. 'It's nearly midnight.'

'I know,' he said regretfully.

They were lying in close embrace. Their lovemaking had made the bed look as if there had been a wrestling contest.

'Odile, this was . . .'

'Shhh! Say nothing.'

'But . . .'

'Please, Franz. Nothing.'

'All right. But I want to see you again.'

'You will.'

'All right,' he repeated. 'With such a promise, I will let you go.'

She got out of bed and dressed quickly. He also climbed out and began to dress.

'What are you doing?' she asked.

'I'm escorting you back. Do you think I'll let you walk back alone?'

'I am in my own house.'

'Your house, but not controlled by you.'

'There really is no need, Franz. I'll be fine.' She went to the door, unlocked it and opened it.

And looked straight into Grüber's face.

She gave a start of surprise. Meckler, his tunic not quite buttoned, came to see what it was all about, then grew angry when he saw Grüber.

'My God, man!' he snapped. 'Must you always be creeping around? Haven't you got your own bed to go to?'

'I was going to my room when your door opened. I was quite startled. Perhaps I can escort the lady to her quarters.'

'I shall do that, thank you, Herr Grüber!' Meckler said roughly as he finished buttoning his tunic. 'Come, Odile.' Taking her arm, he brushed roughly past Grüber.

The Gestapo man watched them go, his villainous eyes blank. They all knew his own room was a long way from there.

* * *

Back in her bedroom, Odile got undressed and washed herself. She then set an alarm clock, which she muffled by putting a folded handkerchief between the knocker and the bell; but she did not put on her nightdress. Instead, she put on totally unfeminine clothes and leaving a pair of soft boots under the bed got in beneath the first layer of bedclothes.

She lay in the darkness and waited.

In his own room, Meckler got fully undressed and climbed into bed a very happy man. The Asbach, he thought, before he fell asleep, had been worth keeping for the right moment.

Grüber was not having a good night of it. The raging jealousy he felt drove him to an arousal for which he had no immediate female body to give him relief. In the morning, he decided, he would demand the return of Agnès. The Malzeys did not control what went on in the château.

When Agnès returned, he would revel in that young body for all the days he'd not had her. He would find new and inventive ways to make up for the lost time. The Malzeys would not be getting her back; ever. As for that aristocratic tart Odile, she would soon know what it was like to have Helmut Grüber inside her, whether she wanted him there or not.

And Meckler. Meckler was no doubt feeling smug. Well, Meckler would be pulled off his high horse one day soon, Knight's Cross notwithstanding. Heroes could fall.

Two kilometres from the château, silent, armed people were converging on the secret entrances to some of the hidden passages that led into the building itself. They would enter the dark labyrinths and there they would wait, until the time was right.

Several other small bands were taking up positions well away from the Waffen-SS troops that formed the defensive screen of the château, but close enough for when the time came to mount their own attack.

A third group, to the west, were preparing for their assault upon the airfield.

Then suddenly all movement in all the locations stopped. The waiting had begun.

Ketelheim woke up with a start. He switched on his bedside lamp: 0200 hours. He listened. There was nothing untoward. Then why had he woken? He turned off the light, waited for his eyes to become accustomed to the dark, then drew open his curtain slightly. All was quiet on the airfield. Must have been a dream, he thought.

He closed the curtain, sensing unease, but not understanding why. After a while, he lay back in the bed.

He still had no idea why he had woken so suddenly.

At precisely the same time that Ketelheim had been startled out of sleep, Pendrake lay on the hard bed at Able Three, his eyes wide open in the dark. Everything he could possibly have done in the time allowed had been done. The men had come through. It was now up to them. No point worrying now.

He drifted off to sleep, listening to Bingo Wilson frequently shifting position on his own bed.

It seemed only seconds later that someone was shaking him.

'Time, sir,' the unknown voice said, shining a torch in his face.

'All right. I'm awake.'

The torch moved on.

'Turn that bloody thing off!' Bingo Wilson said.

'Yes, sir,' the aircraftman said and proceeded to shine it on Kelly.

'Hey! Hey!' Kelly said. 'OK, OK. You can turn off the sun.'

In the next hut Mackenzie, Williams and Hargreaves were undergoing the same treatment, as well as all those in the aircrew huts dotted about the place.

They moved without haste but purposefully, as they got ready. No one spoke. There was no need to. They ate the prepared sandwiches and drank the hot tea that had been brought to them; then they went out to their aircraft.

Stanley appeared at Pendrake's hut just as he was leaving. He hung back for the others to move on ahead.

'I should tell you,' Stanley began, 'do this well, and there could be more Cobra Squadron missions. You never know with these things.'

'Glad you came, Spy,' Pendrake said. 'Here.'

'What's this?'

'A letter to Section Officer Lewis at the Cobra station. It says a few things.'

Stanley took the envelope and put it in one of the pouch pockets of his tunic. 'I'll hang on to it till you get back, then you can give it to her yourself if it's still appropriate. See you later.'

They didn't shake hands.

* * *

One by one, the black Typhoons ripped apart the night as they burst into life. All engines started smoothly. Twenty aircraft would be going. Subdued lighting came on to illuminate the flare path; despite its deliberately low intensity, the whole place seemed unnaturally bright. Take-off would have to be rapid so that the airfield could be shrouded once more in darkness in as short a time as possible.

The aircraft would lift off in pairs by flight in reverse order, with Pendrake going off first, leading Three Flight. He taxied out to the runway, instrument lighting dimmed as far as he dared. A dark shape following told him Bingo Wilson was right there with him. Then they were on the runway.

He pushed the throttle to its full travel. The Typhoon with the mangled hand gathered speed swiftly. The tail inched off the ground. He held it for a brief moment. The aircraft wanted to fly. A gentle backwards pressure and she was off. He bought the wheels up, and banked gently on to the heading for the track to target.

He glanced back. The airfield was nowhere to be seen. All the aircraft had got into the air and the lights immediately turned off. When airspeed reached 380mph, he throttled back and held it there. To his right, a shape that was Bingo Wilson in Cobra Two was keeping station.

They were on their way.

In Odile's room at the château, the muffled alarm went off. She stopped it quickly and got out of bed, grabbed at her boots and put them on. Next to where she'd placed the boots was a powerful torch. She picked it up and went to the connecting door to Mariette's room.

'Mariette!' she whispered.

'We're coming!'

Odile went to the entrance to the secret passage, which was at the back of a false wardrobe attached to the real one. She waited as her parents, Mariette, Agnès and Philippe, whom they had managed to warn in time, entered her bedroom.

They all trooped through to the passage, Odile leading the way. Mariette brought up the rear and shut the wardrobe, then the entrance. No one who entered the room would know where they'd gone. They went far enough to be well away from the building. Odile retrieved her automatic pistol, surprising everyone except Mariette, who already knew. They settled down in the dark to wait.

Soon they saw a pinprick of light approaching. It was the first of the Resistance fighters, a woman.

In his room, Grüber slept fitfully. Every so often, he would jerk awake, thinking of revenge on Odile, on Agnès, on Meckler.

Meckler slept soundly, dreaming of Odile, while in the other bedrooms the senior officers who had attended the tactical meeting had put away their logistical, strategic and political worries to sleep equally soundly, lulled by the château's excellent wines.

Ketelheim was awake again. This was ridiculous. He was as jumpy as a rookie pilot about to go on his first mission. Something was itching at him, but what?

He decided it was pointless going back to sleep and began to dress. He picked up the phone and called the duty officer.

'Wake my mechanics,' he ordered. 'I want my plane made ready.'

'*Now*, sir?' came the startled reaction.

'Of course now! Do you think I'm in the habit of making funny calls in the middle of the night?'

'No. No, Herr Oberstleutnant!'

'And wake Oberfeldwebel Prinz. Get his plane ready too.'

'Yes, sir!'

The duty officer will be thinking the old man's finally gone mad, Ketelheim thought as he put the phone down.

'Old,' he said to himself. 'I'm twenty-seven. Perhaps I have indeed gone mad.'

They made it to the coast of France without alerting any radars that might have been searching. No night fighters came probing. They gained height on instruments to clear high ground, but maintained low altitude across the sleeping countryside. To remain undetected as long as possible, they neither made nor received any radio transmissions. In any case, there was little need at this stage, as each flight knew precisely what to do, without further instructions.

It wouldn't be long now, Pendrake thought, before the thunder of twenty Napier engines woke someone up.

A sudden flash over to the right told him someone

was indeed awake. A flak battery missing by a wide margin. Probably fired long after the squadron had passed. But the phones would be ringing and radio traffic hotting up. It was time for Keane's flight to go.

Right on schedule, One Flight curved away from the invisible formation to head for the airfield. The others forged on.

The phone rang in Ketelheim's bedroom. It was the duty officer, sounding astonished and clearly wondering whether his CO had second sight.

'Message just came through, sir! A large formation of aircraft has crossed the coast and is heading this way! A battery fired, but hit nothing.'

Ketelheim was galvanized. He had *known* something was about to happen. 'Did you wake Prinz?'

'Yes, sir. He's on his way to his aircraft.'

'Good. I'll join him. Wake up every pilot. Hurry!'

He slammed the phone down and rushed out of the room.

Pendrake felt warm. He reached to his right for the cockpit heating lever to reduce the temperature slightly. He glanced at the watch in its holder, on the left-hand section of the instrument panel. Time soon for Two Flight to break away.

A minute later, Dodson led his flight out of formation to make for the hell of the flak-infested woods.

Ketelheim spoke rapidly to Prinz. 'Keep your cockpit lighting low and follow my instructions. Keep your nerve *at all times*. We're going high to see what

278

the radars have for us. You know how to use your equipment. It will soon be dawn and we'll be able to see them and hit them like fish in a barrel. OK, Jürgen?'

'Yes, sir.'

'Good. Get in and let's go.'

They were on their take-off run when Keane's group arrived.

The rockets came off the Typhoons like emissaries from Hades. The air was filled with the roar of their powerful engines, the whoosh of the rockets, the enormous explosions when they hit. A salvo ripped apart a section of the runway.

Then the cannons started a deadly, coughing stutter. The ultra-high-explosive shells began their own murderous accompaniment as they impacted against aircraft, buildings, trucks and gun emplacements. They mowed down running people, sleeping people, mechanics, pilots, drivers. The duty officer to whom Ketelheim had spoken was hit while he was still on the phone. He never finished what he'd been saying.

Astoundingly, the surprise had been so complete that not a single flak gun had so far opened up. Ketelheim and Prinz had managed, against all odds, to get off the ground.

Ketelheim watched in mounting despair as he banked his aircraft steeply to get out of the way, seeing the great explosions and widening blaze of fires spreading about the airfield.

He wondered whether any of the other pilots had managed to get off, perhaps using the emergency runway, or even the grass, if it was not too soft. The

Fw-190 had a nasty habit of flipping over on indifferent ground and smashing its canopy on your head. At least in the 109, the weak landing-gear would snap, leaving you with an enforced belly landing. You'd be the right way up, which was a lot better than being trapped upside down with fuel leaking all around you.

Ketelheim thought he saw something flit across the fires like a great bat, then it was gone. What the hell was it?

He was beginning to feel angry.

For three terrible minutes, the Typhoons wreaked havoc, then, saving ammunition, One Flight headed for the woods to help Dodson and the others.

'This is Night Owl,' Ketelheim called. 'Did anyone get up?'

'Schiller,' came a voice.

'Neumann.'

'Hartz.'

'Möhn.'

'Anyone else?'

Silence greeted him.

Six, he thought bitterly. *Six out of twenty-five.*

He didn't know how many of those attacking aircraft there had been, but he would pursue with his six. Perhaps some 109s would come looking when the light got better.

What had happened to those wretched coastal radars? Didn't any of them work any more?

'Night Owl,' he called to his other pilots. 'Form on me. Let's go after them.' He contacted various ground-control stations and radars to get a lead on the enemy aircraft. None came up with anything. *'They're here!'* he shouted. *'Do something!'*

Meanwhile, he trusted his own instincts and headed towards the château.

Pendrake had arrived at the back of the château, with Wilson close behind. The flak platforms were his first priority. Pulling up slightly from his low altitude, he released a salvo of rockets and broke sharply just as Wilson fired.

The gunners barely had time to assimilate the direction of the swelling noise of the approach, the sudden dark apparitions, and the streams of white hurtling towards them, before their world turned into fire.

Eight rockets tore into the gun platforms, ripping them apart in great gouts of flame that slashed through the paling darkness. Ammunition exploded in sympathy, adding to the destruction. Bodies flew through the air.

Pendrake wheeled away in preparation for another run as the second pair of Kelly and Mackenzie unleashed a total salvo of sixteen rockets at the château itself. They had to haul away quickly as great catapulting lumps seemed to fly past them. The third pair roasted gun emplacements in the grounds.

All six repeated the attack, leaving that part of the château a crackling, burning shell. The Malzey apartments were not hit by a single round.

But the flak was waking up in the woods, over which Dodson had now been joined by Keane's flight. All over the wooded expanse, Meckler's men were taking a beating. Rockets lit up the gloom like something out of Dante. Tracers streamed from the diving, wheeling aircraft, still barely distinguishable, lacing the air with red-gold pulses that seared earthwards like demented lightning. Explosions erupted as men died where they slept or were consumed within their vehicles. Anti-aircraft ammunition exploded while gunners tried to load, turning them into burning lumps of flesh that mixed with their disintegrating weaponry.

But now, something exploded in the air as some flak gunners, out in one of the vineyards, scored a kill.

The château grounds had been pulverized, and Pendrake's Typhoons headed for the woods.

It was up to Halloran's people now.

Of the nineteen remaining Typhoons, those still carrying rockets were wheeling in the still weak approaching light, and unleashing into the woods. They were like a flock of huge bats, flitting between the spouts of fire that came at them as they hunted. Then the flak claimed another. It spiralled into the trees. Even if the pilot had still been alive, he would not have had time to bail out.

'Cobra Squadron,' Pendrake called, 'let's go home.'

And then he saw the fighters.

14

'Break! Break!' he heard someone call urgently. Not to him, for in the distance something flamed silently.

'109s!' another voice called.

'And 190s! Gawd! Look at them!' It was Elmore.

When the first rockets hit, Grüber, with the instincts of a born survivor, had leapt out of bed and rolled away from any flimsy barriers like windows. In desperation, he hid in the bathroom. It saved his life. A rocket had entered a window and exploded on the bed. All that was left of the room was the bathroom, whose solid door had somehow contained the by then dissipating blast. For a while, Grüber was totally deaf.

In a daze, he at last moved cautiously out of the bathroom, and stopped. There was no floor. Choking dust was everywhere. Then he saw that he could creep along a narrow ledge to the now non-existent door to the bedroom. Some of his clothes lay in the still-intact corridor.

He eventually made it, chose some, and put them on. Then he saw something he needed.

His gun. He picked it up. It was fully loaded. Someone was going to pay for this.

*　　*　　*

Meckler was thrown out of bed by the first explosions. Instincts of the battlefield taking over, he got dressed swiftly when he realized he was still alive and unhurt. Although there was plenty of dust in the room, it was intact; but he could smell burning.

He rushed out of the room gun in hand, tunic open and bare-headed. His booted feet crunched on broken glass. Several paintings lay in untidy heaps along the masonry-strewn corridor. He'd heard the departing aircraft, but no answering sounds of anti-aircraft guns close by, although the distant crump of his flak batteries in the woods could be distinguished.

Surprise had been total, he thought clinically. He had failed. He knew whose head would roll.

He wondered what had happened to Odile and her family.

'Cobra Squadron!' Pendrake called. 'Take them!'

He moved the throttle to the 'wall and then slid the supercharger lever forward. The Typhoon leapt for altitude. But he did not intend to go high. He was going to drag them down into his arena. He cut the supercharger and found himself curving behind a darting 190 that seemed unsure which of the Typhoons to go for. At last, its pilot picked one. Pendrake stayed glued to him.

The range closed quickly. The 190 pilot was not checking his tail. The Focke-Wulf looked like a ghostly moth in the dawn light.

Pendrake went in closer until the 190, still intent on its own prey, seemed to fill his windscreen.

He fired.

The high-explosive shells tore into the unsuspecting

aircraft. It jerked upright as if it had itself felt the blow and slowly turned over on to its back, streaming dark smoke. Then it suddenly changed into a puff of flame, a metamorphosis that was as sudden as it was spectacular.

Ketelheim had seen Jürgen Prinz go after one of the black aircraft which he himself had belatedly recognized as a special mark of Typhoon, a type he'd never come across before.

He had called to his eager wingman, who, perhaps incensed by the unexpected attack on the airfield and mesmerized by what he'd mistakenly believed were plenty of easy targets, had plunged in without thinking. In that single moment of unreason, all the discipline that had marked Prinz's flying career so far had disappeared.

Then Ketelheim had seen the ominous black shadow lining up precisely behind the 190, and knew his young wingman was being stalked by a highly skilled practitioner of the art of air combat. He had recognized something of himself in the implacable way in which the Typhoon seemed fixed to Prinz's 190.

'Jürgen!' he'd called. 'Break! Break!'

But he'd been far too late. With an awe-inspiring economy, the black Typhoon had fired the shortest of bursts. But it had been enough. Jürgen Prinz's young life was over.

Ketelheim looked for the black aircraft that had done the deed, determined to take his revenge. But it had gone, and was somewhere among the others. There had been no distinguishable marking on it and even when the light got better, he knew that all he would see would be its faded national insignia.

But he would know it when he saw it again. He would recognize the flying skill.

Pendrake had broken swiftly away after his kill and gone after another 190 that seemed to be pursuing a Typhoon low down. But the Typhoon pilot was well aware that someone was on his tail. It broke sharply left, disappearing momentarily in the gloom below. When Pendrake saw it again it was curving to the right, while the 190, outmanoeuvred, was desperately trying to recover the situation.

But the Typhoon had hauled itself tightly round and was now pulling in behind its erstwhile pursuer. A brief flash of tracer and the 190 exploded, going straight into the trees.

'How do you like *that*?' a disembodied voice exclaimed.

Elmore had made the kill.

Pendrake smiled grimly and went looking for more prey.

Keane, with Wojdat close in, spotted another Typhoon; it appeared to be dancing in a wall of fire coming up from the ground. The light was getting better and better, and the blackbirds of the night were beginning to gain visibility.

'Josef, do something about that flak. I'll watch your back.'

'Roger.'

Wojdat flung the Typhoon on to its back, rolled upright and hurtled towards the flak battery. He had laid down a ferocious fire at the airfield and it had been his cannon shell, though he could have had no way of knowing, that had cut short the life of the duty officer in mid-phone conversation.

The gunners were still intent on downing their target and so were quite surprised when the hellish cannon fire began ripping them apart. The gunfire stopped reaching skywards.

'Many thanks!' someone called with relief. It was Knowles, the New Zealander from Two Flight.

'You are OK?'

'Josef?'

'Yes.'

'Thanks, mate. A few holes in the wings, but otherwise OK.' Knowles brought his aircraft close. The 'few holes' made a section of his left wing look like netting.

He tucked in on Wojdat and together they went to rejoin Keane, who was waiting up top.

Ketelheim had spotted a solitary Typhoon streaking just above the treetops. As the light got better, he was able to see it quite clearly. High above him, some 109s that had come to join the fight were having a fracas of their own. He had now lost Prinz, Möhn and Hartz. That left just himself, Schiller and Neumann. He couldn't see them anywhere, although he'd heard Schiller exclaim loudly, using foul language. Schiller had scored.

Three out of twenty-five.

It was a disaster of monumental proportions.

He felt a cold anger as he dived on the Typhoon like an avenging hawk. The black aircraft drew swiftly closer. The pilot was obviously not keeping a good lookout. Perhaps he was wounded. Ketelheim felt no mercy.

Had she been there to observe him, Mariette would not have recognized the charming man with whom she'd picnicked.

Ketelheim had no intention of letting the Typhoon escape.

Hargreaves was trying to make it back to base. His left arm, hit by a flak splinter, would not move. His radio was out, so he could warn no one of his predicament. When he'd been hit, he had just been pulling out of a dive and had eased the throttle back. It now gave him a power setting that allowed a good turn of speed, with fuel economy, so there had been no need to try to reach it with his good right hand. The aircraft handled perfectly. He was low down, and the trees still screened him.

But the pain had dulled his instincts, for though enough remained to make him check behind, it was just as the first shells from the pursuing 190 struck the aircraft.

A savage bang on the armour-plating behind him threw him forward, causing him to shove at the stick. The Typhoon toppled into a steep dive as more shells exploded viciously against it.

Hargreaves never saw the trees that claimed him.

'That was for Jürgen,' Ketelheim said in his mask as he hauled the 190 upwards. He had to jink suddenly as the tumbling, flaming carcass of a 109 fell past on its way to earth.

The Messerschmitts were not having a good time of it. The fight had now gone out of reach of Meckler's flak batteries. Briefly, he wondered what had happened to Franz. The château had been successfully attacked. Was Franz even still alive?

But where was the man who had shot down the boy from the chemist's shop with such clinical skill?

The man was right behind him.

Pendrake had seen the Typhoon go down before the swiftly diving Focke-Wulf and felt a strange recognition. He knew he had never met this pilot in combat before; but there seemed to be an inevitability about the approaching confrontation.

Just as he was about to fire his first shells, the pilot of the 190 spotted him and rolled swiftly, pulling sharply away in a dive.

Pendrake did not follow. Instead, he pulled up slightly, then banked hard right, almost on the canopy, to pull down to where he judged the 190 would be. And there it was, curving hard to come back at him.

Pendrake rolled upright and turned into the incoming aircraft. They flashed past each other. Neither fired.

No point wasting ammunition, Pendrake thought grimly. This pilot was no novice. He knew he had met the ace.

Ketelheim was also certain he had met Jürgen's killer. It took nerve to face an oncoming aircraft and to hold fire.

'You are a cold one,' Ketelheim said quietly.

He looked swiftly about him. There was no one in sight. The sky seemed to be theirs alone.

'All right, my friend,' he murmured at the black aircraft as he watched it flash past above him, knowing its pilot was about to pull down on to his tail. 'May the best man win.'

He felt a sense of admiration for the other pilot, who was as implacable as he was. The Typhoon looked beautiful as it danced with him, never once allowing itself to become vulnerable.

They used up great segments of sky as they fought for advantage. The crew of an isolated flak battery were so mesmerized when the ballet arrived above them that they chose not to fire and instead paused to watch. The whirling aircraft moved on.

Pendrake watched as the 190 curved above him upside down, then stood on its wingtip trying to turn into him, coming in close from the starboard quarter. He saw the golden emblem clearly.

Marvelling at the fantastic view out that the canopy afforded him, he rolled into the approaching Focke-Wulf, then pulled on the stick. As he fell towards the ground, he was aware that the 190 had missed again. Again no shots were fired.

He kept low down, forcing the other pilot to come after him, leading him towards a large expanse of wood.

Ketelheim could not believe it when he saw the Typhoon roll into a ninety-degree bank, to slip between a colony of trees. Instinctively, he pulled up to avoid colliding with the branches. But where was the Typhoon?

The sudden slamming on his aircraft gave him the answer he did not want. As the shells exploded about him, he felt an unbearable pain savaging his body. His hands let go of the controls. The 190, still in the climb, lost speed, stalled and fell back upon itself.

Just before it exploded among the trees, Ketelheim whispered one word.

'Trudi,' he said.

Pendrake had known exactly what he intended to do when he'd entered the wood. There had been an exit to his right and he'd taken it, just as the 190 had baulked upwards to avoid the trees. He'd then continued his turn and had again begun to climb, nicely on the tail of the fleeing 190.

Choosing the moment well, he'd made sure that every shell counted. This enemy pilot had not been the sort of man to be given a second chance.

Pendrake circled the place of dying once, then went to look for his squadron.

In and around the château, the sound of small-arms fire was a chilling dawn chorus.

Odile, leaving her parents with Mariette, had returned to her home. She was followed by Agnès, who refused to remain, and Philippe, who had been given a weapon by one of the Resistance, some of whom had followed too. They streamed through the building. Odile became separated and turned a corner, to find herself face to face with a dishevelled Meckler. He stared at the clothes she wore, and at the gun in her hand. He pointed his own gun at her.

'*You! You fooled me! You used me!* And now, look what you have done. I am finished.'

She stood before him, completely unafraid. 'What did I do to you? You came to my country and occupied it. You took my house from me. *Your* people abused *my* people in *my* home. You abused *my* country. What did you expect?'

He continued to stare at her. 'And last night? Did you also pretend? Did I share my special drink with you for nothing?'

'If you believe that . . . and if you believe that I am wrong to fight for my own beliefs, then . . .' She lowered her automatic. 'Shoot me.'

For long moments, he just looked at her, remembering how she had felt in his arms. Outside, and within other parts of the building, the ferocious rattle of small-arms fire continued.

Then Meckler lowered his own pistol.

'Oh, Odile,' he said. 'Why couldn't we have met . . .'

'*Veräter!*' someone screamed. 'Traitor! They are all dead, Meckler. It is your fault!'

Two shots barked from behind him and Franz Meckler's eyes opened wide as he pitched forwards, falling almost at Odile's feet.

Shocked by the suddenness of it, she looked up to see the venomous eyes of a bedraggled Grüber, glaring at her.

'And as for you,' he hissed, gun zeroed upon her as he came forward. 'I will have my revenge upon you until you scream for death.'

She backed away from him as he continued to approach, stepping over Meckler's body with total indifference.

'*Stand still!*' he barked.

She stopped.

'Drop the gun. *Drop it!*'

She did so.

'Now,' he said. 'I shall teach you a lesson you will remember until the moment of your death. Remove your clothes.'

She stared at him in disbelief.

'*Remove them!*' he screamed.

Slowly, she began to unbutton the rough, workman's jacket she was wearing. Then she saw movement behind Grüber. *Agnès. Agnès with a long, wicked-looking knife.*

Odile did not pause, so as not to warn him. He licked at his lips as he waited for her to bare her body to him.

But now, Agnès was rushing forward. Grüber began to turn. Agnès gave an inhuman scream of rage and hatred as she launched herself upon the man who had tormented her for so long. The knife plunged deep into his chest, came out, and went in again repeatedly. He screamed, a high-pitched wail that seemed to echo for ever. Blood gushed all over him, and upon Agnès. She kept plunging the knife in as if that was all that mattered to her in all the world. As Grüber began to collapse, the gun fired. Once.

Agnès reeled away, a great wound just below her left breast.

'*Agnès!*' Odile shouted in horror, and ran to help

the stricken girl. But it was of little use. Agnès was dying. 'Oh, Agnès,' she said softly.

Odile cradled her in her arms. Agnès never spoke as she died. Odile laid her down gently, then turned to where Grüber lay dead, looking like a butchered carcass.

She spat upon the body. 'For Agnès, and for Jeanne-Anne.'

A slight movement made her look. 'Franz! You're all right! Here. Let me help.' She crouched to attempt to prop him up.

'No, no,' he said weakly. 'I am not all right.' He coughed, and a great stream of blood came out of his mouth. 'See?' he gasped. 'I have seen many such wound ... wounds before. Go, Odile. Let me ... let me die. I've ... I've been waiting a long time.'

'No, Franz. I cannot ...'

'Go, my love. Go and save your country. Mine is finished.'

She kissed his forehead gently as he died, and stood up to move away. She turned, and gave a start. Michel Montcarneau was standing there, a sub-machine-gun in his hand. The sounds of small-arms fire came more sporadically now.

'Michel! You're safe!'

He nodded slowly then turned as a man, wearing two pistols in shoulder holsters and also carrying a sub-machine-gun, approached. 'Fer de Lance,' Montcarneau said.

Odile and Halloran nodded at each other.

'Boucheron's dead,' Montcarneau continued, 'and that so-called wife of his. Our people in the cellars are safe.' He looked at each of the bodies. 'What happened here?'

She told them about Agnès and the Gestapo deputy, watching as the faces of the two men registered disgust and outrage.

'And this one?' Montcarneau pointed with the gun at Meckler and looked at her keenly.

She wiped the beginnings of tears from her eyes. 'Someone who should not have come here,' she said. 'Not at this time.'

'And Mariette? Is she all right?'

'I'll take you to her. Come, Monsieur Fer de Lance.'

As Halloran went with them, he briefly touched the small crucifix Jeanne-Anne had given him.

'Cobra One,' Pendrake called. 'Heading home. On me.'

No one replied. There was no need to. Those still alive would all be heading towards the homeward track, marked out on the map at Able Three.

Soon, he could see them arriving. It was a glorious sight in the new day. Of the twenty aircraft that had set out, sixteen were returning. A lot better than he had feared. They had acquitted themselves well. Hargreaves and Williams had gone. As had Charlton, who would now never wear his officer's rank.

Pendrake looked about him with a pride tinged with sadness for those he'd lost, as his flock followed him home. There would be more letters to write. Then a new feeling came to him; one that gave him an immense rush of well-being. He would be seeing Karen Lewis again.

In his mind's eye, he saw her running towards him as he landed back at the home airfield.

Only Theo Neumann survived to make it back in his battered Focke-Wulf 190. He was forced to use the emergency strip, but landed badly. The plane hit a bump, turned over on to its back, settling down on the cockpit. Fuel began to leak from ruptured pipes. It exploded while he was still vainly trying to get out.

The Golden Knights had ceased to exist.

OTHER TITLES IN SERIES FROM 22 BOOKS

Available now at newsagents and booksellers or use the order form provided

continued overleaf . . .

*   *   *

*   *   *

All at £4.99 net

All 22 Books are available at your bookshop, or can be ordered from:

22 Books
Mail Order Department
Little, Brown and Company
Brettenham House
Lancaster Place
London WC2E 7EN

Alternatively, you may fax your order to the above address.
Fax number: 0171 911 8100.

Payments can be made by cheque or postal order, payable to
Little, Brown and Company (UK), or by credit card (Visa/
Access). Do not send cash or currency. UK, BFPO and Eire
customers, please allow 75p per item for postage and packing,
to a maximum of £7.50. Overseas customers, please allow £1
per item.

While every effort is made to keep prices low, it is sometimes
necessary to increase cover prices at short notice. 22 Books
reserves the right to show new retail prices on covers which
may differ from those previously advertised in the books or
elsewhere.

NAME ....

ADDRESS ....

....

....

☐ I enclose my remittance for £_____
☐ I wish to pay by Access/Visa

Card number

☐☐☐☐ ☐☐☐☐ ☐☐☐☐ ☐☐☐☐

Card expiry date

☐☐ ☐☐

Please allow 28 days for delivery. Please tick box if you do not
wish to receive any additional information ☐